AuthorHouse™
1663 Liberty Drive
Bloomington, IN 47403
www.authorhouse.com
Phone: 1-800-839-8640

First published by AuthorHouse 4/14/2010

ISBN: 978-1-4490-8582-7 (e)
ISBN: 978-1-4490-8581-0 (sc)

Printed in the United States of America
Bloomington, Indiana

This book is printed on acid-free paper.

Your Invitation!

Come as you are!!

by
Knecht Sylvia

authorHOUSE®

Hello! It is nice to meet you, and I am very glad for God's mercy that we are now united in His Kingdom. I am praying that the fruit off the vine of Christ gifted to me from God, will nourish your spirit, mind and soul as I am in obedience sharing them with you while producing fruit in you that will nourish my spirit, mind and soul uniting us in one family, the body of God's purposes and promises.

Please keep an open mind as you read, you have not picked up a book, you have been attached, linked on to my journey. Understand please that this will not be a structured read as when you read a novel, but will flow like a wedding dance, us being united in the dance through our groom and with our groom Jesus. My prayer is that in this dance unanswered questions will be resolved, and we will be brave enough to take some first steps into things life has thrown our way. Jesus has opened up the staircase of God's throne room, now our steps are on the Kingdom's path. Remember heaven is only a prayer away, making it always within our reach.

I have to confess I find it very hard to live in this very dirty world, in the midst of all this spiritual pollution. Every day I need to start by soaking myself with the fresh anointing God pours out, keeping me clean, washed white as snow, sparkling like a diamond from the shinning of his Son. So be sure you are taking frequent baths in God's Word, because it is in these baths where life can be kept clean. And after your bath dress yourself in the garment of praise and thanksgiving in all conditions.

Before we get into the meat and potatoes, I would just like to finish whipping the gravy by saying thank you to my special friend Dot, who took the journey with me to bring it to you. And even though we all have a different dance step and style, I would like to share that mine is a square dance, and I am looking forward to crab you all hand by hand, as our Caller Jesus Christ guides are every step as he leads us home. So my friend, grab a partner and skip through God's loop. And I am so glad we got to share this dance.

Let nothing disturb your peace. Because with every step quicken by God, we get revitalized, our strength is energized, we are aroused to accelerate, revive, stir, stimulate, awaken, kindle, activate, completing the action of His Word in us.

Praise the Lord!

DANCING MY LIFE TO THE TUNE OF GOD'S VOICE.

This is the journey of a simple woman sharing her heart from God.

I am happy to proclaim that I am a grateful member of the family of Christ, a blessed disciple. We as the church are going to be noticing big changes in the way thing are getting run. One of the churches main prayer is for harvest workers, but if we are doing this in judgment, pride, jealousy, criticism, etc. We are being hypocrites to biblical teaching.

We the church need to be on our knees in true repentance, so that our union can be restored, then as brothers and sisters we will rally around the cross of Jesus. Instead of brother fighting brother over culture and traditions, let the walls come down, to seek unity it is in Christ we must agree.

Why even bother with the church? Is what some of you are wondering. We need the church because we are created by God, and Christ his only Son is the church, so for you already in the church it would be pleasing to our Father to let loose the clique and cult attitude and you staying away it would be pleasing to our Father if you would pick a church that worships God in a way that is comfortable for you and start making a difference. Don't stay away too busy, or angry, someone there will need you as much as you will need them.

The church is not just a structure you enter Sunday morning, evening, or mid-week, for a bible study. The church is you, the temple of the Holy Spirit. It is your listening ear to someone on a Monday, your simple smile and hello for someone on Tuesday, your patient attitude in a line of a store on Wednesday, me controlling road rage on Thursday, all of us forgiving someone on Friday, preparing for the Sabbath on Saturday, relaxing and listening for God in unison at church (hint, hint) on Sunday. This simple woman is pushy as well. Back to the church it is a twenty-four hour a day seven day a week affair. As you are going to the washroom in the middle of the night, and a name is placed in your heart, send a blessing from God their way, you have now had church. Here is an invitation extended out to you to come and worship, opening our hearts together as one allowing God's light to shine. The church (Jesus) is waiting on you.

I wanted to date the events from God in my life. First I went to February 21, 1997 that is the date of my rebirth. Then I thought no, it goes back to my natural birth. But no again, then I thought how smart am I? It goes back to conception, but no again. The truth is my events from God in my life start at the beginning before time, and will last beyond time. It is an eternal blessing, which has never begun as we understand began, and it will never end because I will always be alive in Jesus.

Here is the reason it is possible for me to share this testimony with you, it is because of Psalm 116: I love the Lord because he hears and answers my prayers. Because he bends down and listens, I will pray as long as I have breath. Death had its hand around my throat; the terrors of the grave overtook me. I saw only trouble and sorrow. Then I called on the name of the Lord: "Please Lord, save me!" How kind the Lord is. So merciful, this God of ours! The Lord protects those of childlike faith; I was facing death and he saved me. Now I can rest again, for the Lord has been so good to me. He has saved me from death, my eyes from tears, my feet from stumbling. And so I walk in the Lord's presence as I live here on earth! I believed in you, so I prayed, "I am deeply troubled Lord." In my anxiety I cried out to you, "These people are all liars!" What can I offer the Lord for all he has done for me? I will lift a cup symbolizing his salvation. I will praise the Lord's name for saving me. I will keep my promises to the Lord in the presence of all his people. The Lord's love ones are precious to him; it grieves him when they die. O Lord, I am your servant, yes, I am your servant, the son of your handmaid, and you have freed me from my bonds! I will offer you a sacrifice of thanksgiving and call on the name of the Lord. I will keep my promises to the Lord in the presence of all his people, in the house of the Lord, in the heart of Jerusalem. Praise the Lord!

Let the fire be lit. A very important principal when learning history or reading a story, is simply this — start at the beginning and move to the end. This may seem obvious, even so many people tend to read the Bible in bits and pieces, never taking the time to tie them together. When we do this it is like doing one of those connect the dots/number puzzles and missing a few or going to the wrong number, it will not give you the right picture. The mixing of various topics is one of the causes as to why we find so many different church groups, religions, and cults.

When we read/study or even meditate God's Word (the Bible) God should make remarkable sense. If we believe it or not is entirely up to us. Hopefully you will, but that is your choice. It is in God's Word where we major in some majors — in this idea we are to learn some important points. Right from the beginning and reading to the end, there is no doubt about it; the Bible is a unique word. It is not just one book, it is actually a collection of books, sixty six in all. It is written in a very long years span (time period) over forty generations. It is written by over forty authors some being kings, peasants, philosophers, fishermen, poets, statesmen, scholars, doctors, prophets, apostles, and the list goes on..... It is written from different places, in different moods. Written on three different Continents; in three languages (Hebrew, Aramaic, Greek.) Its subject matters include hundreds of controversial topics, yet it speaks with harmony and continuity from beginning to end. It is one unfolding story connected together with each and every word within it. The reason for this is because it is the Living Word. So when we read the Bible (to study is different), this is hopefully what we will witness without theological jargon, its simplicity and its importance for each and every step of our journey, in the unique way only our Father can guide us. 2 Timothy 3: 16 All Scripture is God-breathed and is useful for teaching, rebuking, correcting, and training in righteousness.

Prophets: God tells man what he wants to record, and they write it down as they listen. Repeating to others, and recording what has been told to us from God is what is known as the gift for the prophetic. Some people think of a prophet as those who tell the future, but the Bible teaches us that a prophet is a messenger who passes on God's words to the people. There are times the message will pertain to the future, but more often it is connected to daily living. 2 Peter 1: 20-21 Above all, you must understand that no prophecy of Scripture came about by the prophets own interpretation. For prophecy never had its own origin in the will of man, but men spoke from God as they were carried by the Holy Spirit.

God: Is a Spirit; he is eternal; he is the I AM — the self existent one; he is the God most high; the Sovereign ruler of all; he is the only God; and this is the way it was in the beginning, is now, and always will be.

Creation: God created everything with great intellect and power. Some beings have more capability than others, but each created as perfect beings, without any evil, but not like robots either; each have will, which gives them the ability to choose. The most powerful, intelligent and most beautiful Spirit ever created was a cherub. His name translated "Lucifer," which means shinning one, or morning star. Isaiah 14: 12 How have you fallen from heaven, O Morning star, son of the dawn! You have been cast down to earth, you who once laid low the nations!

Lucifer was referred to as an anointed cherub. (Anointing meaning, the rite of pouring oil on someone to set them apart to God for a special task.) This act is considered sacred and not to be taken lightly. Ezekiel 28: 14-15 You were anointed as a guardian cherub, for so I ordained you. You were on the holy mount of God; you walked among the fiery stones. You were blameless in your ways from the day you were created till wickedness was found in you.

It seems that Lucifer's job kept him in the presence of God at all times. Perhaps he somehow represented the rest of the angels and led them in worship and praise of their creator-owner.

God can do everything super naturally, and he has and for that we can glorify Him. But we must also give him glory when he does not do things super naturally for then is when he is taking the time to talk to us telling us what to do and how to do it. And through this we learn to listen and obey the voice of our wonderful and loving Abba Daddy.

Here are some sayings lot of us are familiar with, I would like to quote them to you and comment on them. Now the comment is my opinion. So please keep an open mind and by all means feel free to have your own opinion.

1: It takes a whole village to raise one child: I totally agree with this, but also believe the child from the very start of life needs to know where they fit in. So they may learn from the beginning what their function will be in this body. Even though it sounds impossible, remember in the body of Christ through Jesus everything is possible. And some things are a must in order to work proper. Take our human body for example: it is born with all its parts, and each part has a function. As it matures it understands more fully the functions of these parts, learning to use them to its fullest, but none the less it is born all attached to how it is to grow. And our Spirits work in the same aspect.

2: A Loving and mutual respect for a family unit: This takes total unity and acceptance; because family does not always run smooth. So as others deal with life and stumble, we must respect their emotions, just as when we hit a stumbling block in life, we would be grateful for unconditional support.

3: Wisdom is available to the person who seeks it: The harder we discipline ourselves into what we want to learn the more we learn. But as well the more we pray for knowledge in Spirit and the more we are willing to surrender to God's voice and will, the higher the revelation of God's purpose for us we will be gifted with.

4: Acceptance, forgiveness, loving detachment, without understanding: There are times when we do not understand why someone else or even ourselves has done what has been done. We do not have to accept sin but we must forgive the sinner and release them to God in love, in order that we ourselves may be free from bondage. In order for these things to take place in our lives one major thing must take place: Blame has to stop before hate dies. So let us pray a prayer and move on: Lord Jesus, I give you my life, my mind, my heart, my dreams, my emotions, my thoughts, I give them all to you. I surrender spirit, soul, mind, and body. Do with me as you Will. Amen.

Open your heart: To the ancient paths. My heart knows the God who is the possibility of creating anything he chooses. The God that can be anything he wants to be. He could have been a God of cruelty (which unfortunately is how at times the world views him) taking delight in creating an endless number of creation to torture and maim. But God must follow his nature, and we are blessed to be a creation from this great love. We are overwhelmed with the disastrous Tsunami's of the world, as their destruction washes out everything in their path. But at the same time Tsunami's of love and pleasure are poured out over us from heaven and we don't even notice them coming through, filling everything with peace, mercy, grace, healing, building everything up in their paths. Psalm 33: 11-12 But the plans of the Lord stand firm forever, the purpose of his heart through all generations. Blessed is the Nation whose God id the Lord, the people he chose for his inheritance.

Let us then pray with a fearless and faith filled action, praying in the Spirit and from Scripture as long as God has us there. Hebrews 4: 12-13 For the Word of God is living and active. Sharper than any two-edged sword, it penetrated even to divide soul and spirit, joints and marrow; it judges the thoughts ant attitudes of the heart. Nothing in all creation is hidden from God's sight. Everything is uncovered and laid bare before the eyes of him to whom we must give account.

(God speaking) Get in the car, turn the key, now as you start moving I will direct you and anoint you with my grace and for my glory. Trust in me, be in me. Remove all obstructions and distractions, the only instructions coming from the throne room of God. Ecclesiastes 3: 1 There is a time for everything, and a season for every activity under heaven.

If God plants potatoes don't wait for beets or you will miss the harvest. Be willing to harvest what God has planted not what we want to eat. Romans 8: 28 And we know that in all things God works for the good of those who love him, who have been called according to his purpose.

We were created for God's purpose, so our purpose is God. And our purpose in everything comes from our Father himself. Ephesians 3: 10-12 His intent was that now, through the church, the manifold wisdom of God should be known to the rulers and authorities in the heavenly realms, according to his eternal purpose which he accomplished in Christ our Lord. In him and through faith we may approach with freedom and confidence.

We need to be instructed; which can come from God, from church, and even from the world. This is why it is so important to recognize the voice of Abba Daddy, so no matter what the source it is channeled through we know it is God speaking.

Hang out with like minded people, people on fire for God's living word. Because we are to feed others with our fruits, as we eat from others harvests, this way we look after one another instead of ourselves. The fruit from a vine or a tree is to be given away, it does not eat from its own branches. So let's turn our offences into manure and throw them to the ground, so they might fertilize new fruit for enjoyment.

As I reflect back to February 21, 1997. That special miraculous day, when life as the world knows life died, and a new life one of total non-understanding, was reborn with a fullness I had never known possible. A new life filled with peace, love, hope, joy. At this point I called the minister of the church I was attending. And a fellow al anon member, I needed help in understanding this feeling of everything I had been through in the past forty-one years was worth it. To get to this wonderful shining of fullness I have been gifted with, (from an emptiness that can't be explained). In an instant I had a new outlook on how I saw things. When dusk arrived I witnessed the most beautiful sunset ever, it was the covenant of God's promise of my inheritance and adoption to his family. At this point I had a revelation of how important unity really is, I have been blessed with many different people and I now see how each and everyone is important, and being used by God himself to guide me. Right from the start of this journey when my heart stepped onto God's way, this is only because God took my old shattered , broken heart and replaced it with a new one as he baptized me with his Holy spirit. I was convinced I could do all, and I wanted to do everything to honor God. So I tried to quit smoking. Guess what? I failed. I started to learn I can do all comes from Christ, who gives me strength, and everything needs to be God's will in God's time. But low and behold in my failure I still kept growing very much to God. It took another six years before God finally removed smoking from my life.

Here are a few things I had to deal with and accept on this exciting journey. By the grace of God I am who I am. It is my actions alone I should be testing who I am and where my relationship with Jesus stands, to establish who I am in myself (from God) without comparing myself with or to someone else. Making the ultimate goal of this journey knowing Christ in all his fullness, not building a healthy self esteem. Now I can step in to the tune of relaxing and enjoying who I already am. Galatians 5: 22-23 But when the Holy Spirit controls our lives, he will produce this kind of fruit in us: love, joy, peace, patience, kindness, goodness, faithfulness, gentleness, and self-control. Here there is no conflict with the law.

Victory: As the churches are trying so hard to keep tares (weeds) out of their fields, their efforts are fruitless because it is God's will to allow Satan to continue sowing them. (I heard a lot of "oh know we are not's," but the truth is "oh yes we are.") Matthew 13: 30 Let both grow together until the harvest. Then I will tell the harvesters to sort out the weeds and burn them and put the wheat in the barn. If we separate them before God's time we will destroy the wheat along with the weeds. If we do not understand this wisdom we may destroy emerging prophets and other ministries.

Sometime we need a "Jacob" nature so we can experience the kind of encounter with God when he wrestled with him. We must not esteem peace and harmony above the purpose of God. We must certainly value peace and unity, but not at the expense of the ultimate purpose of God. Only the people who now are found in cemeteries are in perfect order and harmony, because all healthy living things grow; all growing things change; and change brings challenge.

In trusting the Lord to lead us into the truth rather than trusting that Satan will lead us into deception, in this way will the clear blessing of prophecy be gifted to us. Matthew 10: 40-42 Anyone who is welcoming you is welcoming me, and anyone who welcomes me is welcoming the Father who sent me. If you welcome a prophet as one who speaks for God, you will receive the same reward a prophet gets. And if you welcome good and godly people because of their goodness, you will be given a reward like theirs. And if you give even a cup of cold water to one of the least of my followers, you will surely be rewarded.

If only the leaders of our disjointed world would listen to God's Word, and direct their people in accord with God's Will. Then they would know the meaning of peace, and they would rejoice in the ways of God. The Lord himself has even magnified his Word above his Name. So let not our names be our identity, for we will be judged by our words, not our titles or reputation. To be able to speak the Lord's Words on his behalf is one of the greatest responsibilities a person can receive. So it must be handled with the greatest of care and integrity.

If we are seeking the recognition and approval of men then the degree of our ministry and word will be corrupted. Galatians 1: 6-10 I am astonished that you are so quickly deserting the one who called you by the grace of Christ and are turning to a different gospel – which is really no gospel at all. Evidently some people are throwing you into confusion and are trying to prevent the gospel of Christ. But even if we or an angel from heaven should preach a gospel other than the one we preached to you, let him be eternally condemned! Am I now trying to win approval of men, or God? Or am I trying to please men? If I were trying to please men, I would not be a servant of Christ. A person who fears God more than man will be perceived as a threat to the world and its interests. So a true prophet in fact will be a great threat to people's perversion's. But at the same time bring great hope for their Salvation.

So I need for Christ to search me, and teach me my heart.

1 Kings 18: 17-18 When he saw Elijah, he said to him, "Is that you, you troubler of Israel?" "I have not made trouble for Israel," Elijah replied. "But you and your fathers family have. You have abandoned the Lord's commands and have followed the Baals.

Teach me my anxious thoughts, and trial me.

1 Kings 19: 12 After the earthquake came fire, but the Lord was not in the fire. And after the fire came a gentle whisper.

Remove all hurtful ways which are buried in my heart, so You lead me, allowing me to step into the everlasting promises of your ways.

Joel 3:16 The Lord will roar from Zion and thunder from Jerusalem; the earth and the sky will tremble. But the Lord will be a refuge for his people, a strong hold for the people of Israel. If we know the Lord, we will recognize his voice regardless of the manner in which he speaks.

The purpose in this world for me is to get to heaven. Bringing as many souls with me as I can.

1 Corinthians 1: 5-7 For in him you have been enriched in every way – in all your speaking and in all your knowledge – because our testimony about Christ was confirmed in you. Therefore you do not lack any spiritual gifts as you eagerly wait for our Lord Jesus Christ to be revealed. All of these complete testimonies of Christ can only be presented by all the gifts and ministries functioning together as one unit.

My thinking has become peaceful, calm and centered. I hear with love. I love and approve of myself, as god supports and loves me.

John 17: 22-23 I have given them the glory that you gave me, that they may be one as we are one: I in them and you in me. May they be brought to complete unity to let the world know that you sent me and have loved them even as you loved me.

Covenant prophesying is to be in harmony with the full revelation of God's person, nature and commission, as manifested in the rest of the gifts and ministries distributed to the church.

Hebrews 1: 1-2 In the past God spoke to our forefathers through the prophets at many times and in many ways, but in these last days he has spoken to us by his Son, whom he has appointed heir of all things, and through whom he made the universe.

I had a dream: I lost all my bottom teeth, they just crumbled out with no pain. There was someone gentle with me so I did not panic, and then our veterinarian was going to change his whole schedule around to operate on me. I said no there is no pain and I must go to work, so I went to work. When I woke up I had a small sore in the middle of my bottom lip which did not hurt. Then as I was reading the Bible that day, I read, Isaiah 6: 5-6 I said, "There is no hope for me! I am doomed because every word that passes my lips is sinful, and I live among a people whose every word is sinful. And yet with my own eyes I have seen the King, the Lord Almighty." Then one of the creatures flew down at me, carrying a burning coal that he had taken from the alter with a pair of tongs. He touched my lips with the burning coal and said, "This has touched your lips, and now your guilt is gone, and your sins are forgiven.

I am releasing the past, so that I may be free to move forward with love in my heart. My mind and soul are clear, and open to the Spirit for this wonderful journey I have stepped onto.

Beyond: When we call on Messiah, it is not some abstract belief about Jesus' essence, but rather the belief that Jesus is 'the life' through whom the Word of God is spoken, and the Will of God is being lived out, through us in accordance with the Holy Spirit. A life which the reality of God is being experienced.

Isaiah 44: 24-28 "This is what the lord says – your Redeemer, who formed you in the womb; I am the Lord, who has made all things, who alone stretches out the heavens, who spread out the earth by myself, who foils the signs of false prophets and makes fools of diviners, who overthrow the learning of the wise and turn it into nonsense, who carries out the words of his servant and fulfill the predictions of his messenger, who says of Jerusalem, 'it shall be inhabited,' of the towns of Judah, 'they shall be built,' and their ruins, 'I will restore them,' who says to Cyrus, 'He is my shepherd and will accomplish all that I please; he will say to Jerusalem, "Let it be rebuilt," and of the temple, "Let its foundation be laid."

Now Cyprus of Persian was not a man which someone would discern that the Will of God would be accomplished through, a man who either knew the Torah nor the name of Yahweh. Wow, who are the messengers? Who are the chosen ones? We must be able to look beyond what we understand! And start getting the way God works or we will miss the mark. So let's continue in Isaiah.

Isaiah 45: 1-13 "This is what the Lord says to his anointed, to Cyrus, who's right hand I take hold of to subdue nations before him and to strip kings of their armor, to open doors before him so that gates will not be shut: I will go before you and will level the mountains; I will break down gates of bronze and cut through bars of iron. I will give you the treasures of darkness, riches stored in secret places, so that you may know that I am the Lord, the God of Israel, who summons you by name. For the sake of Jacob my servant, of Israel my chosen, I summon you by name and bestow on you c. title of honor, though you do not acknowledge me. I am the Lord and there is no other; apart from me there is no God. I will strengthen you, though you have not acknowledged me, so that of the rising of the sun to the place of it's setting men may know there is none besides me.

I am the Lord and there is no other, I form the light and create darkness I bring prosperity and create disaster; I the Lord do all things. "You heavens above, rain down righteousness; let the clouds shower it down. Let the earth open wide, let Salvation spring up, let righteousness grow with it; I the Lord, have created it. Woe to him that quarrels with his Maker, to him is but a potsherd on the ground. Does the clay say to the potter, "What are you making?" Does your work say, 'He has no hands?' Woe to him who says to his father, 'What have you begotten?' or to his mother, 'What have you brought to birth?' This is what the Lord says – the Holy One of Israel, and it's Maker; concerning things to come, do you question me about my children, or give me orders about the work of my hands? It is I who made the earth and created mankind upon it. My own hands stretched out the heavens; I marshalled their starry host. I will raise Cyrus in my righteousness: I will make all his ways straight. He will rebuild my city and set my exiles free, but not for a price or reward, says the Lord almighty.

Here lies the Church.

One Palm Sunday as I sat in church, I was blessed with a shower of lights, full of living colours. Colours that danced, sang, and were more beautiful than I have ever seen. They were over me around me even in me. A personal covenant promise from God to me. I could feel Jesus fill my entire being.

Hymn of Thanksgiving: A day is coming when people will sing, "I praise you Lord! You were angry with me, but now you comfort me and are angry no longer. God is my Saviour; I will trust him and not be afraid. The Lord gives me power and strength he is my Saviour. As fresh water brings joy to the thirsty, so God's people rejoice when he saves them." "Give thanks to the Lord! Call for him to help you! Tell all the nations what he has done! Tell them how great he is! Sing to the Lord because of the great things he has done. Let the whole world hear the news. Let everyone who lives in Zion shout and sing! Israel's Holy God is great, and he lives among his people."

I would like to share the time I went into meditation listening to a praise and worship CD. Abba Daddy scooped me up into his arms, and I felt like I was being cradled like a newborn baby, in the most loving, most gentle arms. I was safe, and loved like I never remembered. Acts 2: 25-28 King David said this about him: "I know the Lord is always with me. I will not be shaken, for he is right beside me. No wonder my heart is filled with joy, and my mouth shouts his praise! My body rests in hope. For you will not leave my soul among the dead or allow your Holy One to rot in the grave. You have shown me the way of life, and you will give me wonderful joy in your presence."

I trust the process of God. All I need is always taken care of, even if not in my understanding. I am safe.

New Anointing: The invitation from the throne is "Come as you are." It does not however say or even allow us to "stay where we are," once we have come. Romans 6: 1-10 What shall we say then? Shall we go on sinning so that grace may increase? By no means! We die to sin; how can we live in it any longer? Or don't you know that all of us who were baptized into Jesus Christ were baptized into his death? We were therefore buried with him through baptism into his death in order that, just as Christ was raised from the dead through the glory of the Father, we may live a new life. If we have been united with him like this in his death we will certainly also be united with him in resurrection. For we know that our old self was crucified with him so that the body of sin might be done away with, that we should no longer be slaves to sin – because anyone who has died has been freed from sin. Now if we died with Christ, we believe that we will also live with him. The death he died he died to sin once for all, but the life he lives, he lives to God.

Hope: For revival, unity, peace, etc. Lays in an ALL –embracing attitude of forgiveness of the people who we consider enemies. Forgiveness is not mere religious sentimentality, it is as fundamental a law of the human spirit as the law of gravity is to the world. If you break the law of gravity your consequence could be a broken neck. If you break the law of forgiveness your consequence could be a broken spirit. Forgiveness is our problem, not God's. But remember in order to receive forgiveness we must first forgive.

There are people who follow the rules and miss God, and there are people who break the rules and find God. God does not look at our outward appearance, so listen for the melody of the gospel of grace and missing God is not a problem.

Legalism might seem hard at first glance, but actually freedom in Christ is the harder way. It is relatively easy not to murder, hard to reach out in love to someone unlovable. Easier to avoid a neighbours bed than to keep a marriage alive. Easier to pay taxes than to serve the poor. When living in freedom, we must remain open to the Holy Spirit for guidance. We become more aware at what we have neglected rather than what we have achieved. We can no longer hide behind a mask of certain behaviours, for certain circumstances.

"The action of prayer to bring heaven down to earth always results in bringing hell up from bellow."

It is easy to get swept into a justified prejudice over what is happening around us in the world. This is why Jesus COMMANDS, "love your enemies." Who are the enemies? To each one of us it is something different, that's why if our activism, however well-motivated drives out love, we have misunderstood Jesus' gospel, stuck with law not the gospel of grace.

We as Christians have a completely different set of weapons when we go out to war, we carry weapons such as 'weapons of mercy, forgiveness, grace.' Not political correctness or moral superiority. We as Christians ought to be marching unto war demonstrating the 'fruits' of God's Spirit: love, joy, peace, patience, kindness, goodness, fruitfulness, gentleness, and self-control. The harder much harder war to engulf in.

Government, can shut down stores on Sunday, but they cannot compel worship. They can arrest and punish wrong doers, but cannot cure hatred or make someone love. It can make laws to make divorce harder to obtain, but cannot force husband and wife to love one another. It can provide subsidies for the poor, but cannot force the rich to show them compassion and justice. It can ban adultery, but not lust, cheating, or pride. It can encourage virtue but cannot produce righteousness.

Being a true Christian is total release to God Almighty. I am the sacrifice. I am only to give myself totally to God, and not allow myself to be controlled by anything else, not even other people.

"The stone that you builders despised turned out to be the most important of all." Because of the stone (Jesus) we live and move and exist as one family all of us God's children. So I Shout Holy, Holy, Holy! The Lord Almighty is Holy. His glory fills heaven and earth and the whole universe, and I am sure still even beyond.

I will no longer fear, and put all my trust in God's Will for me, and pray I will always be bold enough to obey God.

But the Lord says, "Can an axe claim to be greater than the man who uses it? Is a saw more important than the man who saws with it? A club does not lift up a man; a man lifts up a club.

It was a wonderful awakening in this journey when I realized that Jesus was the first gift ever given to me through pure love. Not out of guilt or necessity, (birthday, anniversary, mother's day) imagine just there for the taking. The true miracle being, my acceptance of this wonderful gift with an open heart. And believing that I am worthy of the Holy Spirit living in me.

"Faith that is firm is also patient. Justice will be the measuring line for the foundation and honesty will be the plumb line."

Trapped in a game called Church: The churches one and only foundation is Jesus. She is his new creation the Spirit of the Word. From heaven he came and saw her to be his holy bride, with his own blood he bought her. And the great church victorious shall be the church at rest.

Are you religious? Do you sometimes feel like you have been trapped into playing the game called 'church'? Can the Bible offer understandable answers to the spiritual questions being asked by a generation that is tired of religious rules and church-ianity?

Being Christian is not about trying to find God or please him through your own futile efforts. Being Christian is trusting through God's marvelous grace and mercy he has reached out and found you. If ever you will receive a gift, this is the one. Because our society seems to claim there is no absolute truth of any kind, and this my friend is a lie, because once you have received Christ he is truth.

Religion reaches up to God. Christianity is God living in our hearts. We have an absolute truth as Christians, which is, that God found us while we were searching he was finding. In our religious efforts, we deal with God on our own terms, when it is convenient for us, putting us in control. Christianity is responding in thanksgiving, and willing to serve at any time because of what God has done for us. A hard to admit even a downright crushing blow, a very easy path to step onto, is instead of responding to God's love we reach out to it on our own terms –keeping God at arm's length.

To have a living faith means more than a mental consent to a statement of belief, or an opinion. A living faith is full of power from the Holy Spirit, which put us in touch with God our Father. Romans 1: 16-17 For I am not ashamed of this good news about Christ. It is the power of God at work, saving every one who believes – Jews first and also Gentiles. This good news tells us how God makes us right in his sight. This is accomplished from start to finish by faith. As Scripture say, "It is through faith that a righteous person has life."

I would like to share what the gospel is "not". The gospel is not laws and burdens, or religious do's and don'ts. It is not man made ideas. The gospel is not something man could have created: we do not act in this way, no matter hard we might try.

Am I ready to share the gospel? Sharing is not preaching, not even teaching. It is living from it then sharing your life in it. The good news is realizing the power the gospel gives to the meaning of life, which leads us in God's true purpose and focus.

The Gospel is not anti-intellectual, actually it is very intellectual in a simplistic, humiliating way. There are people who reject the gospel, searching for a more sophisticated, intelligent belief system, thinking the gospel is for the ignorant or that it is even suspicious. This is total nonsense however, because yes even though Christianity is entered through a door of faith, Jesus himself commands us to love God with all our minds plus more. Mark 12: 30 And you must love the Lord your God with all your heart, all your soul, and all your mind, and all your strength.

So how then would it be possible to worship God – but keep him very small? Trying to fit him into our box of our brand of Christianity? My friends trust in the fact that Christianity is not a mindless religion.

God's creation is rebelling against him. Seeing no need to turn to God. Instead asking what right God has to interfere with their lives? Wanting to do as they please, and be their own boss. Having drifted so far from God they no longer see or even care about the consequences of their actions. And here is the result. In this selfishness everything they touch corrupts.

Romans 2: 1 You may be saying, "What a terrible people you have been talking about!" But you are just as bad, and you have no excuse! When you say they are wicked and should be punished, you are condemned yourself, for you do the very same thing.

I know longer ask: why was I born? Instead I thank God for my life, actually, every breath is thanksgiving and testifying to the Father's unfailing love. Praising him for everything he has done for me and through me. I am the most blessed person on the face of this earth. How about you? Let's worship him with a prayer right now. "O, God of peace who taught us that in returning and in rest we shall be saved, in quietness and confidence shall be our strength; by the might of your Spirit lift us, we pray into your presence, where we may be still and know that you are God."

Remember that it is your own face that you see reflected in the water and it is your own self you see in your heart.

Remove fear/Grab victory/ Shout rejoice: Faith; being sure and certain of what we believe and do not see, birth to your destiny, leaping into the arms and character of God. Our desire will equal our reality, remember God wants to give us the desires of our heart. So my desire is to be guided into discipleship, praying for the anointing into authority . The authority for me to enforce Gods mercy, grace, healing, love into the created world. After being saved we become one body accomplishing God's Will.

Luke 4: 16-21 He came to Nazareth where he had been reared. As he always did on the Sabbath, he went to the meeting place. When he stood up to read, he was handed the scroll of the prophet Isaiah. Unrolling the scroll, he found the place where it was written, Gods Spirit is on me; he's chosen me to preach the message of good news to the poor, sent me to announce pardon to prisoners and recovery of sight to the blind. To set the burdened and battered free, to announce, "This is God's year to act!" He rolled up the scroll, handed it back to the assistant, and sat down. Every eye on the place was on him, intent. Then he started in, "You've just heard Scripture make history. It came true now in this place."

Why do we seek God's Word? To eat and drink from the glory of heaven. To be formed more into the image of Christ. To refresh us in revelations, to facts we have heard over and over again. We are always under construction in becoming the masterpiece from God.

Romans 10: 1-13 Brothers, my hearts desire and prayer to God for the Israelites is that they be saved. For I can testify about them that they are zealous for God, but their zeal is not based on knowledge. Since they did not know the righteousness that comes from God and sought to establish their own, they did not submit to God's righteousness. Christ is the end of the law so that there may be righteousness for everyone who believes. Moses describes in this way the righteousness that is by the law: "The man who does these things will live by them." But the righteousness that is by faith says: "Do not say in your heart, Who will ascend into heaven (that is, to bring Christ down) or Who will ascend into the deep?" (that is bring Christ up from the dead). But what does it say? "The word is near you; it is in your mouth, and in your heart ." That is , the word of faith we are proclaiming; that if you confess with your mouth, "Jesus is Lord", and believe in your heart that God raised him from the dead, you will be saved. For it is with your heart that you believe and are justified, and it is with your mouth that you confess and are saved. As the Scripture says, "Anyone who trust in him will never be put to shame." For there is no difference between Jews and Gentiles- the same Lord is Lord of all and richly blessed all who call on him. For, "Everyone who calls on the name of the Lord will be saved."

The new church will be formed in truth, formed by God alone. (I am now going to sing for you) "GLORY/GLORY HALLALULIAH! GLORY/GLORY HALLALULIAH! GLORY/GLORY HALLALULIA! His truth is marching on!" We can only know what we have seen or heard. God is creating the predestined Church that only God knows, and we must be willing to receive. Remember that our Father is very secure and is willing to answer all our questions. As people are stepping back Jesus is appearing more. We need to remove all fear, replacing it with praise, rejoicing, Thanksgiving in everything. The Victory is Gods, so come on messengers of authority "Shout Grace!" Wisdom, victory, power of conviction, truth, faith, integrity, righteousness, already all unveiled.

Light: It is not what we do, that can bring us closer to God, or make us righteous, actually in this state of spirit we will accomplish nothing. It is being in relationship with Abba Daddy, When we are living strictly with God, then the things we do and say come out clean from our hearts, and in this state of spirit all we want to do is please Abba Daddy, so we 'want' to do right, not 'have' to do right.

Isaiah 26: 1-6 At that time, this song will be sung in the country of Judah. We have a strong city, built and fortified with salvation. Throw wide the gates so good and true people can enter. People with their minds set on you, you keep completely whole, steady on their feet, because they keep at it and don't quit. Depend on God and keep at it because in the Lord God you have a sure thing. Those who lived high and mighty he knocked off their high horse. He used the city built on the hill as fill for the marches. All the exploited and outcast peoples build their lives on the reclaimed land.

As I was working in the garden one day, my right hand hurt so bad I could hardly move it. I held on to the pain all afternoon and into the night. Then I had a great idea, I asked for the pain to please be removed. And low and behold the pain left and I was able to move my hand again. Thanks be to God. This was the way God chose to heal at this time God heals in many very different ways so please do not get discouraged when your healing is not to the direct order of your wish, always trust all prayer is answered for the purpose of God and what is best for all not just comfortable for one.

The next day after the memory of this miracle was still very fresh in my mind I drove into to town to do errands. I saw my mum, who at this point in my life I had not talked to for at least a year. I was stopped at a red light at the same intersection she was making a left hand turn, causing us to see eye to eye for a moment. She looked hurt and lonely, just as I was. At this point my spirit was washed clean from all the anger and misunderstanding I was hanging onto. I said Hi! Mum as she drove past. And once more thanked God.

In our lives, in our mind in our heart we have so much that blocks your love from us. I would like to stop and pray together once again: Abba Daddy, "Where shame and embarrassment darken us, where fear or timidity has held us captive, where secrecy and disgrace has twisted us away from you. O God, send your Spirit. Wash us in your healing forgiveness. Strengthen us to grow as we should. Bring us into the Light of your Son. Amen.

Today my parents and I have a good relationship, because I have the strength to face all conditions by the power that Christ gives me. Be on watch and pray always that you will have the strength to go safely through all those things that will happen, and stand before the Son of Man.

Don't hide just seek: Someone who seeks help because of difficulty, is led to an understanding in God's place for their existence, and they are encouraged in faith and taught to pray. Someone who seeks when full of anxiety, is led to see the connection between God's Will and others who are in their lives. Like for instance somebody who lives in the same house, or from the same neighbourhood, or from work. Taking the anxiety and learning how to express it with connection acts such as forgiveness, compassion, affection, turning it around to full service. Discovering God's Will and love at the centre of every encounter. "A Saved People," defined, shaped and centered not by military, political or environmental forces but by the act of God. Salvation is God acting decisively from history so that each person, both individually and corporately is free to live in faith for eternity. Again: Salvation is God doing for us what we cannot do for ourselves, overcoming the power of bondage, leading us through the forces of evil, establishing us his children on facts as his precious ones. Salvation is an event that demonstrates beyond argument that God saves his people. Even today its meaning stands firm in terms with the hard edged historical reality that we owe our present existence to an act of God that rescues us from that which we are doomed, and sets us in a new way of life against all worldly odds, and that makes us whole for a life of faith. The word 'Salvation', in the course of its Biblical usage develops both a sense of rescue from destruction and restoration to health, meaning to be whole. It does not matter how closely evil hedges around us. God will clear for us all the spaces we need to move around it.

Psalm 118: 4-7 Let those who fear the Lord say, "His love endures forever." In my anguish I cried to the Lord, and he answered me; I will not be afraid. What can man do to me? The Lord is with me; he is my helper. I will look in triumph on my enemies.

We need to be careful not too hid behind an experience of only ritual, remember always seek reality, not getting lost in the institution but being found in Salvation. The Song of Songs function by taking up the theme of Saving Love, the kind of love that rescues from non-being, and creates, being-in relationship. Life changing love, massive and overpowering in the history of the Exodus. A love without lust that is celebrated in personal relationship in a language that everyone can understand and experience. The love lyrics of the Song of Songs are to guard against every tendency to turn a living faith into a lifeless religion. They make sure that we proclaim, the truth of God, and that we do not exclude faith in God, providing correctives to our tendencies to reduce faith to a tradition. Insist that however impressive the acts of God and however exalted the truth of God, they are not to great or high to be experienced by ordinary people like you and me. 'Faith and Truth' workable in this habitual world.

When I first got saved we owned a restaurant. One day a robin was trying to get in via a closed window. This went on all afternoon and evening obviously drawing a lot of attention from the guests. The next day the robin was back again and still trying to get through the window. So we covered the window, but that robin just went the next window, so we covered that one as well, and this went on till all seven big windows were covered. Yes it finally stopped. So I thought till after the lunch hour when I stepped out to the patio, and there was the robin sitting next to the flower boxes next to the window calling his heart out. The next day the whole thing started all over again. Now there were no curtains on these windows that could be drawn, so each window had a different unique covering made up special, one had a cut up cardboard box, a garbage bag on another one, and a serving tray on another and so it went for each window. But this day none of these obstacles seemed to be a deferent for this robin, this day it was determined and there was no stopping it. So we finally just had to remove the robin.

Now it is clear how hard God tries to get into our hearts and no matter how many obstacles are in his way he never gives up. So my friend I pray we stand firm, and never remove God.

Changing God's message? Hear me close: The church seems to be adding spiritual 'technologies', extra Biblical ideas and teachings to enhance ministries and increase manifestations of the Power of the Lord, and as a comforting tool the church is deleting things as well. The only reason for these changes that I can see seems to be an insufficient faith to believe that the simplicity of the revelation delivered to the saints and recorded in Scripture really do work.

Ezekiel 13: 2-8 "Son of man, prophecy against the prophets of Israel. Tell those who make up their prophesies, 'Listen to the Word of the Lord.' This is what the Lord Almighty says, 'How horrible it will be for the foolish prophet.' They follow their own ideas, and they have seen nothing. Israel, your prophets are like foxes among the ruins of a city. They haven't repaired the gaps in the wall or rebuilt the wall for the nation of Israel. So Israel will not be protected in battle on the day of the Lord. These foolish prophets see false visions, and their predictions don't come true. They say, 'The Lord said this,' but the Lord hasn't sent them. Then they hope that their message will come true. Prophets of Israel, haven't you seen false visions and predicted things don't come true? Don't you say, 'The Lord said this,' even though I have not said anything?" This is what the Almighty Lord says, "Your predictions are false, and your vision are lies. That is why I am against you, declares the Lord Almighty."

Pray that we would be those who stand in the gap, following only the ways of the Lord, building a strong kingdom on the foundation of Jesus for his return.

Romans 12: 6 God in his kindness gave each of us a different gift. If your gift is speaking God's Word, make sure what you say agrees with the Christian faith.

To be a 'Happy' people, is to make peace with our gift, and with God. Seeking the presence and heart of God, and allowing suffering to become the character change it was intended to produce. Stepping in to a deep abiding peace full of joy that will not be easily shaken by burdens.

Galatians 6: 2 Help carry each other's burdens. In this way you will follow Christ's teachings.

When hearing from God, ask, is there any reason for this message in my own life? If there is no adequate answer to be found, I can then believe that what I am hearing is for someone else. Now I pray for revelation, and continue on praying concerning the revelation I have received.

Why all this praying you ask? Well because I am known to suppress my emotions, rather than healthy emotion release. And so I tend to place my emotions in a 'closet' in my heart without dealing with them while I go about my daily business. Very destructive this behaviour. Locked in the closet the feelings have nowhere to go. As these emotions build up, they become this huge mass undefined pain and confusion that at some point can no longer be controlled or understood. When the closet is full, the pain locked away here starts to overflow, making it very difficult to hear God clearly. 1 Peter 5: 6-7 Be humbled by God's power so that when the right time comes he will honour you. Turn all anxiety over to God because he cares for you.

Well my friend I have been doing all the talking up till now and I am out of breath so to speak, plus God has asked me to shut my mouth for awhile and we want to hear a story from you. So just sit back relax and tell me a story of God in your life. I am a good listener, and God is even a better one.

Well I am going to take you back to that restaurant we once owned. There was a time just before closing the restaurant down I was getting discouraged about business being slow, then had a very busy weekend. Man it was busy and the money was great. Here is when I realized how rich I already was, not with money, but in Christ. I am one of the wealthiest people on earth, if you measure me in Christ.

Proverbs 6: 16-19 There are seven things that the Lord hates and cannot tolerate: A proud look, a lying tongue, hands that kill innocent people, a mind that thinks up wicked plans, a feet that hurray off to do evil, a witness who tells one lie after another; a man who stirs up trouble among friends.

These are not to be used as judgement towards others, or for tools on how to change someone else. These are tools for us to use on us and us alone.

I would like to praise God at this time for how he has changed my life, and has opened up my study. Bringing the revelation into my life on how his Word is alive, for me today, not just in history but in truth of: it was, it is now, and it is to come. Allowing me to be a glove for him to reach others. Learning who Sylvia really is. Sylvia is, a creation from God, the daughter (in-law because I am the bride of his only son Jesus) in his family whose purpose when working with the Holy Spirit, is released into Christ's unity as a part of one body.

Here is how it feels having the Holy Spirit living in me, it is like he is hugging my heart. I hope he is hugging your heart as well right now.

Rejoicing to be different in God: Is our talk of the kingdom of God? Or are we just putting plastic flowers in peoples drab lives? Well intentional attempts to brighten a bad scene? Not totally without use, but not real in any determination or living sense. If so we slowly but irresistibly begin to adopt the opinion, God is not so much alive, but rather a legend, believing the kingdom will be wonderful once we get past this world, but as for now we had best work on the terms that this world gives us. Have we led ourselves to be distracted, diverted and seduced? Have conditions changed? Changed so much in our day and age that prayer is no longer to be the first act? The giving form, the serving form.

The role of community in prayer should be the first act in everything. When people get together and join their prayers in the act of worship, it is neither disorganized, careless, or helter-skelter, rather it is dramatic and basic. It embraces the whole of society in a powerful grip, moulding ideas in the spirit, instructing values and acting as a clue for binding the community together. The prayers of the people for the people are the most important thing we can do.

It is the Psalms that provide the language, the strong desire, energy for the community as it comes together in prayer and from there is called into being. Helping to shape the activities of the prophets. The Psalms indicate; the prophets follow. The inner action of prayer takes priority over the outer action of proclaiming. The involvement of prayer in kingdom work is plain to understand; because it is in prayer where it all originates then allows us to become participants. If we seek to follow the example of the preaching and moral action of the prophets without also seeking the example of the prophets deep praying and worshiping, we become an embarrassment to the faith and a burden to the church.

Our characteristic speech form should not be myth, it should be prayer, as we hear the voice of God. Forming our life on a deeply committed position on the acts of God. There is always something that needs doing about the human condition, in all of us. But attempts from men and women are not what primarily needs to be heard. Instead it is what God is saying and doing. And in order to get in on that action we must pray. Our purpose is not to know the ins and outs of the human race, but instead be part of what is going on with God.

We need to become experts in setting human existence in response to God. Having a prayer for every occasion not just a story, because yes for sure stories are very useful but prayer my friend is essential. Because in prayer we deal with God and his Will first then the world. We need to experience the world not as a problem to be solved but in a reality in which God is acting. Hebrews 4: 12-13 For the word of God is living and active. Sharper than a double-edged sword, it penetrates even to divide soul and spirit, joint's and marrow it judges the thoughts and attitudes of the heart. Nothing in all creation is hidden from God's sight. Everything is uncovered and laid bare before the eyes of him to whom we must give account.

My husband had a surprise birthday party for me once the reason this one was so special to me is because it was given with me in mind. When having to deal with groups of people even family members and close friends, I prefer to have them come into where I already am rather than me walk into the midst of them. This is the reason I am always early no matter where I go because this way again people coming to me not me entering into a group. So back to the party I was there already actually I was working it was at our restaurant. And they all came into me saying surprise one at a time it was the time of my life as I was drinking in every blessing from so many of the special gifts from God in my life. The band that played every Saturday on the patio even came and played as a gift to me for my Birthday. Thank You God for the special people you have put in my life, even my family though they drive me nuts at times.

2 Corinthians 12: 9-10 But his answer was: "My grace is all you need for my power is greatest when you are weak." I am most happy, then to be proud of my weakness, in order to feel the protection of Christ's power over me. I am content with weakness, insults, hardships, persecutions and difficulties for Christ's sake. For when I am weak, then I am strong.

It is amazing to me how much like untamed animal's we have become. We need God to teach us how to obey his voice all over again, there are so many different ways to hear this voice but one very important way is through the special people he has purposed for our lives, and me for theirs. I am so thankful and grateful for the grace and mercy , which returned me to God's fresh and unique life, with a clear and practical understanding that will help me to walk in obedience, where all bondage can be broken healing hurts and wounds.

One of the best things from the Good News, is that with my head hung in shame and disgrace because of sin God always rescues me and forgives me when I repent and start listening to him again. And I am also grateful and thankful in the hard part from the Good News, when I need to forgive as much as I have been forgiven because this keeps me free as free can be. And tame under the freest trainer around, Jesus Christ.

Wilderness suffering remains the path to glory: A good reason to journal is the provision it provides to means of training my senses to see clearly, true from false. And be able to review things which I believe the Lord has spoken and compare those things to the ways in which reality actually unfolds. Journaling as brutally embarrassing as it may get, helps to inform us in solid black and white terms stripping us naked in bare truth to when it is God we heard or the occasions we heard exactly what we wanted to hear, OUCH! Writing things down really helps to keep us from being dominated by the emotions of the moment. The problem with feeling is that feelings by themselves are changeable and often chemically induced. By keeping record I am reminded of the consistent direction the Father has set for my life and what has or will never change, no matter how my feelings may vary. Journaling puts something solid in front of me, leaving me free to focus on one thing and one thing only, intimacy with Abba Daddy. It is discipline, yes, but hey discipline in a way of life.

Now as if this was not hard enough we now are going to take this one step further. Are you ready? What I believed I have heard must be checked against the perceptive or understanding of someone else, and not those who flatter me but someone with courage and security to challenge me. All this lining up with God's Word…..

Hearing God is not a science or a method but rather a function of a relationship. In this mind set hearing from God is a fluid dance of elements that move together in different ways to connect him at every level of our being. God is 'Alive' not an object or an impersonal force.

God spoke to Moses mouth to mouth as with a friend. So only seeking God through dreams and visions might mean we are so crippled in Spirit that this is the only way we can be reached. If we are not hearing the voice of God, along with dreams and visions, it could be evidence of dysfunction, not an advanced Spirit? When we limit ourselves to yearn for mystical experience only, rather than a complete relationship, we are cheating ourselves from the True Gift. "Jesus, teach me to be your friend". Ecclesiastes 5: 7 In spite of many daydreams, pointless actions, and empty words, you shall still fear God.

The new leadership about to emerge in the Body of Christ stands crushed, broken and humbled before God. They can be entrusted with the treasures of heaven because they will not assume power, a position, property, rights, in the Name of Jesus or abuse God's creation. They come with pure word (God's Word) uncoloured by the brokenness and ambitions from the human race. They are not perfect: Far from it! But love does cover a multitude of sins, and mercy truly triumphs over judgment. Our human nature, short of the Cross, cannot sustain the power and love God sends us. James 2: 12-13 Talk and act as people who are going to be judged by law that brings freedom. No mercy will be shown to those who show no mercy to others. Mercy triumphs over judgment.

My son had minor surgery done on his big toe. After the surgery the toe kept getting worse and worse. So bad in fact that a nurse had to come to our home and change the dressing every day. Now the bigger problem to this situation turns out to be the fact he was signed up for a six week survival camp with the cadets. This was a paid and certified course. He wanted this bad. All my special friend where praying for him. I went into a total surrender to God in the hospital washroom, and on my knees, opened myself up to God alone, and he filled me with strength, hope, love. I physically felt it. After that my son's toe was on a quick mend. He even got to go to camp. How great is our God!

Deception: A hidden reality not easy to detect. When we deceive others we are first deceived ourselves. Most of us do not begin with evil intent. The Devil, is a Spiritual being. And more time than not his usual mode of temptation in not obvious evil but to apparent good.

We are deceived when we glamorize congregations. Like for instance glitzy, enthusiastic churches cross our paths, and we start wondering what we are doing wrong. After some true examination it turns out that there is no such congregation. As we hang out long enough we will detect the gossip that never seems to stop spreading, material things that malfunction, sermons that misfire, disciple who quit, choirs that lose their tones and even tunes. Because every congregation is made up of sinners. And if this is not bad enough they have a sinner for a Pastor.

One of the oldest truths in spirituality: That it is in our moral righteous attitude where the danger is most likely for us to serve sin. It is when we are being good where the chance of being bad can creep up on us. When we are being responsible, being obedient, we must be careful that we don't replace our will for God's Will because we can easily be deceived that they are identical. It is the progression of being a good pastor, prophet, teacher, apostle, evangelist, we have the most chance of developing pride, arrogance and insensitivity. We need to remember and believe that God works his purpose through who we actually are, in our rash disobedience and our heatless obedience, and generously uses our lives as he finds us, to do his work. It is done in such a way that it is impossible for us to take credit for any of it, causing us to grasp in surprise pleasure at the victories God accomplishes. In spite of us. A lot of what the world refers to as religion is not gospel. Actually it is mostly idolatry. And even self elevation, a downright ego trip in some cases.

Religious activity is very common and even popular in our society in this day and age. In our country Canada there is absolute religious freedom, which means we have the right to be religious any old way that pleases us. But the question is does it resemble Biblical originals? Or is it based on a consumer religion? We need to be careful that we are not turning to religion as a product that will help us live well. And when it does not suit our purpose or comfort go shopping for the best deal, to the life we want not to the life we were created for.

There is only one shopping mall for Christians and that would be the Bible. And one of the many items available here is prayer, which is a connection of putting together separated parts and joints that cannot move on their own. But in harmony and in agreement and support of one another they respond to the Word of God. Here we allow exposure to what is unmanageable by us, and submit our live to him. Focusing on the awareness that God constitutes our work and lives.

Jonah 1 : 17-2:9 The Lord sent a big fish to swallow Jonah. Jonah was inside the fish three days and three nights. From inside the fish Jonah prayed to the Lord his God. Jonah prayed: "I called to the Lord in my distress, and he answered me. All your white caps on your waves have swept over me." Then I thought, 'I have banished from your sight. Will I ever see your holy temple again?' Water surrounded me, threatened my life. The deep sea covered me completely. Seaweed was wrapped around my head. I sank to the foot of the mountains. I sank to the bottom, where bars held me forever. But you brought me back from the pit. O Lord, my God. As my life was slipping away, I remembered the Lord. My prayer came to you in your holy temple. Those who hold on to worthless idols abandon their loyalty to you. But I will sacrifice to you with songs of thanksgiving. I will keep my vow. Victory belongs to the Lord!

A very special family member tried to commit suicide. Thank God for her special friends who were there to stop her, and loved her enough to come and tell me even though this threatened their very close friendship. And again thank you Father for the friends you have gifted me for this time to pray and love me through it all, and answering those prayers by sending the Holy Spirit to become one with the circumstance. This person is alive and well Praise the Lord!

I would like to sing with you now a favourite song of mine. Hope you like it as well.

-Have you seen Jesus my Lord? He's here in plain view, take a look, open your eyes. He'll show it to you.

-Have you ever looked at the sunset with the sky mellowin' red? And the clouds suspended like feathers? Then I say you've seen Jesus, my Lord.

-Have you ever stood at the ocean with the white foam at your feet? Felt the endless thunderin' motion? Then I say you've seen Jesus, my Lord.

-Have you ever looked at the cross with a man hangin' in pain? And the look of love in his eyes? Then I say you've seen Jesus, my Lord.

-Have you ever stood in the family with the Lord there in your midst? Seen the face of Christ on your neighbour? Then I sat you've seen Jesus, my Lord.

That was fun thank you for singing with me and the angels.

Church: is the whole family in heaven and earth. Ephesians 3: 14-19 For this reason I kneel before the Father, from whom his whole family in heaven and on earth derives its name, praying that out of his glorious riches he may strengthen you with power through his spirit in your inner being, so that Christ may dwell in your hearts through faith. And I pray that you being rooted and established in love, may have power, together with all the saints, to grasp how wide and long and high and deep is the love of Christ, and to know this love that surpasses knowledge - that you may be filled to the measure of all the fullness of God. …

Christ is the church the firm foundation and he gave his own life for it to belong to everyone. Dedicating and cleansing it with the washing of his Blood and the water by the Word, uniting all of us to himself a glorious church, not having spot or wrinkle or any such thing. But that we should be holy and without blemish. For no one should hate their own flesh; but nourish it and cherish it, just like the Son for the Father. So church is a learning place, that is safe in Christ, and all who want to know Jesus should be able to take part in this venture, continually learning how to behave in the house of God. Not in judgment but in love, which is the church of the "living God". The pillar and ground of Gods truth which is found in faith, not our truth because we have no idea what truth should look like.

Big churches with small empty soul people, are of not much use. Small churches with big people full of the Spirit souls' are of much greater value. Now imagine the power of a big church full of big people, WOW! The church should be constantly stretching its family spiritually and personally. Because the church is not just the building it is the life of everyone involved to it. Every creation has a purpose for their life, I feel so special knowing mine is for the Body of Christ. We are all blessed with gifts, talents, and different abilities to accomplish the work for his kingdom. Ephesians 4: 8-16 This is why it says: "When he ascends on high, he had captives in his train and gave gifts to men." (What does "he ascended" mean except that he also descended to the lower earthly regions? He who descended is the very one who ascended higher than all the heavens, in order to fill the whole universe.) It was he who gave some to be apostles, some to be prophets, some to be evangelists, and some to be pastors and teachers, to prepare Gods people for works of service, so that the body of Christ may be built up

Until we reach unity in the faith and in the knowledge of the Son of God and become mature, attaining to the whole measure of the fullness of Christ. Then we will no longer be infants, tossed back and forth by the waves, and blown here and there by every wind of teaching and by the cunning and craftiness of men in their deceitful scheming. Instead, speaking the truth in love, we will in all things grow up into him who is the Head, that is Christ. From him the whole body, joined and held together by every supporting ligament, grows and builds itself up in love, as each part does its work.

The church should not be an organization but an organism, in which God's plan is for the leaders to nurture in the people a dimension of who they were created to be. We should see ourselves as a tool of God's love and power where we are right now, no matter where that is, or what we do for a living. In this way every time we go to church something discernable, something of growth should be taking place inside of us, through the teaching, worship and prayer, keeping us refreshed, renewed, encouraged and edified. If these things are not happening for us when we go to church, then I am sorry to say that we are not being equipped to become all we were created to be. And we might want to ask ourselves if we are in the right church? God has a specific purpose for our lives, and when we ask and then listen, in faith God will guide us in the right direction.

No matter what our loved ones get into, what they do, who they see, what they say, we cannot for any reason use someone else's life or actions to affect our serenity. We cannot blame anyone else for how we feel, or react. All we can do is wait for them to cry out, reach out, for help. And once they do Praise God and accept where God leads them to obtain this help. The only help I can offer anyone is to go through God for their help, and allow the Holy Spirit to talk to their hearts, while we continue praying for them to find peace, hope, love, guidance to fill their hearts. The most important thing to remember is that no matter how much we love someone, or grateful we are that they are a part of our life, our Father is always Number One and only he can mend his children, and when he is our first love then everyone just seem to fall into place.

And my friend I know this from personal experience, one day when the life of my loved ones had my life in total turmoil, my left eye got infected. I got some drops, but it just seem to get worse. The as I was in the Word (Bible) I read Matthew 7:1-5 "Stop judging others, and you will not be judged. For others will treat you as you treat them. Whatever measure you use in judging others, it will be used to measure how you get judged. And why worry about a speck in your friend's eye when you have a log in your own? How can you think of saying, 'Let me help you get rid of that speck in your eye,' when you can't see past the log in your own eye? Hypocrites! First get rid of the log in your own eye, Then perhaps you will see well enough to deal with the speck in your friend's eye.

I realized the log in my eyes were getting out of control, this was such a blessing to have God show me how jealous I was and the fear of becoming less venerable instead of being grateful I could get more humble if the people in my life where blessed with what was gifted to me. And who would be accountable for my feelings, who would there be to blame for the dysfunction in our life if we all got fixed. Not looking past the fact that if we are all fixed these would all disappear. I was so sorry for this and started really praying for the people gifted into my life, that they also be baptized by the Holy Spirit, and we can live together. Guess What? My eye healed.

Prayer of St. Francis: Let's pray it together. Make me a channel of your peace. Where there is hatred, let me bring your love, where there is injury, your healing power. And where there is doubt, true faith in you. Make me a channel of your peace: Where there is despair in life, let me bring hope. Where there is darkness, only light. And where there is sadness, ever joy. O, Spirit, grant that I may never seek so much to be consoled as to console. To be understood as to understand. To be loved as to love with all my soul. Make me a channel of your peace: It is in pardoning that we are pardoned. In giving to all, that what we have received. And in dying that we're born to eternal life.

In the beginning God created: It is incredible to realize that God created everything out of nothing. And I am going to be bold here and state my opinion, a revelation I believe I have received. We always talk about God creating in the past tense but has he stopped creating? I will let you think about this and I will move on.

We also create, but only with pre-existing materials. But when God creates he uses nothing but his Word he creates to take care of our needs, creating the pre-existing material for us to use. Psalm 147: 5 Great is our Lord and mighty in power, his understanding has no limit.

For us to create even the simplest objects takes hundreds of people with combined knowledge and even unrelated joint skills and efforts. No one person knows it all: (this goes for building the church as well.) Hebrews 11: 3 By faith we understand that the universe was formed at God's command, so that what is seen was not made out of what was visible.

It is for us to envision God being all-power full and all-knowing, rather than see him at all places at all time. But over and over again the Scripture teaches us that God is everywhere present. Psalm 139: 7-12 Where can I go from your Spirit? Where can I flee from your presence? If I go up to the heavens, you are there; if I make my bed in the depth, you are there. If I rise on the wings of the dawn, if I settle on the far side of the sea, even there your hand will guide me, your right hand will hold me fast. If I say, "Surely the darkness will hide me and the light become night around me," even the darkness will not be dark to you; the night will shine like the day, for the darkness is light to you.

The fact that God is everywhere at one time needs to be separated from the concept of pantheism, simply put pantheism teaches that God is in everything and everything is in God. In contrast, we will see that the Bible teaches that the Lord is distinct from his creation, he is not part of it. The Bible defines God as being, not some sort of abstract force. Isaiah 40: 28 Do you know? Have you heard? The Lord is the everlasting God, the creator of the ends of the earth. He will not grow tired or weary, and his understanding no one can fathom.

People can never make something flawless. What we produce may be quite acceptable, but it will still have defects. But when God creates everything is without fault. Genesis 1: 25 God made the wild animals according to their kind, the livestock according to their kind, and all the creatures that move along the ground according to their kind. And God saw that it was good.

Psalm 18: 30 As for God, his way is perfect; the Word of the Lord is flawless. He is a shield for all who take refuge in him.

God could have limited his creation of plant life to a few kinds, because just a few would provide our needs quite adequately. But no, we have an overwhelming variety. The Lord is a God who truly cares. 1 Timothy 6: 17 Command those who are rich in the present world not to be arrogant nor to put their hope in wealth, which is so uncertain, but to put their hope in God, who richly provides us with everything for our enjoyment.

God created man with a mind, so we are able to investigate, understand and create. Although we have intellect, we are not all-knowing, actually we are born into the world with little knowledge. All our knowing must be learned.

Emotions: The ability to feel is a very important aspect of being human. Without feeling, our response to others would be like that of a robot, cold and calculated. God created us with feelings, because he has feelings. A heartless, unaffected God without the capacity to feel, love or show compassion would be truly frightening.

Will: the capacity to choose and have preferences is what gives mankind variety, but we often take these decisions for granted. We were given a Will so we can freely follow God, not as a robot, but as one who grasps that God cares for us, and that is how we know God is looking out for our best interest.

1 Chronicles 29: 11 Yours, O Lord, is the greatness and the power and the glory and the majesty and the splendour, for everything in heaven and earth is yours. Yours, O Lord, is the kingdom; you are exalted as head over all.

There was a night when I was still going to a support group. I went to a meeting in a small town. I had not actually attended on a regular basis any more so this was a new group I had never been before. There was only one other lady there, what a special evening it turned out to be. Her and I were walking the same Spiritual path and seemed to be at the same place on our journey. It was awesome. We opened up to each other in pure honesty, sharing thing we would never have shared if there were others present, what a gift. Shows us how God always meets our needs, and his desire for our well being. So once again Praises are in order for the guidance and support from heaven.

Not long after this evening my husband and I were talking at dinner, and he informed me that he might like to start coming to church with me. I was excited about this. It took seven years to come to play so my friend do not get discouraged when hearing God's voice it does not ply out in your time, God's time is the only right time for anything. The way I think things should look like in our walk together with Christ is still very different to what they are. Not only do I feel we are not on the same page most times I feel like we are in totally different books. But I see the hand of God at work. When my husband finally did start coming to church his response to me for this decision was: "You always do things I enjoy doing with me example going to flea markets. I want to start doing something you enjoy doing with you." And his choice was coming to church with me, and then God got a hold of him ha ha ha. Now he has accepted Christ and has been baptized and God is still working.

Psalm 131 Lord, I have given up my pride and turned away from my arrogance. I am not concerned with great matters or with subjects to difficult for me. Instead, I am content and at peace. As a child lies quietly in its mother's arms, so my heart is quiet with in me. Israel, trust in the Lord now and forever.

As I journey on the path with Jesus it is amazing to see how safe from the darkness, and close to the kingdom we are. Because it was here on this path he brought me after rescuing me from myself mostly, setting me free in the release of my sins through his forgiveness.

Romans 8: 18 I consider that what we suffer at this time cannot be compared at all with the glory that is going to be revealed us.

Thank you Jesus, for your promise of never being abandoned again. It is exciting to share the new discoveries of a new day in God's creation, always something new and wonderful to taste and see. The joy to participate in the work of tending to our assigned task of learning more about God.

Romans 4: 1-4 I will extol the Lord at all times; his praise will always be on my lips. My soul will boast in the Lord; let the afflicted hear and rejoice. Glory the Lord is with me; let us exalt his name together. I sought the lord and he answered me; he delivered me from all my fears.

Rejoice and give thanks in and for everything. The worst thing in 'our' lives (not someone else's remember) get, the louder and longer our praises should become through worship.

Isaiah 33: 6 He will be the sure foundation for your times, a rich store of salvation and wisdom and knowledge; The fear of the Lord is the key to this treasure.

I need to take a moment and share together, with you, the repentance for my impatience of God's eternity. If you would like to share something here, I will listen, and pray healing into everything you are struggling with. And I ask you to stand in agreement with me as I pray to always be in God's time, eternity (no time) NOW, in trust and belief always in Abba Daddy.

Psalm 1: 3 He is like a tree planted by the streams of water, which yields its fruit in season and whose leaf does not wither. Whatever he does prospers.

When everyone will prefer everyone else before themselves, peace can reign in every corner of creation. No more battles or squabbles. Learning to hear God's voice and not Lucifer's who will say one thing while hiding the truth from our hearts. Lucifer will often say what we want to hear were as God will tell what needs to be heard for peace and love and joy and the list goes on, to happen. Be very careful to listen to what is being told not being said and this my friend is tricky because we do not like to be told much. Right? Come on now, Right? The phrase "Have you been told today" just flooded through my mind, and what a joy to say yup! Now I can spend this entire day in praise and worship from the Word of God and for the Word of God.

We need to heed the warning to us, mankind, the fruit of our Creator. Do not betray our intimacy through appearance. We need true and honest relationship so we do not destroy or change what God has indefinitely created us to be. Our honour for God must come from the inside (heart) out, because with an outward appearance only we will get filled with emotions, jealousy, offence, etc.

2 Timothy 3: 2-5 People will be lovers of themselves, lovers of money, boastful, proud, abusive, disobedient to their parents, ungrateful, unholy, without love, unforgiving, slanderous, without self control, brutal, not lovers of the good, treacherous, rash, conceited, lovers of pleasure rather than lovers of God – having a form of godliness but denying its power. Having nothing to do with them.

We must continually pray that these characteristics do not sneak into our lives through appearance, stripping us from the complete intimacy of God's purpose for us.

Even though we try to commit sin in secret, though not publicly announced, sin will always be visible to God, consequently visible through creation. So as we attend to our routines, pastimes, work let's do it with worshiping God, and coming together in fellowship, fun, with God kept hearts. Being filled with the peace and joy from God for the living Word and in the living Word. Do not allow yourself to be coerced with power and position.

Understand the intimacy the Lord has for us, and enter into the relationship as the bride with her groom. Constantly check your heart with caution that you are living the Living Word of God. Making sure masked beauty, false splendour, charm, pride, some of many deceptions which are a form of corrupt wisdom are not taking root. Ezekiel 28: 17 Your heart became proud on account of your beauty, and your corrupted wisdom because of your splendour. So I threw you to the earth; I made a spectacle of you before kings.

Something I am really focusing on is the fight and questioning that creep up in me when fantastic changes occur. Learning to just plain enjoy the presence of the Holy Spirit in me, walking together in faith hand in hand with my family toward the kingdom. Understanding, trusting, believing I am a Spirit filled person – not crazy.

When we pray it is not just asking for things from God. Nope, when we pray is also the time to listen for God and do what he is asking us to do. I am learning to open my heart in prayer and in this my mind and mouth seem to close down, this is a good thing believe it or not. The more I prayed the more of a difference I was experiencing, it was not easy to figure out the difference actually I couldn't figure it out, God had to speak to me, and man what a revelation when I heard. It was one night a prayer meeting and here is what God wanted me to do. He wanted me to share with the others the prayer he had given to me. It became doable to pray God's Word, not having to think of words that I thought would be acceptable by the group all he wanted from me is to share, beyond that I was not responsible how it was received or what was going to be done with the words besides anyone but me. The word given that night was, "You need to get rid of all your self-worth and self-confidence, and replace them with God-worth and God-confidence. In truth, faith and belief you must be courageous enough and with boldness

Obey what I the Father ask you to do. Because every time you don't you are robbing someone of a blessing. So as you sit here and pray for souls, come only into my presence, because only through the Holy Spirit can a lost soul come to the throne."

God has called the church to hold the wedding which has been arranged between his only Son and us, sounds like the engagement is being taking to the next step. How would we feel as a bride on our wedding day our husband handed us a book and said, "Darling this was written for you, so that we would never have to speak again." The quality of a relationship depends on the quality of communication, better yet communion. The Lord himself affirmed that his sheep know his voice. John 10: 4 After he has gathered his own flock he walks ahead of them, and they follow him because they recognize his voice.

Every Christian should recognize the voice of the Lord. This does not in any way replace the Scriptures in our lives. They alone are given for the establishing of the doctrine of the church, but they were never given to take away a personal relationship with the Lord. Thank God for the bible because it is one of the greatest gifts that he has given his people, but he does not say that his sheep know his book. It is the Holy Spirit who convicts the world of sin, reveals Jesus, and leads us into all truth.

Philippians 3: 3 For it is we that are the circumcision, we who worship by the Spirit of God, who glory in Christ Jesus, and who put no confidence in the flesh.

If we are looking for the true promised seed of God we must allow God to bring us to the place where it is impossible to do anything without him. This is true faith – total dependency on God. We must also realize our mistakes are meant to be stepping stones not stumbling blocks.

Song of Songs 8: 5 "Who is coming up from the desert, leaning on her lover?" Behold under the apple tree I roused you; there your mother conceived you, there she who was in labour gave birth to you.

Even though cults have been increasing, the power given to the church is being increased even more.

Isaiah 59: 19 From the west, men will fear the name of the Lord, and from the rising of the sun, they will revere his glory. For he will come like a pent-up flood that the breath of the Lord drives along.

As we receive wounds as a blessing as the Lord declares them to be. Then they can become the source of authority for healing others who are wounded. Compassion is the true foundation of all spiritual authority.

We must see all people with God's eye, hear all people with God's ear, and know all people with God's heats.

Rejection is the opportunity to grow in grace, and allow us to die to things such as ambition and pride, which can quickly cover our revelation.

True spiritual authority is an honour and not to be greatly desired or achieved: rather it is a responsibility even a duty to be carried. If we are called to a potion in leadership, then we are also called to absolute dependency on God's wisdom. Even though knowledge may carry more excitement, if we are stepping up into true spiritual authority it will do us well to seek the words of wisdom rather than the words of knowledge. True authority is based upon the grace of God, the more authority we are given, the more grace required. This authority is not a position or a way to control; it is grace.

When the Lord tells us something why does he not just speak loudly and clearly? Why does he send us hard to interpret dreams and visions? Isaiah 55: 8-9 "For my thoughts are not your thoughts , neither are my ways your ways," declares the Lord. "As the heavens are higher than the earth, so our my ways higher than your ways and my thoughts than your thoughts."

We need to change to act in accordance with his ways if there is going to be communication and communion between God and us.

In order for the church to walk by the leading of the Holy Spirit, it needs to learn how to balance two principals: The first one: Freedom of individuals to take their own initiative in response to revelation from God. The second one: Proper submission to the authority God has obtained in our church. The balance is not easy to obtain, and many fall short of it. But they are both essential to protect the church.

1 Corinthians 14: 1 Follow the way of love and eagerly desire spiritual gifts, especially the gift of prophecy.

Many feel that if they would just have a spiritual experience, like for instance seeing an angel, or being caught up in the third heaven that their faith walk in this experience would get rid of the problems they are facing or maybe facing them? There is probably no truth in this. Satan himself saw the glory of the Lord. Satan dwelt in the presence of God. Satan still appears before God even after he has fallen.

Being prone toward narrowness of race, sex, age group, denomination, or movement can seriously warp what we are trying to be seeing. Jesus died to save the whole world, not just who we think might be suitable. Galatians 3: 28 There is neither Jew nor Greek, slave nor free, male nor female, for you are all one in Christ.

People of God are often rejected, but we should never let rejection get a grip on our spirit, instead let our hearts get a grip on God's affection and God's acceptance.

God please help me at this time to give up some more lies that have entered into my heart as reality, I would like to accept abandonment of the voices from the past trying to take over the present, creeping into the future, the voices of the world, Satan and even myself. Let these become strange to me, in return allowing Abba Daddy's voice to become the only voice my heart will surrender to. The only voice that will be familiar to me no matter where or how it is spoken.

We need to re-teach the title "Father". It has become such an individualized word. Instead of portraying safety, comfort, loving, merciful, grace it seems to have become such a common word, very male, very stylish, old-fashion, very religious and even distant. Seeming to draw out a traditional God image of the old man who lives just beyond the sky somewhere over the next cloud maybe. Also justifying the oppression of women by religious institutions.

Now add the intimidating word "Almighty" to this word "Father", and wow it can become quite scary. All because we are viewing the words with the big blue or brown or green eyes of this world. So, what if, we were to put on a blindfold? Seeing from our heart. Showing the world that all-powerful, all-knowing comes out of love not intimidation. It is unfortunate that it is peoples understanding when attributing omnipotence and omniscience to God, we also seem to attribute to the deity the power to remedy any wrongs or prevent any disaster. But this is not truth, because God is 'just' he loves us so much that he will do whatever it takes to bring us back into a relationship with him. God wants so bad to spend eternity with us, and keep us from Hell, he will do anything in love, yes a love we might not understand, but pure love to bring us to receive this relationship, a love he wants to share. A God that gave us the Holy Spirit to live in our hearts – not beyond us, because when the wrath of God is released we do not look beyond the wrath but to see at the same time an even greater anointing of grace, mercy, peace and healing released. Here is the place when to step down from our comfort zone and step up into the anointing, not having to be destroyed in the wrath, nope, just receiving all that God has for us and choosing to come into God's glory, because his promise is to bring us into his glory not destroy us.

In retrospect, the almighty quality of God, possessing the divine ability to interpret every event in life as either a deserved blessing or curse, interpreted in terms of God's all knowing capacity, is successfully being challenged.

We need pray within God's 'Will' more. And understanding God wants to heal, and sickness is not a punishment for sin. It might be a consequence of wrong choices made over time by us, but God wants us to be whole. Same as natural disasters, praying a hurricane out of our path, will just affect someone else. We need to pray that those violent winds be stilled. And

24

trust. God's Will is always the just path in everything. God works for his people. Exodus 14: 3-4 Pharaoh will think, "The Israelites are wandering around the land in confusion, hemmed in by the desert." And I will harden Pharaoh's heart, and will pursue them. But I will gain glory for myself through Pharaoh and all his army, and the Egyptians will know that I am the Lord. So the Israelites did this.

Jesus wants his people safe and whole.

Exodus 14: 21-31 Then Moses stretched out his hand over the sea, and all that night the Lord drove the sea back with strong east wind and turned it into dry land. The waters were divided, and the Israelites went through the sea on dry ground, and a wall of water on their right and on their left. The Egyptians pursued them, and all Pharaoh's horses and chariots and horsemen followed them into the sea. During the last watch of the night the Lord looked down from the pillar of fire and cloud at the Egyptian army and threw it into confusion. He made the wheels of their chariots come off so that they had difficulty driving. And the Egyptians said, "Let's get away from the Israelites! The Lord is fighting for them against Egypt." Then the Lord said to Moses "Stretch out your hand over the sea so that the waters may flow back over the Egyptians and their chariots and horsemen." Moses stretched out his hand over the sea, and at daybreak the sea went back to his place. The Egyptians were fleeing toward it, and the Lord swept them into the sea. The water flowed back and covered the chariots and horsemen – the entire army of Pharaoh that had followed the Israelites into the sea. Not one of them survived. But the Israelites went through the sea on dry ground, with a wall of water on their right and on their left. That day the Lord saved Israel from the hands of the Egyptians, and Israel saw the Egyptians lying dead on shore. And when the Israelites saw the great power the display against the Egyptians, the people feared the Lord and put their trust in him and in Moses his servant.

The great thing about this marvellous journey we are on is that we don't have to be perfect in order for the Holy Spirit to live in our heart, we are accepted for who we are now, and always keep growing. The always keep growing is what keeps being Christian exciting. Developing us to change into Jesus' ways.

2 Timothy 2: 19 "The Lord knows those who are his", and "Whoever says that he belongs to the Lord, must turn away from wrong doing,"

My Father guides me day by day gives me victory over those things that try to hold me back. Don't fear the devil more than you trust God. Follow God, and you will not need to fear the devil. "He who is in you is greater than he who is in the world." Do not be afraid, because as we grow into the changes of God's way we will be tested, so that the fear of God will be with you to keep you from sinning. Fear of the Lord: A healthy respect for God's power, 'fear of the Lord' doesn't mean being afraid, it means understanding God and respecting God so that we live a life of loving obedience.

God will not force his will on us, this is why it is up to us and us alone how welcoming and how wide we open the doors of our heart to let Jesus take over our lives, and be resurrected into God's life. There is nothing we can do to make God love us more. There is nothing we can do to make God love us less. God just loves, a pure love at all time.

Christians should be a colony of the true home (heaven) right here and now in the world. We need to focus our direction towards the establishment of this kingdom colony. The church often holds up a mirror reflecting back the society around us, instead of the window that is open to us in this different (true) way. The church should look like a colony of heaven in this hostile world, allowing anyone who wishes to peak through the window of hope, releasing revival through its front gates.

Even though one out of a hundred Christians reads the bible on a regular basis: be assured my friend that the other ninety-nine will read this Christian.

It is logical that a church should exist for those who need help? Right? Not for those who are by their own services so good that it is them who help the church. So just like a bar keeps whiskey on the shelf, and when you want whiskey you know where to go for it. Just like this the church should keep grace on its shelf so when someone wants grace they know where to go for it. And for those who are looking to replace whiskey for grace it is clear and welcoming for them to make the change.

There will be those who come to church every Sunday, some once a year, and even those who never make it between their baptism and their funeral. But they all have a right to be here, the alcoholic as much as the speckles saint. There is one stipulation for anyone who walks through the door of church and that is they ought not to come under false pretences.

John 4: 25 The woman said, "I know the Messiah, (called Christ) is coming. When he comes he will explain everything to us."

It's the Messiah finding a Messiah seeker. A hungry heart finding our Father's feast. The searching soul finding our Saviours face. A wondering wanderer finding the dwelling place of the Holy Spirit right in their heart. Finding God and God finding us. Wow! Now this is a worshiper in deep worship. Hope you won't mind if we stop and pray together for a moment here? Abba Daddy please make your presence real, that we may live the true meaning of worship. Thank you. Amen.

1Thessalonians 5: 18 Give thanks in all circumstances, for this is God's Will for you in Christ Jesus.

There are times when we must simply ignore our feelings and act on the principles of Christ, doing it despite the lack of joy, simply because God called us to. True praise, grows out of identification and acknowledgment that in his time God makes good out of everything. It is God's Will that in faith we turn our backs on bad and face the good, beginning actively to praise God, just like the Bible tells us to. Romans 8: 28 And we know that in all things God works for the good of those who love him, who have been called in order to his purpose.

Continue to praise God for all things, good and bad. All setbacks, frustrations, even resentments because God's ways are not our ways. Remember? Now here is a challenge from me to you. Are you ready? Actually it is a blast, for just one day try full attack praise and witness as 'every trickle' from every victory flows together forming a 'river of praise'. Wow talk about bringing us back to how worship honestly begins: In choice, confession, trust, truth, obedience, total submission. Most times we cannot see God clearly from the dust that this life has settled on our hearts making us seem dull. This is why it is so important that we worship where we can trust God enough to let him take our hearts and clean them up. Squeaky clean from everything that isolates us from God, a relationship of complete need of our Father.

I am remembering a taize service, I went to, talk about magnificent. I felt like an eagle learning to fly soaring into freedom and peace along with the Holy Spirit there as my guide like a mamma eagle. Shortly after this God called me from the church I was attending to a small non denominational church in the small hamlet where I was living at the time. From the very first service the voice of my Father confirmed the move by saying as clear as could be, "Welcome home Sylvia." At this step of my journey it seemed every time I would meditate which is often, a vision of an eye would appear. Had not a clue what this was all about until God lead me in my Bible reading, and opened up in revelation for my life Psalm 32: 8 I will instruct thee and teach thee in the way which thou shalt go; I will guide thee with mine eye.

Earlier if you remember we looked at Romans 2: 1. A very common first reaction from this verse is: "Now wait a minute, is this passage fair when it says you 'are just as bad'? The 'decent ethical folk' don't always realize they also have a problem called sin. Thinking only towards their own goodness and failing to search their heart. Not realizing that we are all under God's judgment. It is easy to see sin in someone else, but often we fail to spot similar sin in ourselves. Hopefully the closer our relationship with Christ becomes, we will begin to see ourselves as we really are on the inside and seeing the truth in this verse that we are not blameless. This only starts making sense when we start to view ourselves in the light of Christ.

Comparing ourselves to others we might think we are pretty good. But when we enter into the presence of Jesus, it becomes a different story. Inside we all have dirty closets that we don't want anyone to discover, sometimes even ourselves.

Everyone needs the Gospel: Bad guys, good guys, even the religious guys. Yes even the ones who read the Bible regularly, praying, fasting, tithing and worshiping God. Never crossing their minds that we are all under God's condemnation. Growing proud can lead to that pride turning to fraud. Proud of knowing God's laws, then disgracing God by breaking them.

There are many churches where religion comes before a personal relationship with Christ, this is when it becomes easier to be lead into pride and self-righteousness. Failing even to be kind, honest, humble and loving.

Lots of people stay away from church altogether, accusing Christians of hypocrisy. Why? Because they see through the game called "Church", and name it as phoney. There is no one free from sin we all need a change of mind to heart or heart to mind.

I have a question for you. Are Christians on parole, or fully pardoned? A lot of Christians live as if they are on parole (on conditions based on future good behaviour.) But has God put the Christian on parole? **Answer** – We have been fully pardoned into the hands of Christ.

Christ paid the penalty for our sins, he also removed the guilt from our sins. Guilt is an important fact that many of us overlook, or just do not understand. Holding on to guilt stops us from that 'fresh step' into NOW, keeping us in the past. Guilt binds us and makes us open to hurt, becoming a weapon for others to use against us. When a sinner turns to God through Christ, the guilt is removed along with the penalty. In the eye of God we are entirely pardoned for all our past repented sins, God not only pardons us he makes us one of his family.

God's unearned, non-conditional love and mercy are available for everyone. Even those who hate him, when we are truly sorry for our sins and trust Christ, God freely forgives and accepts us, no matter what we have done or felt. And he wants us to do the same my friends.

Redemption means 'releasing from bondage by payment of a price.' A ransom of sort is involved. Jesus gave his own life as that ransom for us all. So what is left to do? Nothing except to receive God's Good News, believe it, have faith. Faith is simply our response to the Salvation Christ obtained for us. We now face God unafraid.

Isaiah 42: 16 But I'll take the hand of those who don't know the way, who can't see where they are going. I'll be right there to show them, directing them through unknown country. I'll be right there to show them what road to take, make sure they don't fall into the ditch. These are the things I'll be doing for them – sticking with them, not leaving them for a minute.

The truth is that sadness does turn into a joyful dance, and every sorrow can be surrendered and exchanged in for joy. But not in silence, the difference comes when we sing praise to God. Thankful for everything, even when we don't know what is going on or why, just knowing God does and will take care of everything in a proper fashion.

One example of this in my life is when my son moved out at 18. He had been out on his own before this but had moved back home, but this is the move I remember giving God thanks for. The gifts of hope, love, serenity that were poured into my heart from heaven, the blessings of the people who were there to help with the move, the ones who prayed for us, and of course God my Father who again guided me to Scripture for his helpful Words for my life, "Let the grind stones of Life Shine you up!"

It would be an honour if you would share a time from your life. Thank you.

Now what does love have to do with paying taxes or staying within the speed limit? Everything, we need to be living our Christ like life in our every daily routine, sharing Christ's love in the everyday contact we have with others in this world.

Where ever there are people there is government of some sort. Romans 13: 1-5 Everyone must submit himself to the governing authorities, for there is no authority except that which God has established. The authorities that exist have been established by God. Consequently, he who rebels against the authority is rebelling against what God has instituted, and those who do so will bring judgment on themselves. For rulers hold no terror for those who do right, but for those who do wrong be afraid for he does not bear the sword for nothing. He is God's servant, and agent of wrath to bring punishment on wrongdoers. Therefore, it is necessary to submit to the authorities. Not only because of possible punishment, but also because of conscience.

These thoughts of obeying civil governments are not simply shared to fill up space. They are to teach us all governments, even cruel, brutal dictatorship, are a part of God's plan and Will with approval. Because along with the saints God's Will is also carried out by tyrants.

It is very difficult for someone to completely disassociate themselves from their community. There is an agreement with membership even in community, purposed with responsibilities as well as gifted with privilege. Duties of this combined community for each individual may be as far as into different nations, or as close to the family next door no matter where it leads it needs to be in harmony the Father wants us in agreement. The reason Abba Daddy needs us in agreement is because disagreements may be different but the results are the same, not seeing eye-to-eye will lead to judgment, criticism and evaluating each other, (in a very spiritual way of course). Careful here not to fall into a trap of helping others to be spiritual, we are responsible for one person's spirituality and one person's only, our own, no matter what the size of the community.

Beware my friend because as soon as we start criticizing one another, we run the risk of slipping into the sin Adam did: Deciding we will become like God.

It is easy to judge someone else especially in their weakness, thinking them to be shallow because of a personal habit or an idea which we do not agree with. The reality is that we ourselves are the weaker one in a critical moment because we are allowing legalism to enter our lives. I wonder if it could be possible to use disagreement to be a key opportunity to practice Christ love in our life? Sounds like something we should go talk over with Jesus, he is always willing to talk over ideas with us, his friends, members of his community.

Be honest and open with others about yourself. Instead of having a spirit of fear, learn to be strong and wise through Jesus, in order for them to enjoy being with you in an open true-to-life bonding.

2 Timothy 1: 7-10 For God did not give us a spirit of timidity, but a spirit of power, of love and self-discipline. So do not be ashamed to testify about our Lord, or ashamed of me in prison. But join with me in suffering for the gospel, by the power of God, who has saved us to a holy life- not because of anything we have done but because of his own purpose and grace. This grace was given us in Christ Jesus before the beginning of time, but who has destroyed death and has brought life and immorality to light through the gospel.

It took me over forty years to find my one true love. I always thought that whoever gives me a white rose without knowing it is my favourite flower, this will be my true love. Well my first white rose came to me from the church, and shortly after that one, three were presented to me from a special sister in Christ. She is known as my angel with the other wing. So my true love turned out to be Abba Daddy, who would of guessed, are you surprised. I know there is no one I will ever love more than Father, Son, Holy Spirit. And no one will ever love me more.

Ezekiel 36: 25-27 I will sprinkle clean water on you, and you will be clean: I will cleanse you from all your impurities and from all your idols. I will give you a new heart and put a new spirit in you. I will remove from you your heart of stone and give you a heart of flesh.

Oh God, how can I ever thank you for the richness of this new life in Christ. Thank you for setting my mind on you. Teach me only to be alive to this new life which you have planned from the beginning. Let me never stop receiving the wisdom and boldness to share all your blessing with others. One of the amazing things of how this new life found me is that I did not read about it then it all happened to me, Nope. It all happened to me then I discovered it all in God's Word. The Fathers Word teaches me that unless I accept the kingdom in the simplicity of a child, it can't be received. So man I never want to grow up! How about you?

1 John 1: 6-7 "If you claim to have fellowship with him yet walk in the darkness, we lie and do not live by the truth. But if we walk in light, as he is in the light, we have fellowship with one another, and the blood of Jesus, his Son purified us from all sin,"

The Song of Songs is an explanation of Genesis 2 in a positive way, it shows the goal of which Genesis is the origin. Its love songs, are a theme of the capacity for encounter with results of a relationship that is whole. A statement of a covenant at work. The coming together of what was separate, the escape from solitude and an arrival of communion, a personal realization of intimacy, frustrated by sin but made possible by salvation.

The reality is that in the relationship between man and woman even prior to its character as the basis of the father-mother-child relationship, the Song of Songs is a description of fantasia, an unquenchable yearning and restless willingness of readiness, which both partners in this covenant rush toward an encounter. Humankind is only complete when male and female are in unity as one. The man alone is not yet complete, for it is not good for man to be alone; female alone is also not complete, because she was taken out of the man. Genesis 2 speaks of the covenant made and permanently sealed, it also sets the beginning for which in the Song of Songs is the goal. Male and female were created for the sake of this covenant and will always be hastened towards an encounter in spite of whatever obstacle or restriction.

There is a desire for closeness in every encounter, a need for break through from the defences of sin, the need to be in touch with one another. Intimacy of every level, from husband and wife to friendship in both love and faith, are full of tension. An example is when fulfillment is delayed, desire becomes bitter. It takes the task of pushing through and patiently praying to keep life passionate and faith zealous.

This is why prayer is the chief work in relation to someone's desire for, or difficulties with intimacy. Anything but prayer fails to deal with either the expressing existence of desire, or the complexity of the difficulty. When we pray with someone we enter into the desires of God, and any difficulty is put in perspective under God. Prayer is the language of covenant taking serious relationships that matter most both physical and divine. In prayer the desires are not talked about they are directly expressed to God. In prayer the difficulties are not analyzed or studied they are worked through with God. Our Father even chose to use a physical body as means of revealing his saving love to us; John 1: 14 The Word became flesh and made his dwelling among us. We have seen his glory. The glory of the One and Only, who came from the Father full of grace and truth.

It is well within the Biblical boundaries to use the Songs keen interest in the body as a means for understanding aspects of intimacy with God.

The first forty plus years of my life I never read the bible at all. And I listened to it more like a Pharisee than a Christian. The first forty plus years of my life I made the mistake of believing God for too little. But now my friend if a mistake needs to be made let it be for believing God for too much. But really how can anyone believe such an awesome Father for too much?

Since the moment I accepted Jesus, I accepted because he called, and through my new heart he killed me of the world, and resurrected me into his life, allowing me to be in a union with him as my roots grow deep and strong into the vine. Now from that vine my faith is built up from his wisdom as the Holy Spirit teaches me to be full of thanksgiving, peace and joy in everything. And just the thought of living with him in eternity is more than enough for me knowing that no matter what will take place it is all under the love of Christ.

Ezekiel 18: 32 For I take no pleasure in the death of anyone, declares the Sovereign Lord. Repent and live!

Here is the place of perfect peace. Jesus carries the burdens not me. It is through the intercession of Christ my burdens are light under the worlds challenges. Me I am just a servant. Burden bearing can be an indicator pointing the way to prayer, but done incorrectly it can become enormously destructive. Keep in mind that there some elements of wilderness suffering that may never end here on earth, they are there to be accepted as blessings. 2 Corinthians 12: 6-10 If I had a mind to brag a little. I could probably do it without looking ridiculous, and I'd still be speaking plain truth all the way. But I'll spare you. I don't want anyone imagining me as anything other than the fool you'd encounter if you saw me on the street or heard me talk. Because of the extravagance of those relations, and so I won't get a big head, I was given the gift of a handicap to keep me in constant touch with my limitations. Satan's angel did his best to get me down; what he in fact did was push me to my knees. No danger then of walking around high and mighty! At first I didn't think of it as a gift, and begged God to remove it. Three times I did that, and then he told me, my grace is enough. It is all you need. My strength comes into its own in your weakness. Now I take limitation in stride, and with good cheer, these limitations that cut me down to size – abuse, accidents, opposition, bad breaks. I just let Christ take over! And so the weaker I get, the stronger I become.

So a persistent and relentless opponent our flesh remains, allowing itself to be constantly disciplined and loved from the Father. Luke 9: 23 He said to all of them, "Those who want to come with me must say no to the things they want, pick up their crosses every day, and follow me."

What is the cross if not an instrument of death? Is it not the place where corrupt flesh dies so that new life can emerge in unison with Jesus? We must welcome this in gratitude and go on with joy undisturbed, with constant blows to pride and ego, and all other element of character that are not yet formed to the character of Jesus. Notice however that the only cross we are to be carrying is our own! Proverbs 17: 10 a reprimand impresses a person who has understanding; more than a hundred lashes impress a fool.

When attack by an evil spirit we must use the Name of Jesus. Philippians 2: 10 So that at the Name of Jesus everyone in heaven, on earth and in the world below will knee.

In this unity even though we may not even be able to speak, we can be assured that the demon will know what we are telling it, and that is get lost!

I know I would love to be as forgiving as Jesus, but I am just like everyone else a work in progress not yet the finished product. So what we might read as pride in character can actually be simple defensiveness. What might appear to be a hard and arrogant exterior could be simply concealing a gentle and wounded heart of love. This is why we need compassion and understanding and a relationship rather than a frontal assault on perceived character flaws. Trust comes hard, but wins the day, and the one who comes in love will be the one to earn it. Ephesians 6: 18-20 Pray in the Spirit in every situation. Use every kind of prayer and request there is. For the same reason be alert. Use every kind of effort and make every kind of request for all God's people. Also pray that God will give me the right words to say. Then I will speak boldly when I reveal the mystery of the Good News. Because I have already been doing this as Christ's representative, I am in prison. So I pray that I speak about the Good News as boldly as I have to.

My friends without a strong support system for one another and from the kingdom we would stay lost because being found is overwhelming at times and impossible to do alone at any time. *Jeremiah 1: 9-10* Then the Lord stretched out his hand and touched my mouth. The Lord said to me, "Now I have put my Words into your mouth. Today I have put you in charge of nations and kingdoms. You will uproot and tear down. You will build and plant."

Hey Jesus himself says to us: *Mark 9: 23* What do you mean, "If I can?" Jesus asked. "Anything is possible if a person believes."

See it in heaven and copy it on earth. This has always been the best way to live, not the easiest but the best. It is the lifeblood of all sincere prayer: "Thy Will be done, on earth as it is in heaven". No one can do Gods Will unless God first reveals His Will from the Throne. God reveals we copy. God initiates we respond.

I would like to share a favourite poem of mine hope you enjoy it as well.

The Will of God

Thou sweet, beloved will of God
 My anchor ground, my fortress hill,
My spirit's silent, fair abode,
 In thee I hide me and am still.

O will, that willest good alone,
 Lead thou the way, thou guidest best,
A little child, I follow on,
 And, trusting, lean upon thy breast.

Thy beautiful sweet will, my God,
 Holds fast in its sublime embrace,
My captive will, a gladsome bird,
 Prisoned in such a realm of grace.

Upon Gods will I lay me down,
 As child upon its mothers breast;
No silken couch, nor soft bed,
 Could ever give me such deep rest.

Thy wonderful grand will, my God,
 With triumph now I make it mine;
And faith shall cry a joyous yes
 To every dear command of Thine.

So did you like it? Let's pray here and then continue on. Please teach us, O God, how to be peace makers. How to confront violence with love, how to courageously and patiently promote your Will and your Word among the hostile and angry masses. Amen.

The purpose of denominations should be to form believers into distinct families, not to build up walls that separate the body of Christ. God does not want us to judge other denominations, building walls of attitude toward them and justifying this in Jesus' Name. God wants us to love one another because we are one united body through Christ and in Christ. Lots of these walls are built through fear of people's needs changing, of God's calling us into his purpose and people are moved to move on. We should rejoice in these movements instead of building up walls or closing doors. We should be in harmony for our differences, blending together in unity for Christ and of Christ. Jesus said the way the world will know that we are his disciples is by our love for one another. John 13: 34-35 "A new commandment I give you: Love one another. As I have loved you, so you must love one another. By this all men will know that you are my disciples, if you love one another."

If we are not doing this if we are closing ranks and just loving our own we are not reaching out to those who are different. We are just fighting amongst ourselves. And in doing this we will end up destroying ourselves.

Right now at this moment as we are stepping to the tune of Jesus' song, some of us up, some in, some out, some down, no matter where you are let's just say goodbye to expectations, jealousy, judgment, and everything else that is troubling your heart and keeping you out of this fantastic line dance we have started in harmony. There is nothing worth keeping us from being separated from one another, from Christ, and becoming a family in unity with God. The church needs to be built in acceptance, joy, forgiveness and love. This is not a onetime event however that will last a lifetime but it is a daily event with the new anointing from God. Every morning is gifted to us Lamentations 3: 22-24 The faithful love of the Lord never ends! His mercies never cease. Great is his faithfulness; his mercies begin afresh each morning. I say to myself, "The Lord is my inheritance; therefore, I will hope in him!"

God wants us to love each other no matter what – the way he loves us no matter what. Forgiveness is what has to take place on a regular basis. We all have faults and weaknesses that keep us from being all God wants us to be. We need the Holy Spirit's guidance and help to grow to be more Christ like in the face of these shortcomings. This involves our willingness to be honest and open with God and others and to be obedient in following through on what God reveals to be his Will in our lives. The only way I can figure out how this could work is by serving one another and the Father, and willing to repent of our sins, building the temple of the Holy Spirit whose dwelling place is in our heart, on the foundation of Jesus.

Are we still friends? Good, because we are going to push through even more; are you ready? Let's do it! Let's open our hearts and bring hurts, regrets, poor attitudes, bad feeling, fears, you get the drift. And now bring them all to the foot of the throne. And watch them as they are burnt up with the fire of the Holy Spirit knowing we have been forgiven and washed clean by the Blood of Christ.

Let us come together every Sunday morning with pure and joyful hearts, ready to praise, leaving everything in our hearts, mind, soul, outside by the church door, (this way if you choose you can pick them up again on your way out). Now we can fill our church, heart, mind, soul with the Spirit of God so we can go and shine the light of Jesus into our community. (Hope so full that it is impossible to pick up what was dropped off on your way in).

When God speaks in an audible voice you can be sure the powers of Hell will rise up to challenge that voice. The voice comes when the divine ministry that is about to be performed is extra ordinarily difficult to accept or believe, or when the task about to be under taken is so hard that it will require the clarity and assurance of an audible voice in order to endure and complete the task. The voice when spoken to me starts out by asking "Do you trust me?" What does it say to you? Whatever the words the trick is always act on the voice when you hear it, even at the risk of looking foolish in front of others. Philippians 3: 12-21 I don't mean to say that I have already achieved these things or that I have already reached perfection! But I keep working toward that day when I will finally be all that Christ Jesus saved me for and wants me to be.

No, dear brothers and sisters, I am still not all I should be, but I am focusing all my energies on this one thing: Forgetting the past and looking forward to what lies ahead! I strain to reach the end of the race and receive the prize for which God through Jesus Christ, is calling us up to heaven. I hope all of you who are mature Christians will agree on these things. If you disagree on some point, I believe God will make it plain to you. But we must be sure to obey the truth we have learned already. Dear brothers and sisters, pattern your lives after mine, and learn from those who follow our example. For I have told you often before, and I say it again with tears in my eyes, that there are many whose conduct shows they are really enemies of the cross of Christ. Their future is eternal destruction. Their god is their appetite, they brag about shameful things, and all they think about is this life here on earth. But we are citizens of heaven, where the Lord Jesus Christ lives. And we are eagerly waiting for him to return as our Saviour. He will take these weak mortal bodies of ours and change them into glorious bodies like his own, using the same mighty power that he will use to conquer everything, everywhere.

God is not some sort of crusty, distant super- professor. He is our best friend, many times our only friend.

Psalm 24: 1 God claims earth and everything in it, God claims world and all who live on it.

God never leaves anything unfinished and he never changes, he is not like us, but my goal is to be more like him.

Psalm 100: 3 Know this: God is God, and God, God. He made us; we didn't make him. We're his people, his well tended sheep.

God has also given us the choice to obey or disobey him. There is a big difference between a person who is programmed to say, "I will obey," and someone who does it by their own free will. Having this choice allows the word obey to have great meaning and depth. Choices are what make a relationship genuine. We were created to reflect God's grandeur–to honour him. Revelation 4: 11 "You are worthy, our Lord and God, to receive glory and honour and power, for you created all things, and by your will they were created and have their being.

We think patience is the ability to wait, but really it is the ability to keep a good attitude while waiting.

Psalm 33:11 But the plans of the Lord stand firm forever, the purposes of his heart through all generations.

Even overstatement from the Word of God produces an un-desired reaction. Example: When Eve tried to defend God even though the Lord does not need defending. When she did this she added to God's demand. Genesis 3: 2-3 the women said to the serpent, "We may eat fruit from the trees in the garden," but God did say, "You must not eat fruit from the tree that is in the middle of the garden, and you must not touch it, or you will die."

God did tell them that they should not eat of the tree. He never however said they could not touch it. When you add to God's Word you always take something away from it. Here Eve made God to be more demanding, and in doing so marred God's character. Getting people to add or subtract from God's Word is the sort of math the Devil specializes in, he just loves the resulting confusion. No matter how small the addition it creates a crack in the dike, and that is all Satan needs.

If we are disobedient to God, we are like children playing in the street against their mother's instructions. The youngsters assume they know better than their mother what is safe and fun. They are showing that they do not entirely trust their mother's knowledge of safety. They are disregarding her authority. In this same way when we feel we know better than God what is good for us we are sinning. Our choices make a statement. When we act like this we are showing we don't quite trust our creator, that we are not sure God is telling the truth. James 4: 4 You adulterous people, don't you know that friendship with the world is hatred toward God? Anyone who chooses to be a friend of the world becomes an enemy of God.

Let's pray that we will never reject a pure perfect word, to experience with a forbidden one! Romans 1: 24-25 Therefore God gave them over in the sinful desire of their hearts to sexual impurity for the degrading of their bodies with one another. They exchanged the truth of God for a lie, and worshiped and served created things rather than the creator

Who is forever praised. Amen.

Why did God ask Adam and Eve questions about the events that took place in the garden? Would not an all-knowing God know what went down? What do you think, was the Lord really that limited that he had to ask if they had eaten the fruit from the forbidden tree? The truth of the matter is that God did know exactly what had happened, the questions were directed for the pure reason to help Adam and Eve sort out in their own minds to what had taken place. They disobeyed their Father. Which meant they had trusted Satan. The sad truth being they both chose to sin, both of their own accord. Now God was giving them the opportunity to own up, and they blew it. They refused to admit their guilt, instead here is what they said: Adam-"The woman 'you' (even God gets blamed here) put here with me, she gave me some fruit from the tree, and I ate it." Eve-"The serpent deceived me, and I ate." Let's hear what they should have said: Adam-"God I have failed you miserably. I have disobeyed your clear direction to not eat of the fruit, I have sinned. Please forgive me." Eve-"Lord God, I too have sinned by disobeying your command. I want to see our relationship restored to what it was. Please tell me how."

Adam and Eve had done wrong, now they have spoken wrong, good thing we were not the judge, jury and executioner because we would have given the thumbs down and squashed them both. But not God, no, God still shows compassion beyond anything we can even imagine.

Even though Adam and Eve's sin brought a curse on the whole human race. God in his love also gave a promise. Genesis 3: 14-15 So the Lord said to the serpent, "Because you have done this, cursed are you above all the livestock and all the wild animals. You will crawl on your belly and you will eat dust all the days of your life. And I will put enmity between you and the woman, and between your offspring and hers; he will crush your head, and you will strike his heel!"

The Lord is saying here that he would someday deliver man from Satan. There will be a male child born of the woman, who will crush Satan's head, a fatal wound. True Satan would also hurt the child, but only with a strike at the heel, a temporary injury that would heal. (already from the very beginning was Jesus promised to us).

Remember no matter what happens to you the majestic God is in control of your life.

Habakkuk 3: 17-19 Though the fig tree does not bud and there are no grapes on the vines, though the olive crops fail and the fields produce no food, though there are no sheep in the pen and no cattle in the stalls, yet I will rejoice in the Lord, I will be joyful in God my Saviour. The Sovereign Lord is my strength; he makes my feet like the feet of a deer, he enables me to go on the heights.

We are on the way! God has great plans for our lives. We might not see it at times, but know it is always for good. I have an awesome friend who is known for her advice of 'time will tell.' I am sure this is a huge revelation for my life through her wisdom from God. See how we are all so connected? How we ask? Why we ask? Because he said so. God needs us to be good productive soil where his Word can produce an abundance of sweet juicy fruit. He needs believers through whom he can reveal his mighty power.

I was always under the impression that God being un-mortal, powerful, super natural, he would have total control over my life, which for me would work perfect because I know how to react in that atmosphere. But instead he lets me lead my life with choices and just loves me through it, now man this concept is new to me. Plus to top it all off he never leaves my side. Let me tell you in a world that has always told me what to do and a world that has left me abandoned many a time this is all very hard to take in.

My friends another real cool truth is this, the Devil will give up when he sees that we are not going to give in.

Deuteronomy 4: 29-31 from there you will search again for the Lord your God. And if you search for him with all your heart and soul, you will find him. "When those bitter days have come upon you far in the future, you will finally return to the

Lord your God and listen to what he tells you. For the Lord your God is merciful—he will not abandoned you or destroy you or forget the solemn covenant he made with your ancestors.

Here are some very helpful and much appreciated pointers I have picked up on my journey, hopefully they are helpful for you as well. Be content with what God has given you, and called you to do. When searching for truth, finding it in the pure untainted Word from Abba Daddy. Be peace makers not peace keepers, this is hard my friend because it requires us never to compromise whatever is necessary for peace to hold rank, at all times upholding the standards of God. Do not allow your conscience to be seared, but always recognize sin and repent, never holding onto any guilt. Never stop listening to the watchmen who have been sent to you. And fellow watchmen never lose the boldness and courage to keep bringing it. These are just a few of some sure fired ways to walk in the way of our Lord.

We were created to be the Bride of Christ, prized possessions of God, the apple of his eye. This is why we must be ready for judgement even invite judgement. Even so the Lake of Fire will be uncovered we have still won the war and remain the proud owners we were created to be through our Fathers love. Created to live in this love for eternity. So as the world is at war with curse and blessing, which has been won already let's welcome God's time, ready in victory from the Living Word of God that breathes life and truth into us.

Jeremiah 6: 11-20 "But I am full of the wrath of the Lord, and I cannot hold it in. Pour it out on the children out on the streets and on the young men gathered together; both husband and wife will be caught in it, and the old, those weighed down with years. Their houses will be turned over to others, together with their fields and their wives, when I stretch out my hand against those who live in the land," declares the Lord. "From the least to the greatest, all are greatly for gain; prophets and priests alike, all practice deceit. They dress the wound of my people as though it were not serious. 'Peace, peace' they say, when there is no peace. Are they ashamed of their loathsome conduct? No, they have no shame at all; they do not even know how to blush. So they will fall among the fallen; they will be brought down when I punish them," says the Lord. This is what the Lord says, Stand at the crossroads and look; ask for the ancient paths, ask where the good way is, and walk in it, and you will find rest for your souls. But you said, "we will not walk in it." I appointed watchmen over you and said, 'listen to the sound of the trumpet!' But you said, 'we will not listen.' Therefore hear, o Nations; observe, o witness, what will happen to them. Hear, O earth; I am bringing disaster on this people, the fruit of their schemes, because they have not listened to my words and have rejected my law. What do I care about incense from Sheba or sweet calamus from a distant land? Your burnt offerings are not acceptable; your sacrifices do not please me."

Here is what pure love looks like: Father, Son and Holy Spirit left the throne, and came to the Garden and joint-full created us in perfect cooperation of their offices. Nothing here about us but it is all for us.

So in the power of obedience, we give the Father permission to fill us with revelation, love, glory, mercy and healing.

The Lord cares for every single creature of his creation, supplying the needs from sparrow to man alike. So why are we filling the means of our own needs, desires and entertainment? All we are really doing then is destroying to extinction the wonderful creation of God. Revelation 4: 11 "You are worthy, our Lord and God, to receive glory and honour and power, for you created all things, and by your will they were created and have their being."

Everything and everyone created was created for the exclusive purpose for God's pleasure.

Psalm 36: 6 Your righteousness is like the mighty mountains, your justice like a great deep, O Lord you preserve both man and beast.

We must follow God's goals for our lives, allowing true, pure love judgement to be administered. Now the manifestations will be granted, filled with grace, mercy, and eternal life with our Creator.

Every morning I wake up it is for God's strength to pilot me, support me, his wisdom as my guidance. It must be his eye to look before me, directing me, his hand to guard me, from myself mostly, my ears to be sharp in hearing his voice so his words are what will be spoken through my lips. Totally surrounded by Jesus and full of the Holy Spirit, and if this is not enough hear this my friend, Jesus is the mouth of 'everyone' who speaks to me, in every eye that sees me, in every ear that hears me. How obvious is it that I am the most blessed person? I wake up every day through a mighty strength, the invocation of the Trinity. And the greatest part about all this is that it is available to anyone who receives it.

Another small but powerful poem that helps me not just to remain on the path but skip on it rather than move along head down feet dragging, both ways we will get us to where we want to be, but me I like the fun:

Wait! For the day is breaking (bursting).
 Though the dull night be long.
Wait! God is not forsaking (leaving).
 Thy (my) heart. Be strong - be strong!
Wait! Tis (it is) the key to pleasure
 And to the peace of God.
O Tarry thou (linger yourself) his leisure -
 Thy soul shall bear (must support) no load (baggage).

Waiting is something we have lost the art of. We want to microwave everything, meanwhile God is stuck in the marinating days and wow those sure are tender times.

There is only one difference between a spiritual sheepdog who guards and guides his masters sheep, and the wolf that devours them. The wolf has unhealed wounds.

Forgiveness is basic Christianity, if we fail to forgive we are straying from God's path, now we are entering the place where the hurts can find us.

The declaration that we will not submit to men, but only to God, is evidence of extreme rebellion. Such a mentality is complete deception, because The Trinity speaks and works through its entire creation. True fear of God that is not controlled by the fear of man is free to recognize, honour, and submit to all who are anointed by God to the authority in God's grace. 1 Samuel 15: 23 for rebellion is like a sin of divination, and arrogance like the evil of idolatry. Because you have rejected the word of the Lord, he has rejected you as king.

If we are spending our time trying to put out fires God has started, we will be in conflict with the purpose of God. The quality of the church is tested by God as we are walking through the throwing of matches! Whatever is left after the fire is what God approves. 1 Corinthians 3: 10-15 By the grace God has given me, I laid a foundation as an expert builder, and someone else is building on it. But each one should be careful how he builds. For no one can lay any foundation other than the one already laid, which is Jesus Christ. If any man builds on this foundation using gold, silver, costly stones, wood, hay or straw, his work will be shown for what it is, because the Day will bring it to light. It will be revealed with fire and the fire will test the quality of each man's work. If what he has built survives, he will receive a reward. If it burns up, he will suffer loss; he himself will be, but only as one escaping through the flames.

Throwing these matches ourselves is one of the most arrogant things we can do.

A high priest carries the stones of all the tribes in his breastplate (heart). We to walk in a calling each and every one of us to carry the whole church on our heart. Not just our own congregation, denomination or movement either.

Luke 11: 34-35 Your eye is the lamp of your body. When your eyes are good, your whole body is also full of light. But when they are bad, your body is also full of darkness. See to it, then, that the light within you is not darkness.

It is up to us to use our eyes for the Lord, who has already used his before ours. So really there is no other choice for our eyes but to be used for God alone. If you were looking for a sure fired way to stay in full light this is it.

I would like to take a minute and look at how lust has taken over in every area of every area, nothing is sold without using lust, everything on the television seems to introduce lust, even a lot of marriages are formed from lust not love. Lust is a sin that we are told we will not overcome, but we are to flee from it. These are the hardest sins the ones we overcome and get out of our face we have no need to deal with any longer, but man to flee. Wow my friend see how important it is that we stay in the surrounding support of the Trinity, it is our only hope.

We are worshipers seeking the worship that will grow us in grace and wisdom from Jesus, not from physical or emotional experiences.

John 13: 23 One of them, the disciple whom Jesus loved, was reclined next to him.

This place is still available. And me well my friend I'm there! You too? It is so much better when we know God's ways, not just see his acts. To be so intimate with God that we feel his heartbeat, so that our hearts would beat in unison with Abba Daddy himself. This is how we will be trusted with great revelations and power.

Go! Step by step and each step reveals a miracle, every step marks the path of this journey with another miracle. Don't you be the one who will miss thousands or even more miracles by waiting for the huge manifestations. Live in the simplicity and truth that as long as we are with Jesus and the Holy Spirit is alive in us everything and anything is a miracle.

A mature Apostle does not need to seek a specific revelation for everything they are to do; decisions can be made as a trusted ambassador, who has the mind and heart of Christ, because they are so dependent on Jesus' every step in their life the prophetic direction just flows naturally.

God will always be King of kings and Lord of lords. His authority will always rule over us, but God is also preparing us to rule like Jesus not under God but in God's voice. God is pleased when our directions are his decisions in the normal way of our living. We are only independent when we are depending on our Father. This might not make sense to what we have learned from the world, but in the Spirit realm this is the way of existence, and to be honest a way of survival while here on this earth.

Unfortunately there are those who fake the manifestations from God, but there are more that do not. The Holy Spirit truly does move among God's people. Knocking them to the floor, filling them with God's joy in which they might appear to be drunk. This is not done however for our entertainment. The important message in these demonstrations of the Spirit, is that the Lord is not trying to change us, he is actually killing us. The only way to be alive in spirit is to be dead to ourselves.

It is so important my friend that we dramatically open up to the ability to hear directly and accurately from God, as we proceed to the end of the age. Stepping into the standards of the Holy Spirit for us now, so sounds like it is pretty important that we listen to what we hear, and you think we could stop here, but, guess what we are to act on what needs to be done. The more we learn about God the more awesome he becomes.

The purpose of prophesy is to help the church prepare us for eternity by making a clear truthful path for us to follow and to prepare us as much for revival as for conflict.

Most of our wisdom that comes from experience is from our mistakes, not victories. If someone does not take note of mistakes at the beginning of their life, they will catch up to them in the end. And here my friend is where they become even more devastating. We have to embrace our mistakes not cover them up, in order to learn from them. Proverbs 24: 3-4 By wisdom a house is built, and through understanding it is established: through knowledge its rooms are filled with rare and beautiful treasures. Knowledge can fill a house, but wisdom builds it.

Someone said to me once and I agreed that: "God is kind, but he's not soft. In kindness he takes us firmly by the hand and leads us into a radical life style change."

When Mother Theresa past away the night of her funeral God woke me up to go watch it on television. As I turned on the television a banner reading "Works of love are Works of peace." It is amazing how someone we don't even know can lift us up into God's Word, speaking a prophesy that is not understood at the time perhaps but will come together in other prophetic words that will come down the road. Again, the witness to a Whole Body in Jesus.

Here is a question for you. Are human beings truly free? As far as my own understanding goes I am pretty sure that even Satan challenged God on this. We have freedom to descend of course, Satan himself, Adam and everyone who has ever lived has proven that. But do we have the freedom and ability to ascend? To believe God for no other reason than, well, for no reason at all? Can we believe when God appears to us as an enemy? Or is our faith like everything else a product of environment and circumstances? As for me my friend I am praying for the strength, courage and wisdom to believe in the Living God, just because! Amen.

God's true concern for us is our faith, rather than our pleasure and comfort. So concerned he sent us Jesus, from heaven, now we can know him not just imagine him. People have actually embraced Christ, we have world knowledge about Jesus and this is what makes Jesus more historically specific than God and enables us to get to know God our Father through Jesus Christ his Son.

This means however that in order to be true believers we must be honest believers, people of faith not people drugged on the narcotics of religion, or a religious straight jacket into which Christians must be bound.

As a true and honest believer I should not deny the reality of a Christian experience. So that even the past experiences promised through God by grace, can be released today, without compromising the truths or integrity to those called in this day and age. We need to recognize that past, present and future understandings working together are the very shape of Christianity and Church that will inevitably be given to us through obedience, forming an unbreakable relationship with God.

In doing so we are believers who live in exile from the traditional way in which Christianity has many times been proclaimed. And a believer in exile is a new status in many religious circles. Leaving us with a responsibility to learn from God the true, and new calling for the church in all it manifestations.

The time has come for the church to invite its people to step forward onto a frightening journey into the mystery of God, and away from the pre-modern theological concepts that continue to mark our life and keep us in a religious box, not a creation of God.

The 'hunger of God' is in all of God's creation, not the hunger for the answers the church has traditionally given. The yearning 'hunger' of truth for believers and non believers alike, who have found themselves in exile from the form in which that faith has been proclaimed in the church throughout the ages.

When someone offends us which lets be fair is more often than we are willing to admit. It is up to us to do the right thing. What? You say. Now come on don't put the book down. At least hear me out, ok. When offence is taken we must go directly to the source. Most often we go off and complain to someone else, (preferably someone who will see things in our point of view), right? This is the easier way, and even the most comfortable way, but unfortunately solves nothing, it only steps us back into sin.

I had to break out of a friendship from someone very dear to me. Her choices were the highlight of one huge gossip ring in the church, it came to a point of a very false attachment to her, so the only thing that seemed right for me to do for both of us was for me to lovingly detach. I then removed myself from the gossip plus the self righteous attitude that came over me from the choices she made. None of this being my business. Now that it is all back in the hands of God I pray her every good thing God has purposed for her life.

No matter how annoyed we are in a situation at the end of the story it was always God's Will for us, but because we tend to do things our way God needs to direct us for our own good into his direction for us. There was a Sunday evening some friends and I went off to the city in search of an evening service, (not an easy hunt) it was a long weekend. The church we had chosen was closed because of the long weekend, so of course the very first emotion to show up was annoyance. Then, stopped to think is there maybe another church that offers a Sunday night service? So yup there was another church that came to mind, so off we went. Good thing we pushed through and did not give up and go back home because it turned out to be a dynamic service, and the healing in faith by the grace and mercy of God was speechless. The faith and trust from the day I was baptized in the Holy Spirit was renewed, and added to this was the promise that what is given by God nothing can take that away. It can be given away so hang on to it my friend, and hang on tight. When we listen to and obey the voice of God he will always lead us back to his side. And he will be with us no matter what.

God created us, and still he allows us the freedom to choose him. And in the return from this choice is where true healing begins, the healing of being whole.

James 5: 16 Therefore confess your sins to each other and pray for each other so that you may be healed. The prayer of a righteous man is powerful and effective.

A diet of relationship through confession, praise, and worship, draws others to Christ, this diet equals a restoration of heaven right here on earth. Only by maintaining a focus on God will take our praise to the heights of this restoration. 1 John 1: 5 This is the message we have heard from him and declare to you: God is light; in him there is no darkness at all.

As long as we look with commitment on God's light, we will have no trouble keeping our praise pure. God asks us simply to fall at his feet and worship, to acknowledge that we cannot heal ourselves, that we are dependent on him every single moment. Going deeper in our lives with our Father is a more solitary life, in unity with one another. I would like for us to be encouraged to follow the lead of the leper in Matthew 8: 2-3 A man with leprosy came and knelt before him and said, "Lord, if you are willing, you can make me clean." Jesus reached out and his hand and touched the man. "I am willing," he said. "Be clean." Immediately he was cured of his leprosy.

We are called to be a home for the Holy Spirit, a prepared heart, where he can live, and from there pour out God's life and love. So make sure that we are not giving the world our best, leaving merely the leftovers for God.

1 Thessalonians 5: 16-18 Be careful no matter what; pray all the time; thank God no matter what happens. This is the way God wants you who belong to Christ Jesus to live.

Praying continually, and being full of heavens joy involves 'Abiding' in the Fathers presence. Me I love to pray, (talking with God, listening to God) in every situation. My mouth might not be movin' but be assured my friend my heart is grovin'. In my heart I pray all the time, even when there seems to be no apparent reason, because every breath I breathe is a Blessing. I love to fellowship with my Abba Daddy. Just today my grandson responded to my saying "I love being in the Spirit". Oma you are always in the Spirit, like to say if it is Jesus I am looking for I know his dwelling place, I see him in you. What an honour.

Glory be to God!

God is my Father and yours. He knows all about us. We can come boldly to him, we can come timidly to him, he always understands exactly what we mean and the attitude in which we mean it. In an attitude of prayer all the time, it is pretty hard to worry or think of negative or evil things. Prayer is simply expressing the hearts sincere desire to God, in silence or aloud, in song or grunts, spiritual language, however it is expressed God's desire is that it is as natural as breathing.

I may not always be happy, but I always have joy! Joy/joy/joy down in my heart! And this kind of joy comes when we are in the presence of the Lord. Just be yourself: he'll understand exactly what you mean because he is the one who made you this way in his fashion. We were created to have fellowship with Jesus, so as this becomes our natural environment the happier God will be and the more joy we will experience.

There is a difference between prayer in faith, and faith in prayer. Luke 18: 6-8 Then the Master said, "Do you hear what the judge, corrupt as he is, is saying? So what makes you think God won't step in and work justice for his chosen people, who continue to cry out for help? Won't he stick up for them? I assure you, he will. He will not drag his feet. But how much of that persistent faith will the Son of Man find on the earth when he returns?"

Prayer is answered in God's way not ours. We pray, then fret anxiously, waiting for God to hurry up, (and do something we understand) all the while God is waiting for us to calm down so he can do something through us.

Faith in prayer is very common. Prayer in faith is so uncommon that our Father even questions if he will find it on earth when he returns? Prayer in faith is a commanded duty; it is making known our request unto God in full confidence that, if we ask according to his Will: He hears us; and that according to our faith, his answer will be granted, for his purpose and glory. After asking, we tend to sit back and wait on God when he is often waiting on us. You may need to forgive your spouse, child, parent, friend, sibling, yourself, before God can use you for his deliverance. There are times we too prefer the darkness of denial to the light of truth, just for the simple reason it is more normal to what we are use to reacting to. It is true that the truth does hurt sometimes, but it is still truth. Denial does not change it, or make it go away. When Satan has managed to take gains, let's admit it and determine to take them back.

If the death and resurrection of Jesus Christ is not enough proof, then all the experiences of all Christians who have ever lived, will not prove anything either. The core of our message is not what we have experienced, it has to be the truth. Satan can imitate (even outshine) any Christian experience. But he is helpless against the truth of the Gospel; the death and resurrection of Jesus Christ.

I am a Christian today because the Living God has chosen to have a relationship with me, and I in return have chosen to have one with him.

We are fully pardoned even our guilt is gone. We are not on parole earning freedom, continuing to pay the debts for our sins. Does this mean we can live any which way we want to and not be concerned about obeying God? Just the opposite! Being pardoned by God makes you a new person, one that puts their trust in God for the power they need to live as they should every day. In fact, only when we trust Jesus can we truly submit to his authority and obey him.

If there is no Biblical foundation in the importance of our faith, then we as Christians can be claimed to be heretics (skeptic). If it is possible to be justified by what we do, to be saved only when we keep God's laws, then Christianity is false. Again Christianity is relationship one that is firmly rooted in the Bible. Already in the Old Testament the covenant of this relationship was taught. Genesis 17: 1-8 When Abram was ninety-nine years old, God showed up and said to him, "I am the Strong God, live entirely before me, live to the hilt! I'll make a covenant between us and I'll give you a huge family." Overwhelmed, Abram fell flat on his face. Then God said to him, "This is my covenant with you, you'll be the father of many nations. Your name will no longer be Abram, but Abraham, meaning that I'm making you the father of many nations," I'll make you a father of fathers – I'll make nations from you, kings will issue from you. I'm establishing my covenant between me and you, a covenant that includes your descendants, a covenant that goes on and on and on, a covenant that commits me to be your God and the God of your descendants. And I'm giving you and your descendants this land where you're now just camping, this whole country of Canaan, to own forever. And I'll be there God."

With Abraham it was all faith. He believed God. He acted on the relationship he had with God, he did not just sit back and do nothing. Belief may be for the study, but faith is for the road.

The faith you have is the faith that shines. Faith is not just knowing what you believe, or even that you do believe. Faith is life lived to a response to God's revealed Will. Faith my friend means 'Risk!'

What are we wanting from this life we are living? Confidence? Peace? Love? Hope? Happiness? Security? Accomplishments? Even though these desires are expressed in different words and ways, they are all pretty much the same goals. Felling one equals another. But the truth is when we are made right in God's sight, by faith, this gives us real peace with God.

It is never just us and the problem, God is there too. No matter what happens, knowing in God's Will all is well, and God loves us. When we rely on the Holy Spirit, every trial and problem is used for building faith, confidence, hope, happiness. How do we rely on the Holy Spirit you ask? Well my friend we 'Wait'! Do nothing.

Faith in Christ, is power to take 'it' when things (it) gets tough. Waiting does not mean do not act to solve a problem. Waiting and doing nothing in our own strength, is the way to show our reliance on the Holy Spirit. Waiting, meditating, praying, praising, worshiping, can give God's love a chance to calm the troubled waters inside and around us.

The blasts of winter from earth may get stormy and uproot our desires, relationships, even our passions. Dividing us from emotions, or in some cases bring hidden emotions out into the open, which seems to lead into a whirl wind, causing us to run as fast as we can in an opposite direction. Which sounds scary and believe me it is, but think about the opposite direction, we are running away from flesh and into the arms of our heavenly Father, and it is only God that can support this struggling heart until it ceases to sigh over the things here on earth and begins to unfold its wings for heaven. Moving us into the act of our faith and then experience more and more the healing power of Jesus.

2 Corinthians: 3: 16-18 But whenever anyone turns to the Lord, then the veil is taken away. Now the Lord is the Spirit, and wherever the Spirit of the Lord is, he gives freedom. And all of us have had that veil removed so that we can be mirrors that brightly reflect the glory of the Lord. And as the Spirit of the Lord works within us, we become, more and more like him and reflect his glory even more.

As we shed our masks even more, we become more genuine. We allow the Spirit of Christ to work in us, helping us to be sensitive and appropriate in our honesty and openness, which are vital to being genuine.

Being genuine is not fool hardy frankness or harsh honesty. If anything this is how judging, criticism often get there start. So we need to be honest in the leading from the Holy Spirit, because the person who shares their life with God, and whose life is shared by God, proves to be faithful.

We need to be accepting, because all of us are self-conscious. Our image to self is directly related to how we feel, what we do, the thing we like. So to criticize a person's opinion, taste, or idea, you criticize them. No matter how much you intend not to. Being accepted sound difficult because it is, but it makes as aware of how accepting God is towards us, just as we are. John 7: 24 stop judging by mere appearance, and make a right judgement.

To really understand one another involves empathy, insight, compassion towards everyone's situations. (even our own) When empathy is offered we are mentally trying to enter the thought and idea of the person involved to the situation. Empathy is actually communicated more in the ways of action and facial expressions than any statement offered.

The real point is that we acquire an attitude of understanding towards one another, then there will be a better chance of less disappointment and less judging, and less blame. There really is nothing to lose except maybe some pride, fear, defensiveness.

The only meaning of 'I' in our walk with Jesus should be, how can 'I' fulfill 'my' responsibility to help and serve others. Striving to live a life that will not cause someone else to stumble. These battle may be lost, but even so we can never stop fighting for the good of others, in the body of Christ. A great way to stay sane and in peace would be to regulate your life to please every Christ like idea, all this requires is to be willing and ready to do what appears necessary to help another child of God within the sphere of influence. Now not to be a stumbling block is great, but even better is when we are stepping stones, always actively in search of ways to help one another. You realize I hope that being a stepping stone implies that you will be walked on, which does not seem too appealing or glamorous, but comes nowhere close to being crucified.

If you are operating on a platform of self-awareness, we will most probably find ourselves to be inadequate, so step down, now step over on to God's platform and you will find all things to be adequate guaranteed. So who is working in whose ministry? I think I now can realize it is not my ministry, but God's ministry working through me. It is amazing to find the effectiveness of God's ministry in us continues even when we ourselves are failing or making mistakes.

Dance has been a form of worship throughout history, the ritual movement of dance puts the entire body at the service of the Spirit, expressing adoration, joy, enthusiasm, to the God who creates and redeems the body. Exodus 20-21 Then Miriam the prophetess, Aaron's sister, took a tambourine in her hand, and all the women followed her with tambourines and dancing. Miriam sang to them; "Sing to the Lord, for he is highly exalted. The horse and its rider he has hurled into the sea."

All the way back to the time when Miriam and the maidens danced their way out of the Red Sea. They rejoiced with their bodies the song of deliverance and rescue.

Dance is a way of prayer, the body put to the means of adoration, mind and muscle coordinating to the glory of God.

Love changes everything for us, and in us, our ideas about ourselves, our attitudes toward ourselves, our value and our goals. The impact of God's love in our life gives it meaning, makes it good for something, eternally.

We don't need to pray out loud for everyone we meet, or even say "I'll pray for you" to everyone who announces a problem. But we must pray for everyone we meet. (see how prayer is never ending) Before, after, during conversation prayer must be made not in formal but keeping God in the presence of everything, constantly working at the center as intercessors before God on behalf of each person.

Busyness, it is an illness of spirit. A rush from one thing to another. And not do we just miss things in between, we miss a lot of what we are busy in not getting the whole or true purpose. So why do we find our self in this destructive spirit over and over again? Could be because there is no stability of trained integrity and no confidence in the authority of grace.

The Eucharist is the act of worship that remembers the unhesitating act of Salvation, enacts the events in a ritual meal in which participation by the demonstration a faith involvement in God's action. God truly delights in us, his creation. With the help of a vocabulary learned in the Song of Song's we see God's people along with ourselves not through the dirty lens of our own muddled feelings, and not through the smudgy window of another's criticism, but in terms of God's Words. We don't see how good we can look, how delightful we can feel, or how strong we can be until we hear ourselves addressed in God's love. We are now able to rebuild a sense of worth by extending the acts of Eucharistic joy in prayer. Not that prayer is a quick cure or instant therapy, for it is a lifelong practice; but it does seem to have the advantage of actually starting in the center instead of puttering around the edges. Prayer that is conceived by the Spirit will have honest character, compassionately it will view the person being prayed for in the environment of the covenant, drawing it all into Salvation. It is in prayer where genuine beauty and worth are obvious.

But what we call ugly is only matter that is out of balance, to what we think it should be. The Eucharist instinct is for wholeness, for being satisfied with nothing but our Fathers best for us is confirmed in prayer.

Another strand of prayer is a passionate involvement in the action of improvement and reconciliation. Matthew 28: 28-29 This is my blood of the covenant, which is poured out for many for the forgiveness of sins. I tell you, I will not drink of this fruit of the vine from now on until the day, when I drink it anew with you in my Father's Kingdom.

A raised banner marks a place where battle is joined; it also marks a sight of victory. When the banner is love, both conflict and consummation in our every day affairs are parable of God's victorious relation with us. God's love is an assault on our indifference and a victory over our rebellion.

Prayers do not calculate their changes by evaluating a person's past; they are awakened to action by the word of promise. Christ's love brings action to lives as it announces the springtime of resurrection. Prayer is the place where doubts that result from disappointments and failure are dispelled and a warm faith in resurrection love is created.

Struggling with evil exclusively on an external level often covers our own sin, leading to self righteous piety instead of real purity. Hiding from the garbage that's already in us from our point of contact with a fallen world. We lose our sense of compassion, we become judgemental, end up condemning the world rather than identifying with its fullness and bring the Good News of Salvation Jesus did. The important issue is not to keep the garbage out, but to deal with it. This is where we must be careful that my Spirit is in gear, not neutralized through passive involvement. Titus 1: 15-16 Everything is pure to those whose heart is pure. But nothing is pure to those who are corrupt and unbelieving, because their minds and conscience are defiled. Such people claim they know God, but they deny him by the way they live. They are despicable and disobedient, worthless for doing anything good. Only he who believes is obedient, and only he who is obedient believes.

1 Corinthians 2: 15-16 We who have the spirit understand these things, but others can't understand it at all. How could they? For, "Who can know what the Lord is thinking? Who can give him counsel?" But we can understand these things because we have the mind of Christ.

Truth and love are two sides of the same coin therefore are not able to be separated. Love that that holds no truth can turn to slush and sap. Truth without love can be harsh and cruel. They are both joined together perfectly in Jesus.

A prophetic word tears down what the Lord has not authorized as it is releasing power to plant and build the purpose of God. There is something in the genuine prophetic word that kindles things in the heart of God's servants, releasing power to set things in motion. A prophetic word tears down false doctrine and obstacles raised up against God's purpose, it restores his people to the foundation in him which is necessary for the unfolding of his plans and intentions. 1 Corinthians 14: 3 but when a person speaks what God has released, he speaks to the people to help them grow, to encourage them, and comfort them.

So a genuine Word releases power and encouragement for building 'up' the people of God, to accomplish his Will. In maturity people are consumed with concerns for others. Prophetic words are not a secret, hearing from God is the birthright of every Christian in a living relationship with our Father. All of us hear from him, be it through a sermon, a devotional, a song, etc., and on a personal level. Beware not to latch onto a gifted or charismatic person, standing on the words of that gifted one rather than on the eternal Word of God. Deuteronomy 5: 11 Never use the name of your God carelessly. The Lord will make sure that anyone who uses his name carelessly will be punished.

Traditionally, we understand this to mean that we must not use the Lords name in connection with profanity. Which is true. But in 'vain' actually means 'without purpose' or 'void of anything good'. We must not claim to be speaking a word from God, when it is not in fact his word. Deuteronomy 18: 20 But any prophet who dares to say something in my name that I didn't command him to say or who speaks in the name of the other gods must die.

In our culture we do not put people to death, but the sternness of the warning remains. Something to watch for is when pride is threatened, a false prophet takes offence, and offense taken indicates lack of humility. Does the Word of God being spoken stand the test of Scripture? God has spoken once for all with finality in the written word. No valid prophetic word will ever convey new revelation that is not already contained in Scripture, and it will not in any way contradict the written word. Colossians 2: 18-19 Let no one who delights in false humility and the worship of angels tell you that you don't deserve a prize. Such a person, whose simple mind fills him with arrogance, gives endless details of the visions he has seen. He doesn't hold on to the Christ head. Christ makes the whole body grow the way God wants it to, through support and unity given by the joints and ligaments.

This verse speaks of arrogance. The Scriptures never disappoint, but the words of people often do, even when we believe they are coming from God. We must stake our lives on the eternal word of God alone, while we thoroughly test everything else. Make sure when a word is given that it reflects the revealed nature and character of God. Again this guides us to the Bible, where the final revelation has been recorded for all ages.

Have I pulled down the window curtain, and am I allowing someone else (besides God) even me, to create my reality? Simply because they have told me so? Stand in truth. Open the curtains, open them wide, my friend, scream, do whatever it takes to wake up, before we all fall asleep. At the same time be gentle and accept the reality that there are some people with blinders on. We are in battle, but much of the warfare is beyond our sight. It's a spiritual battle in which God reveals and Satan blinds. Who sees and who doesn't is not our responsibility; our responsibility is to proclaim the clear unaltered truth. In truth we can render Satan's veil powerless. Acts 26: 18 You are to open their eyes and turn them from darkness to the light and from the powers of Satan to God, so that through their faith in me they will have their sins forgiven and receive their place among God's chosen people.

As we venture into prayer, every word spoken and even unspoken, at any moment, is capable of becoming the true meaning of what we are praying, involving us with a Holy God who wills our holiness. So we must be careful that what we are praying is not just some religious small talk, or spiritual elevated gossip. We need to be well aware that prayer is not an enterprise to be entered into lightly, because when we pray we open our hearts and take them into God's neck of the woods. Psalm 29: 5-9 The voice of the Lord is majestic. The voice of the Lord breaks the cedars: The Lord breaks in pieces the cedars of Lebanon. He makes Lebanon skip like a calf, Sirion (Mount Hermon) like a young ox. The voice of the Lord strikes with flashes of lightning. The voices of the Lord shakes the desert; of Kadesh. The voice of the Lord twists the oaks and strips the forest bare. And in the temple all cry "Glory!"

Praying may well lead us to speak in a quivering voice, uttering different sounds, on our face, on our knees, even soul-shattered. Isaiah 6: 3-5 And they were calling to one another - "Holy, holy, holy is the Lord Almighty; the whole earth is full of his glory." At the sound of their voices the doorposts and thresholds shook and the temple was filled with smoke. "Woe to me!" I cried, "I am ruined! For I am a man of unclean lips, and my eyes have seen the king, the Lord Almighty."

In prayer we have a more than average chance of ending up in a place that we quite definitely never wanted to be, angrily protesting, preferring death to the kind of life God insist on recklessly throwing us into. Jonah 4: 1-4 but Jonah was greatly displeased and became angry. He prayed to the Lord, "O Lord, is this not what I said when I was still home? That is why I was so quick to flee to Tarshish. I knew that you are a gracious compassionate God, slow to anger and abounding in love, a God who relents from sending calamity. Now, O Lord, take away my life, for it is better for me to die than to live." But the Lord replied, "Have you any right to be angry?"

We want life on our conditions, not God's conditions. Praying puts us at risk of getting involved in God's conditions. Praying most often does not get us what we want but what God wants, sometimes quite different with what we conceive to be our best interest.

Prayer is never the first word; it is always the second word. God has the first word. Prayer is not an 'Address' (appeal), but a response. Prayer is for us to rejoin into God's conversation, not God's into ours.

Rejection=Blessing: Praise the Lord. Being rejected by family either earths blood, or God's blood, (natural family, church family). Yes even the church rejects, even though it hurts bad being rejected by loved ones I can say from experience, this is the best time to go directly to our Father and see the beauty of his answered prayer just for me. And feel the true peace sitting at the feet of Jesus as he catches my tears. 1 Timothy 1: 16-17 but God was merciful to me in order that Christ Jesus might show his worst of sinners, as an example for all those who would later believe in him and receive eternal life. To the eternal king, immortal and invisible, the only God-to-him be honour and glory forever and ever! Amen.

I had to give God permission to do anything he wishes to me, in me, or through me that will glorify him, I once claimed these rights as mine, and surprise, it came out all wrong. But now they belong to God, and are under his control, so even though there are times I have no understanding at all within my own life, I can trust in faith everything is just as it should be. Not the way I want it to maybe be, but definitely the way it must be.

It is awesome yet so frightening when God confirms our lives, the possession of my confirmation as a warrior in God's army as an Ambassador, what an honour to be a representative for the glorious Kingdom of God, into which I am a member. 2 Corinthians 5: 20 We are Christ ambassadors, and God is using us to speak to you. We urge you, as through Christ himself were pleading with you, "Be reconciled to God!"

I am learning to trust that the boldness to carry out this duty comes from God's Word, and from the unity and support from the Kingdom. I must never stop seeking God's face, or listening to his voice, no matter how the world, my family, the church, the devil, myself, take their toll. I know God will always be there, and if it is not the time to be free from any of these chains God will stay chained to me, for his glory to be known in his perfect moment. Really my friend no matter what we are never alone. 2 Corinthians 5: 16-17 No longer then, do we judge anyone by human standards. Even if at one time we judged Christ according to human standards, we no longer do so. When anyone is joined to Christ, he is a new being: the old is gone, the new has come.

The Christian life is easy, when we just let Christ do it. Romans 11: 6 His choice is based on his grace, not on what they have done. For if God's choice were based on what people do, then his grace would not be real grace.

When we persevere in brokenness holding nothing back we develop an aroma of sweetness and bear a healing anointing in which the people of God find needed rest and security, to form our character to the accepted fullness of the promise we received in our early days. Our true destiny in him. First comes calling and success, then exile and wilderness and finally return and fulfillment. No one is exempt.

Surprisingly enough how to hear from God has little to do with learning how to interpret dreams or how we exercise the power of heaven. It has everything to do with character development. For example the prophets from the Bible times trained under older, more experienced prophets, not in order to impart what the young prophet was gifted to do, rather to expose them to what they could not do. It was a program designed to produce humility through menial tasks and failures. Imagine us today

Being put through such a program. But my friend at the end of this program the young prophet would know their weakness and their complete dependence on God. First we need to be servants, which develops us into our callings.

We need to be trained in humility before we can be permitted to steward the Living Word of God. Luke 22: 31-33 then the Lord said, "Simon, Simon, listen! Satan has demanded to have you apostle for him. He wants to separate you from me as a farmer separates wheat from husk. But I have prayed for you, Simon, that your faith will not fail. So when you recover, strengthen the other disciples." But peter said to him, "Lord, I'm ready to go to prison with you and die with you."

Satan received permission to sift Peter to the point of exposing his weakness and failures. Jesus knew that Peter would be humiliated and broken at the point of his determination (will) and pride. Power and authority flow best upon a riverbed of compassion born of a brokenness of spirit that results from the destruction of confidence in all things human.

Jesus never abuses, never violates, never manipulates and never even exalts himself despite his divinity. He lets his Father do that. In all these ways we must reflect his nature. Psalm 63: 1 O God, you are my God. At dawn I search for you. My soul thirsts for you. My body longs for you in a dry, parched land where there is no water. So I look for you in the holy place to see your power and your glory.

In wilderness function there is a desperate craving. Wilderness suffering strips away every selfish ambition, every sense of personal accomplishments, every ability of the flesh to achieve. Leaving nothing remaining but a desperate, urgent, holy hunger for the pure Spirit and presence of Jesus. Psalm 63: 8 My soul clings to you. Your right hand supports me.

Dear Lord, whenever we hear your Word. Give us wisdom to understand it. Faith to believe it, and the courage to obey it. Amen.

When it says in Psalm 116: 1-5 I love the Lord because he hears and answers my prayers. Because he bends down and listens, I will pray as long as I have breath! Death had its hands around my throat; the terrors of the grave overtook me. I saw only trouble and sorrow. Then I called on the name of the Lord: "Please, Lord, save me!" How kind the Lord is. How good he is. So merciful this God of ours!

The Bible never once refers to us not dying. Actually it blesses us with two deaths. One death of self and re-born to Christ. And one of this world, when we go home to Abba Daddy.

I cry pretty much every day, in joy, in sorrow, in anger, from fear, in spirit when I don't even know why. But not one of these tears are for nothing, everyone of them is caught and then blessed by God. I will always stumble here on earth but I will also know that God is always there to help me up, or just lay with me for awhile. When you hear the saying "It grieves God when they die." This is not the deaths we just talked about, it is a separation from him, here on earth which leads to separation from him always.

Any time I am in trouble I pray, I even pray anytime I get into trouble, so believe me when I tell you now that I am in prayer a lot.

The prayer in lament (grieving) form is very common in the Psalms. This is to be expected because as humans it appears to be a very common condition.

Taking Jonah as an example: being in the belly of a fish seems like it is the worst trouble imaginable. We naturally expect him to pray a lament (woe to me prayer) what we hear however is the opposite, a psalm of praise. So even though circumstances may dedicate 'lament' prayer, while influenced by circumstances, is not determined by them. We need to stay creative in our praying, choosing praise and worship as a foundation. And if we can do this first, before the angry prayer, the lament prayer, what a lifting of our spirit we will witness.

Our culture presents us with forms of prayer that are mostly self-expression. Pouring ourselves out before God or lifting our gratitude to God as we feel the need and have the occasion. These prayers are dominated by a sense of self. Prayer, mature prayer, is dominated by a sense of God. Prayer rescues me from myself, from a preoccupation with myself and pulls me into adoration and a pilgrimage to God. Want to come?

Psalms is a great schoolroom for us to learn how to pray. Prayer is our response to a God who is speaking to us. God's Word always first, we answer. And not just yes sir, no sir, three bags full sir, but our whole being in response.

Ok, Psalms is the Schoolroom, now let's add Proverbs as the Gymnasium, and the rest of the Bible an Assembly Hall, now our mind, soul and spirit has a whole routine of a structured daily workout. Keeping ourselves equipped for a life full from the kingdom of God. 'Alive' human beings.

Now, this daily workout is not an isolated act, nope, it is set between two other large constructs. Corporate worship, on Sunday (a gaggle of God's works). And a random unscheduled prayer, sometimes willed, and other times spontaneous recollections of what we are saying, or what we are doing, in answer to God. 'Now'.

We need to beware of a consumer approach to spiritual life, where we have options placed out on the table from which we pick and choose according to our appetite and whim. We started from God and our goal is to return to God, all the time being with God. Hanging on to dear life in prayer from start to finish.

No matter where we go, what happens, who we meet, the risen Christ always gets there first. The important prayer now becomes what is He doing? What is he saying? What is our Fathers Will in any and every situation? Mark 16: 6-7 The young man said to them, "Don't panic! You're looking for Jesus of Nazareth, who was crucified? He was brought back to life. He's not here. Look at the place where they laid him. Go and tell the disciples and Peter that he's going ahead of them to Galilee. There they will see him, just as I told them.

Give your life to God, he can do more with it than you can. And never take life to seriously, because you will never get through it without death, but take Christ seriously and man the promise is that you will live forever! The revelation to understand Christ as life has been the most thrilling spiritual truth that I have realized. Yet God's purpose in revealing this exchanged life to his children is not simply so that we will enjoy the grace walk. His ultimate purpose is that he reveal himself in this world through us who abide in him. To express his life through believers is the ultimate intention in the Father. It is, as we, fulfill his divine purpose that we find our greatest contentment.

God has given us the privilege to fill our community with His Spirit. 'WOW'. We have the strength to face every circumstance and situation by the power that Christ gives us. And 'when' - not - 'if' revival comes we will be ready and able in this power and strength to accept and then fulfill our mission.

Now I am asking you please not to forget that we are not just a family on Sunday morning. We are a family seven days a week twenty four hours a day for eternity. Through good and bad. Stay in touch and in this love of God get to know each other. Talking things out, asking forgiveness, do whatever it takes. The key is 'do'. James 2: 17 In the same way, faith by itself, if not accompanied by action, is dead!

So Father we Thank you for our gift of faith. By your Spirit move us to act on this faith so that we may experience more and more the healing power of Jesus. So let us be like John 4: 23-24 Yet the time is coming and has now come when the true worshipers will worship the Father in Spirit and truth, for they are the kind of worshipers the Father seeks. God is Spirit, and his worshipers must worship in Spirit and truth.

Pray always. But remember, praying is not just asking for things from God. But, listening to God and obey what he asks us to do. So please God help us to open our heart and mind, and listen to you and obey your Word and Will. Believe in

Deuteronomy 31: 8 "The Lord himself will lead you and be with you. He will not fail you or abandon you, so do not lose courage or be afraid"

If something is happening in or around us and it has brought us to pray, then guess what it served its purpose.

This is so what I want to be when I grow up: An act of hope, and a firm belief in God. My Father I believe most firmly that you watch over all who pray in you, and that we can want for nothing when we rely on you in all things. That is why I am resolved for the future......to cast all my cares upon you......People may deprive me of my status, sickness may take my strength from me, I may even jeopardize our relationship with sin: But faith and trust will always be with me, because I am going to persevere it to the last moment in this life, and the power of hell can seek, but in vain, to grab it from me. Let others seek happiness in their wealth and in their talent. Let them trust in the purity of their own lives, in the number of their activities, in the intensity of their prayers; as for me my confidence in you is what fills me full of hope. You are my divine protector. In you alone do I trust and pray. I am assured, then, of my eternal happiness. I know too well that I am weak and changeable. I am constantly at battle with the power of temptation against the strongest virtue. Even though stars fall and foundations of the world crack. These things do not alarm me. While I hope and trust in you, I am sheltered in all misfortunes, and I am sure that this truth shall endure, for I rely upon you to sustain this unfailing hope. Finally: I know that my confidence cannot exceed your generosity, and that I shall never receive less than I have hoped and prayed for from you. Therefore I pray in hope that you will sustain me against the ways I deceive myself. I hope in prayer that you will protect me against the deceitful attacks of the evil one. I pray you will cause my weakness to triumph over every hostile force. I hope that you will never cease to love me, and that I will love you unceasingly.

What does God want from us? God just wants us, not our promises, not our good intentions, not even our Christian service, because all these things just seem to take care of themselves when we just rest in God's arms, or sit on his lap, allowing God to work through us. What a joy and a relief. It isn't passive lifestyle, but a peaceful one when we actively rest in God, and God does it all. It's a walk of grace, and it really is amazing. Micah 6: 8 "What he requires of us is this, to do what is just, to show constant love, and to live in humble fellowship with our God."

A good definition for religion is this: man's effort to reach God. Our natures tend to be religious, constantly trying to create new ways to find God, even though this is hopeless. The Bible says that mankind is in a spiritual wilderness, we are lost, and cannot find our way back to God by our own efforts. We cannot get rid of our sin, to make ourselves acceptable to the Lord. The only true way to God was provided by the Lord himself, when in his mercy, reached down and provided us with a way to escape the punishment for sin. It is in Jesus only that we can be rescued.

2 Samuel 14: 14 Like water spilled on the ground, which cannot be recovered, so we must die. But God does not take away life, instead, he devises ways so that a banished person may not remain estranged from him.

The more advanced and comfortable things are, the less we seem to feel we need God. Even though God has granted us free will, his intentions in this was never for us to be independent from him.

How awesome my life would be if I could bring myself to be as faithful to God as Abraham was. Abraham's confidence was in the keeping of God's Word. Hebrew 11: 8-10 by faith Abraham, when called to go to a place he would later receive as an inheritance, obeyed and went, even though he did not know where he was going. By faith he made his home in the promised land like a stranger in a foreign country: he lived in tents as did Isaac and Jacob, who were heirs with him of the same promise. For he was looking forward to the city with foundations, whose architect and builder is God.

Although Abraham's body would die, he knew his spirit would live forever with God in heaven. In order to get rid of sin we must trust the Lord, believe his promise, God will provide. No matter what is happening to us, or around us we need to always have our confidence firmly placed strictly in God, because when we trust God the natural result is, we do things God wants us to do. Another prime example here is Jacob, he often failed in life, but God was always the ultimate focus on his trust.

Exodus 3: 4-6 When the Lord saw that he had gone over to look, God called him from within the bush. "Moses! Moses!" And Moses said, "Here I am." "Do not come any closer," God said. "Take off you sandals, for the place where you are standing is holy ground." Then he said, "I am the God of your father, the God of Abraham, the God of Isaac, and the God of Jacob." At this Moses hid his face, because he was afraid to look at God.

Moses' blood must have chilled, he knew all about the eternal Most High God. He knew God was the creator, owner of every living thing. He knew God was a holy God who separates himself from mankind because of their sin. And Moses himself was a sinner - a murderer.

Exodus 3: 10-12 So now go, I am sending you to Pharaoh to bring my people the Israelites out of Egypt. But Moses said to God, "Who am I, that I should go to Pharaoh and bring the Israelites out of Egypt?" And God said, "I will be with you. And this will be the sign to you that it is I who have sent you; when you have brought the people out of Egypt, you will worship God on the mountain.

I tend to be like Moses at times and find myself puzzled that God does not come to judge my sin, but he continues to entrust me with the great important job of his purpose that he created me for. So even though I seem to continue to struggle with misgivings, I trust in God's promises, because he always keeps them. So when push comes to shove, you will see me doing what God has asked me to do.

We must put our good intentions aside, (by not doing our own thing) but only follow God's instructions for our lives, through the word, because no matter who we are, as soon as we believe in the Lord, we have faith in God's way. Our faith will be honoured by God who will extend us his grace and mercy.

God gave ten commandments to live by, before Jesus was born. And God said, "If you will obey the ten commandments, then you will be special people, with a special relationship belonging to Me. You will know how to live together in peace and order.

Exodus 20

#1 "I am the Lord your God, who rescued you from slavery in Egypt. Do not worship any other gods besides me.
We often think we are keeping this rule because we do not pray to any other gods. But the truth of this rule is: anything else more important to you than God, such as family, work, the way we look, recreation, then this rule is broken. God has to be #1.

#2 "Do not make idols of any kind, whether in the shapes of birds or animals or fish. You must never worship or bow down to them, for I, the Lord, am a jealous God who will not share your affection with any other gods! I do not leave unpunished the sins of those who hate me, but I punish the children for the sins of their parents to the third and fourth generation. But I lavish my love on those who love me and obey my commands, even for a thousand generations."
The Lord is a Spirit so there can be no worship of images, or replacements of anything. Examples: Drugs, alcohol, food, even going to church because we think we have to. Unless we can trust and enjoy God completely we are breaking this rule.

#3 "Do not misuse the name of your Lord your God. The Lord will not let you go unpunished if you misuse his name."
This rule tells us that God's name should always be respected. But in today's culture we have learned to use God's name in a very loose and common manner, and we even use God's name as a swear word. Unless we talk about God as judge of all the

Earth, , as King, and is of our utmost honour. We break rule #3.

#4 "Remember to observe the Sabbath day by keeping it holy. Six days a week are set apart for your daily duties and regular work, but the seventh day is a day of rest dedicated to the Lord your God. On that day no one in your household may do any kind of work. This includes you, your sons and daughters, your male and female servants, your livestock, and any foreigner being among you. For in six days the Lord made the heavens, the earth, the sea, and everything in them; Then he rested on the seventh day. That is why the Lord blessed the Sabbath day and set it apart as holy."
God has set this day aside for us his people to show the rest of the world that God has established a distinct relationship with us. So we must honour the Sabbath as a special sign of distinction. (Families would not be drifting apart as far as they are if they did this.)

#5 "Honour your father and mother. Then you will have a long, full life in the land the Lord will give you".
The Lord wants families to be a place of respect, not chaos and anger. Children are to be respectful and obedient. Parents are assumed to be looking out for the best interest of their family. So we should not talk back, ignore, argue, pout, use the silent treatment, criticize, all these are ways of disrespect.

#6 "Do not murder."
God has given life to man, so it is wrong for one man to take the life of another. But the Lord has more than action of murder in mind for this rule. Because God looks at the heart, he judges murder on a much broader plain than we do. The Lord even considers certain types of anger as murder. Matthew 5: 21-22 "You have heard that the law of Moses says, 'Do not murder! If you commit murder you are subject to judgement.' But I say if you are angry with someone, you are subject to judgement! If you call someone an idiot, you are in danger of being brought before the High Counsel. And if you curse someone you are in danger of the fires of hell."
To meet God's standards we must get rid of our temper, and not let anger lead us into sin.

#7 "Do not commit adultery."
God is saying that the only acceptable time to have sex is after we are married, and the only person to share intimacy with is your marriage partner. But because God looks at the heart he takes it one step further, God knows when we have sinful thoughts. Matthew 5: 27-28 You have heard that the law of Moses says, "Do not commit adultery. But I say anyone who even looks at a woman with lust in his eye has already committed adultery with her in his heart."

#8 "Do not steal."
God does not want anyone to take things that belong to others. Stealing means cheating as well, whether on an exam or our taxes.

#9 "Do not testify falsely against your neighbour."
We should always be honest. Satan is a liar. God has no part in lies, truth comes from God. Titus 1: 1-4 I, Paul, am God's slave and Christ's agent for promoting the faith among God's chosen people. Getting out the accurate word on God and how to respond rightly to it. My aim is to raise hopes by pointing the way of life without end. This is the life God promise long ago-

and he does not break promises! And then when the time was ripe, he went public with his truth. I've been entrusted to proclaim this message by order of our saviour, God himself. Dear Titus, legitimate son in the faith. Receiving everything God our Father and Jesus our saviour give you!

Because God is truth, to him all lying is a slap in the face. False accusation, gossip, all fall under this law.

#10 "Do not covet your neighbours house. Do not covet your neighbours wife, male or female servant, ox or donkey, or anything your neighbour owns."

We must not envy anything other people have, possessions, abilities, looks. To be greedy or jealous is a sin. In today's society many people have a craving to upgrade, a keep up with the Jones' attitude. We believe we deserve this, which is an appeal to our pride, another sin.

God wrote these laws in stone, to show they never change. We might convince ourselves that cheating is ok, but the law still says it is wrong. So the question remains: Just how strict is God about following theses laws? Is it ok if we break one occasionally? What does God expect? God tells us to be accepted by him, we must accept all these laws, every one of them. We might say, "God is not fair." If this is the only way I can be accepted by God, he has made it impossible. There is no way I can keep that list of rules perfectly! Galatians 5: 3-4 Again I declare to every man who lets himself be circumcised that he is obligated to obey the whole law. You who have been justified by law have been alienated from Christ; you have fallen away from grace.

God knows we cannot keep this list of rules. It is no surprise to him. Romans 3: 19 Now we know whatever the law says, it says to those who are under the law, so that every mouth may be silenced and the whole world accountable to God.

We are guilty everyone of us of breaking these laws. Romans 3: 20 Therefore no one will be declared righteous in his sight by observing the law; rather, through the law we have conscious of sin.

So the purpose of these laws are to show us we are sinners. They are like spiritual thermometers. They can show us when we are sick, but they are not the medicine we need to get better.

With these rules no one can boast that God loves them more than another, because we think we are better than others. Through these laws God brings everyone to the point of realizing Psalm 51: 5 Surely I was sinful at birth, from the time my mother conceived me.

And through this we can see how holy and righteous God is, and how much we need God, and that God is always here with us. So, when we focus on obeying the commandments we miss their purpose.

There are two types of sinners. First: The people who believe there is something they can do to make themselves acceptable to God. Example; keeping these rules, keeping the golden rule, going to church, praying, be baptized, give to charity, be nice to others. These are all great thing and yes God wants us to do them, but good does not outweigh bad, none of these things can restore a broken relationship with our Father. Second: Helpless sinners. These are the people who know there is nothing you can do to become acceptable to God. He just loves without condition, without reason, He just loves. Isaiah 64: 6 All of us become as one who is unclean, and all our righteous acts are like filthy rags; we all shrivel up like a leaf, and like the wind our sins sweep us away.

Thank You again God, for sending us Jesus.

When we're reborn, made new in Christ, it should be plain for everyone to see. Ephesians 4: 24 Put on the new man which was created according to God, in true righteousness and holiness.

The change needs to come from the inside-out. Come on now, we have been given the change to our true life and family. Does it matter if their heart was made soft from being hard? Does it matter that the gift of a whole brand new heart was received? We need to come together and shout with the voice of triumph. This life bring many differences; for instance it is easy to be kind and good to those who show us love, and are doing thing we are in comfort with. Right? But wow to love those who are different, do not love us, do not respond in ways familiar to what we are comfortable with. What a way to exercise our new heart, putting it to the practice, because practice does make perfect. Turn some heads my friends and hearts will change.

And please no matter how long and steep the path appears or how heavy the task of the unfamiliar seems, hear God telling you, "Press on my precious one; one step is all I ask." We conquer by continuing.

We need to remember and stay aware of the fact that God knows everything that is going to happen, before it happens. Redemption has been in place since the beginning. We were created to be the Bride, so let there be no doubt about the Salvation plan for the Son of God to give his life to redeem his Bride. So never forget or take for granted how grand Abba Daddy really is. This way as we stay in God we stay safe. 1 John 3: 7-8 So, my dear children, don't let anyone direct you from the truth. It's the person who acts right who is right, just as we see it lived out in our righteous Messiah. Those who make a practice of sin are straight from the devil, the pioneer in the practice of sin. The Son of God enters the scene to abolish the devil's ways.

We have freedom to chose who we will serve, and my friends there are only two choices, God or Lucifer. So don't let yourself be deceived by the wrong choice, or be blackmailed into something fake. God has all power, mercy, grace, and everything that happens is permitted through God first. Isaiah 5: 20-21 Woe to those who call evil good and good evil, who put darkness for light and light for darkness, who put bitter for sweet and sweet for bitter. Woe to those who are wise in their own eyes and clever in their own sight.

The spirit of Jezebel is to lead the people of God astray and the spirit of Ahab is to allow her to do just that as long as it is to his benefit.

Jezebel was a high priest, very devoted to Baal, regardless of her marriage to Ahab, she was first of all wife to Baal. Her mission is to gain control over our reason for creation, to be the Bride of Christ. It is her duty and honour to control us to worship her husband Baal.

Now Ahab allows Baal to be worshiped or God to be worshiped depending on which one will better service his personal purpose, allowing mixture to pervade the people of God. Luke 21: 34-36 "Be careful, or your hearts will be weighed down with dissipation, drunkenness and the anxiety of life, and that will close on you unexpectedly like a trap. For it will come upon all who live on the face of the whole earth. Be always on the watch, and pray that you may be able to escape all that is about to happen, and that you may be able to stand before the Son of Man."

We can't let the spirit of fear control our lives. Fear of loss, death, shame, exposure, because these will cause us big pain, and they will wound us and our loved ones. So in place of fear let's pray in love, love will free us from fear and bring us joy, love will even lead us right into Abba Daddies arms.

Detective work comes in quite handy on this journey, always investigating for truth, because when we chose to believe in a lie, strong delusions from God will be sent. 2 Thessalonians 2: 9-12 The coming of the lawless one will be in accordance with the work of Satan displayed in all kinds of counterfeit miracles, signs and wonders, and in every sort of evil that deceives those who are perishing. They perish because they refuse to love the truth and so be saved. For this reason God sends them a powerful delusion so that they will believe the lie and so that all will be condemned who have not believed the truth but have delighted in wickedness.

Jesus has already been sent to take away the sins of the world. When the words "It is finished," were spoken it was finishes. The very curse on earth of mans sin was placed to rest (the Sabbath from sin). The veil was torn, we can now step right up to the throne of glory, turn around and bring that freedom into our lives releasing it into whoever wants to receive it. We no longer labour under the curse, it did not resurrect with the resurrection only restoration was risen in blessing overflowing to everyone. And if we are not living in the gift of this freedom we are living a lie. Though our bodies are still condemned to death from this world, we are blessed with enough life to fill us with his grace, mercy, and to labour in his purpose from our very creation, and wake up to the full spiritual life that is our true existence here for God, right into eternity.

Revelation 2: 7 He who has an ear, let him hear what the Spirit says to the churches. To him who overcomes, I will give the right to eat from the tree of life, which is in the paradise of God.

I was lost to the true quality of love, in the full character of this world. Then revival came into the living room releasing 'surgeon mercy' who transplanted the heart 'grace' sent from heaven. Now sin sets off the alarm in warning to stay in the gifted freedom, where I find the face of Jesus. There is not a sinner here on earth that is safe from Salvation. No one is too good, or to bad. Ephesians 2: 8-9 For it is by grace you have been saved, through faith - and this not from yourselves, it is the gift of God - not by works, so that no one can boast.

Once again I hear the words sing in my spirit that come with this new heart, Works of Love are nothing but Works of Peace! Ephesians 2: 19-22 Consequently , you are no longer foreigners and aliens, but fellow citizens with God's people and members of God's household, built on the foundation of the apostle and prophets, with Jesus Christ himself as the chief cornerstone. In him the whole building is joined together and rises to become a holy temple in the Lord. And in him you to are being built together to become a dwelling in which God lives by his Spirit. The gifts of God are given to draw people closer to him not to us. We have already witnessed the great works God has done. In order to see the even greater works yet to come, we must be faithful in even the smallest, most unspectacular stuff, God asks us to do. We all volunteer to do the fun things, but not many of us want to go through the discipline and training that it takes to be trusted.

1 Corinthians 3: 11 For no one can lay any foundation other than the one already laid, which is Jesus Christ.

Not only is Jesus the foundation, he is the whole building. In all aspects we are to grow up to him. Our ministries are just vessels through which God himself ministers to his church.

Ezra 4: 24-5: 2 That put a stop to the to the work on the Temple of God in Jerusalem. Nothing more was done until the second year of the reign of Darius king of Persia. Meanwhile the prophets Haggai and Zechariah son of Iddo were preaching to the Jews in Judah and Jerusalem in the authority of the God of Israel who ruled them. And so Zerabbabel son of Shealtiel and Jozadok started again , rebuilding The Temple of God of Jerusalem. The prophets of God were right there helping them.

The work of the Temple of God ceased until the prophets started to prophecy. This is why the prophetic ministry is being raised again, to give inspiration and assistance for those called into leadership.

Prophets seldom hold potions of authority over people, their calling is usually to serve those who are in authority. Leaders will be held back in their ministries or sink into idolatry if they do not have prophets who support and encourage them. Both leaders and prophets working together is essential if the work of God is to be completed, and both must refrain from doing the others job.

James 3: 17-18 But the wisdom that comes from heaven is first of all pure; then peace-loving, considerate, submissive, full of mercy and good fruit, impartial and sincere. Peacemakers who sow in peace raise a harvest of righteousness.

The church is suppose to be a family not an organization, only in this way can we be a true church. Families are built on relationships not programs. Building their foundation on trust not rules and regulations.

A very important reason for a church, actually the most important reason is not for a gathering place for people, but it should be the place where the Lord dwells among his people who are gathered. When the people are in the Lord's dwelling, he is able to build us and fit us together. Our primary goal must be first to gain the endorsement of God not man. In order to obtain the endorsement of God, we must devote ourselves to the truth, integrity and submission to God's Spirit.

1 Corinthians 14: 8 Again if the trumpet does not sound a clear call, who will get ready for battle? When we can produce a distinct sound, the church will hear us.

Spiritual life is having spiritual communication with Jesus. In this form of living people can kill our body, but they cannot kill us, because we are living in a higher level.

Proverbs 18: 21 The tongue has the power of life and death, and those who love it will eat its fruit.

The spirit searches the deep things of God. That is why anyone led by the Spirit is on a constant quest to go deeper. In order for us to be so close to God that he will be constantly revealing revelation to us because we are his friends.

John 6: 63 The Spirit gives life; the flesh counts for nothing. The words I have spoken to you are spirit and they are life.

I am always hungry, no eating actually is a better word, eating is my biggest tackle such a challenge, and since I quit smoking I have put on many/many pounds, but I am also very hungry not just for food but for peace that comes from a pure heart. I am thirsty as well, but not just for fluids (water) is what most people would say, but another secret about me is I do not like water, I do thirst for the passion to serve my Father, and be with him at all times. I use to walk around naked, not from wearing clothes, but from heavens joy that is found in God's voice, but now royal robes of purple are wrapped beautifully around my spirit as songs, poems, serenade me from morning till night. I was homeless, not from shelter made from brick, but from a heart that understands, a home covered in love and that is so inviting that I never want to leave, and many want to come.

Wow, what a stability we have in Christ even when or should I say especially when life's trials attack. How often we stumble, how often we fail, but you Jesus are always there to rescue us, make thing fresh and help us to grow. Now we are ready to triumph in the unity we are bound to with love from the Holy Spirit.

I am now a servant of the Gospel by the gift from God's grace given to me through the working of his power.

Ephesians 4: 1-7 Therefore I, a prisoner for serving the Lord, beg you to lead a life worthy of your calling, for you have been called by God. Be humble and gentle. Be patient with each other, making allowances for each other's faults because of your love. Always keep yourself united in the Holy Spirit, and bind yourself together with peace. We are all one body, we have the same spirit, and we all have been called to the same glorious future. There is only one Lord, one faith, one baptism, and there is only one God and Father, who is over us all and in us all living through us all. However, he has given each of us a special gift according to the generosity of Christ.

To be in exile is never a voluntary experience. It is always something forced upon a person by things or circumstances over which the affected ones have no control. "Exile," is not a wilderness through which we journey to arrive at a promised land. Exile is an enforced displacement into which we enter without any verifiable hope of either a return to the past or an arrival at some desired place. Exile needs to be a defining movement into a new unseen hope, our past left behind, and future out of focus, just pure trust in the mercy, grace and works from God.

It is traumatic to watch God who has given shape, definition, and creation to all life, be removed from his creation by this world which he also created. The God that is so intensely personal, and intimately involved in all our affairs.

Exiled people know there can be no return to the past, so we must be prepared either to give up, or look in a new direction. So we must be willing to dismiss the churches comfortable holding power of the past, a step not taken lightly, because with this step, there is only one other alternative open to us, and that is to step forward into we know not what! Putting our faith on the new insight emerging from the Kingdom of heaven for a new true direction.

Anger seems to hoover just beneath the surface of organized religion. The preaching of religion is marked by finger pointing and facial expressions of hostility while they talk about the wrath of God. Anger lies underneath the glee expressed as church assigns unbelievers to hell. Anger seems to be the reason rule after rule in the church were created to clarify just who is in – and who is out of this religious enterprise. So that religious people can know who their enemies are and can act appropriately against them.

So how about we have some prayer? Abba Daddy please remove every expectation from our heart, and replace it with total acceptance, now the world can feel the peace and safety from Christ through us, which will allow revival to be released, because we are all one creation, created for love, from pure love. Amen.

I know, some people make some choices me included which make this hard to fathom as being possible at times. But it does not matter if we like it or not, the truth is we are all one big family, God's special children.

Maybe we could look at things in a different way. Let's try replacing 'who' for 'what' rather than pretending we have a source of divine revelation to our religious questions. Let's inquire! Is there a depth dimension of life that is ultimately spiritual? If so 'who' is it? Is there a connection, a gap maybe, to both this life and beyond, linking us to a presence? A presence in our heart of our life that could be totally unfamiliar with the present state we now understand, but nonetheless is a divine and an infinite reality? If so 'who' is it? Wow, it's God, expanding us to our full purpose in our consciousness of awakening to him. Opening our possibilities to such a reality, and become aware of this awesome relationship, learning to become intensely aware of 'who' is stirring.

Think back to what your life was like before you met Christ. Not when you first started going to church, but when your friendship with Christ was started. Now thank him for the transformation that he has made in your life – both your instant rebirth into his kingdom and also the gradual remoulding of your character since then and is still being worked on. God's promise is to do everything 'with' us, not everything 'for' us.

Prayer in faith comes from an abiding peace for the person being prayed for – with only the confidence of God's best for the entire situation in his purpose. It is based on a personal relationship, and on a trusted conviction that God is worthy to be trusted. Praying in faith is the act of a simple hearted child of God.

We must find a way to make Yahweh the one on centre stage. Experiencing the phrase "practicing the presence of God," intentionally involving God in every detail in our lives. Confident that we matter to God. Psalm 18: 19 He brought me out of a spacious place; he rescues me because he delighted in me.

Like David believed, truly believed. The invisible world of God, heaven and the angels was every bit as real as his own world of swords and spears, (slingshots and stones) caves and thrones. So must we.

Even though our anxiety and fear sneak into our lives, we need to learn how to turn them into an overwhelming power of joy, just because we are again working together with our father.

We open up ourselves to God as we pray we become the answers to our own prayers. So often we come to God in prayer detached from the very situation we are praying about, as if we have no part in it at all. "God change the situation," we pray. While we fail to take account of the obvious fact that we ourselves are part of that situation. The difficult relationship, a complicated problem. When God changes things, he will begin by changing us and the part we have to play in whatever the circumstances. The very fact that we are concerned about the problem, and are bringing it before God in prayer, makes us prime candidates to be used by him in solving it.

Psalm 6: 6-9 I am worn out from groaning; all night long I flood my bed with weeping and drench my couch with tears. My eyes grow week with sorrow; they fail because of my foes. Away from me, all who do evil, for the Lord has heard my cry for mercy; the Lord accepts my prayer.

A single teardrop on earth summons the King of heaven. WOW!

One of the greatest drawbacks of our cold sophisticated society is its reluctance to show tears. How silly, and unfortunate. An uninvolved heart surrounded by heavy bars of confinement, is the ultimate result of this. A structure that resembles a prison, we need to mimic the prophet Jeremiah, so tender and sensitive. His heart lived in no such dwelling as a prison, his tender heart full of God's Spirit always allowed him to bury his head in his hands and sob aloud. To us it may seem strange that Jeremiah was selected by God to be God's personal spokesman at the most critical time in Israel's history. Seems like such an unlikely choice, unless, you value tears like God does. So let loose and allow some tenderness to conquer this great drawback. You might lose a little of your polished respectability, but you'll gain a lot more freedom, and a lot less pride. These tears might last for a season, your peace and freedom will follow. Tears are the material out of which heaven weaves its brightest rainbow.

I would like to share with you the most blessed Christmas Day of my life to this day. My husband was in a horrible mood, bless his soul he was grieving for his mother who had passed away a few months earlier. My son would not even answer his phone never mind come for dinner, so I had to settle with wishing him a Merry Christmas on his answering machine. So off I went to church. This was not my home church but a church I was very familiar with we had a good relationship in the Lord. The reverend and I were the only ones who showed up the reverend however preformed the entire service communion and all just for us. He said it was the least he could do since I come out to be filled with God's Spirit. He had no idea what was going on with my life he was just obedient and overflowed me with blessing. Now while we were worshiping and giving praise to God, the presence of the Holy Spirit came filled the entire church including us with a beautiful filled Christmas present of joy and peace, encouragement and promise. Then the reverend laid healing hands on my shoulders and I could feel the fire of the Living God physically working within me, and through my spirit. Wow to be this blessed and to be able to dwell in the presence of Abba Daddy is really speechless. I will never forget this dreadful Christmas that ended up one of the top ten moments with God in this thankful life. Blessing it and living in this glory forever and ever.

A Christian is not someone who simply follows the great teachings of Christ. A Christian is someone who is one with Christ in a personal relationship, then follows these great teachings, the more we identify with him, the harder it is to tell the two apart.

Christ does not force his way into our lives, proclaiming he is going to take over. Challenging everything to go his way or else. No, it is up to us to make the choice to go to him. Temptations still come but sin is no longer our only alternative. Another route has now been made available to us, obedient to Christ which in itself will keep us so busy there is not much room or time to get into trouble. The choice is up to us, and the amazing part of this is that we will be loved through both.

Choice is always a part of life in Christian living the choices that are made either lead us towards sin or away from sin. It is how we program our spiritual compass to who we turn towards and call Master. Accept Christ by faith, because unless our faith is constant and real sin will still rule life, and determine to whom we belong. So really it would be in my best interest here to give up my choice and choose to surrender it all to Abba Daddy. Now I know where my path will lead.

The Holy Spirit is not just a concept the Holy Spirit is alive and is a major part of our lives, especially if our interest is to be in the kingdom and not religious. We have a battle on our hands that is for sure, constantly battling between sin and obedience, the very fact of the awareness that we have these choices to battle against, that concern, shows that we want the victory of glory to live within us. There are no rules in this war, we are all one rank with our main weapon being the guidance of the Holy Spirit, and following in unity.

Funny how when we set out to please God, we end up being pleased as well, marching is how this battle will be won, in a two beat rhythm sounding like this: Spirit/Flesh, Spirit/Flesh. It is a very simple way of life one of either committing to the Spirit or committing to the old me, but on a daily bases not just a Sunday stroll with Jesus.

It is impossible I have found to walk with the Holy Spirit and not be on speaking terms, or walk with the Spirit and deny his cause. It is in the Scriptures we are told that the Spirit will teach us what to say, and bring it to our heart when we need it. If we are not on speaking terms how would this be possible? John 14: 26-27 But the counsellor, the Holy Spirit, whom the Father will send in my Name, will teach you all things and will remind you of everything I have said to you. Peace I leave with you; my peace I give you. I do not give you as the world gives. Do not let your heart be troubled and do not be afraid.

I know a secret which I am permitted to share: Prayer is the secret to a full life in Christ, (talk to me Jesus says), prayer is the secret to a ministry full of fruit, prayer is the secret for the true church (a church in strong belief, un-error, lack of sin, Christ like behaviour in our daily living), prayer is the secret of having our heart full of joy. Best piece of gossip you will ever receive!

How do we go about being a stepping stone, and not a stumbling block? By simply being genuine, accepting even when we do not understand, working on being a listener in just our every day conversations, really hear what is being said. To receive the full information of the message being exposed you often have to listen how something is being said, as well with the words themselves. For example: an occasional but important offhand remark or a facial expression. The real trick is us wanting to hear the other person before we can be willing to listen. Proverbs 18: 13 He who answers before listening - that is his folly and his shame.

Christ's kind of love has no motive but the good of others it expects nothing in return, because it only seeks to give. So we have to make sure we are receiving from heaven so we can give to others what has been revealed, this is 'filling in the gap'. 1 John 3: 16-20 this is how we know what love is; Jesus Christ laid down his life for us. And we ought to lay down our lives for our brothers. If anyone has material possessions and sees his brother in need but has no pity on him, how can the love of God be in him? Dear children, let us not love with words or tongue but with action and truth. This then is how we know we belong to the truth, and how we set our hearts at rest in his presence whenever our hearts condemn us for God is greater than our hearts, and he knows everything.

Becoming a stepping stone does not mean however being a doormat it does not mean you submit unquestioningly, serving Christ is not a mechanical attention to duty, but the highest possible motive to glorify God.

Our main interest is what a person could be rather than what a person is, or has been. This isn't always easy or automatic, because it requires growth through change. And growth and change are often painful and not everyone grows at the same pace. We need to take on the attitude of hope and confidence, committed strictly to the Almighty God in faith and obedience, because even in the life of the Christian I am going to slip, and I am going to fail. That is why I need to be non-stop connected to my Father.

We need a hope a power and a potential that comes from beyond ourselves, as you grow, change, become all that God has in mind for us to be. Continually learning to trust, listen to and glorify the Living God. And you never look back..............

Romans 16: 25-27 Now to him who is able to establish you by my gospel and proclaim of Jesus Christ according to the revelation of the mystery hidden for long ages past, but now revealed and made known through the prophetic writings by the command of the eternal God, so that all nations might believe and obey him – to the only wise God be glory forever through Jesus Christ.

When we enter into God's presence to pray, we need to acknowledge our lack of knowledge on how to pray correctly. Truth be-known we can't even pray unless we are being guided by the Holy Spirit to be delivered into God's presence. Now in total direction of God's Will, we surrender our requests trusting that they have been answered, and now be willing to accept the answer God has for us. This is how it is possible to give thanks for everything, because anything that comes from God is only good.

Passionate response putting adrenalin into prayer so now the desires expressed flow through the intercessory Christ. Strong sense of expectation and anticipation exhibit the end product of prayer that develops out of Eucharistic action. What an honour to be able to pray like Jesus. 1 Corinthians 11: 23 For I receive from the Lord what I also pass on to you.

We get to copy the vision from heaven in hope for those who have and are going to by faith, receive our Lord and therefore putting them in a position to be moved in the Holy Spirit. We can sing: Song of Songs 4: 16 Awaken north wind, and come south wind! Blow on my garden that its fragrance may spread abroad! May my lover come into this garden and taste its choice fruits.

We can do nothing till we are set to motion by God's Spirit. Love is present but invisible until stirred; virtue is asleep until awakened to responsive obedience. How many of us leave the act of worship still asleep? Walking out of Church no different than when we had entered, missing out on the awesome experience of the Spirit praying in us. Soaring intimacies of love and faith only make sense when you participate in them. Bystanders can't see the whole of the kingdom. Heaven right here on earth.

The theme of Pentecost is in the covenant relation at Sinai: At Sinai Israel was introduced of this structure and direction. The past clarified is the future established, and the everyday conduct of the people was ordered within the covenant boundaries. Just like for them then, as for us now, life is not a random series of experience, impulsive (frivolous), casual or unpredictable, there is a plot, structure, purpose and design. Each detail of every person's life is part of a large picture the title of this picture being 'Salvation!' At Sinai God revealed his ways and showed how all behaviour and all relationships were included in the overall structure of redemption. The people found out who God was and where they stood in relation to him.

The Sinai covenant is an axle for holding two basic realities together: First; everything God does involves us (Election). Second; everything we do now, matters (Covenant). Because I am chosen, I have consequences. Election a unique identity – Covenant describes how the things I do fit into those designs. Our lives must then be consequential. In short this shows us the relationship that we are of value, and what we do has its purpose. Nothing is random, or inconsequential or meaningless. Sinai was not a special holy place to which the people had come on a pilgrimage. It was where they happened to be when God's Will was clarified and the people's response was recognized.

Are we convinced that God really does work among us where we are everyday? Do we believe that what we do, whether in faith or unbelief, sin or righteousness, obedience or rebellion, is significant? Because not only is it significant it is a part of the structural purpose.

We need to find our area of praying, this like everything else in the complete body of Christ will be different for everyone, with each difference in unity working in perfect harmony. Here again relationship among us is very important we need to know each other's heart in prayer so we can accept the format and understand each other while praying. Mine is listening, and I seem to hear most clear through praise and worship. So even though you might not hear from me in a circle of prayer, this does not mean I am not praying many times what I hear will be spoken out by someone else and it does not matter who speaks it out as long as it gets spoken out, so if God does not ask me to speak specifically I will stay in silence. Plus most time in prayer circle quiet or aloud I will be praying Scripture. I do not enter into a pre-structured prayer time unprepared; I come prepared with an open heart, ready to receive and prayerfully in agreement, and after it is over I end on my own in total praise to God, believing everything has been answered in God's Will and for God's Purpose. What is your area of prayer?

God's love may take many forms, ranging from tenderness to discipline and even anger, but no matter what the form it is always in pure love. We think it is for our sake or in our best interest but I am apt to believe it is for the greater purpose of creation. But no matter what the reason it is always pure this love and we have an obligation to live in the nature of this love.

Most of us are excited when a prophet receives a Word for us. Is the Word being given lined up with what our Father is already doing and with what the Bible tells us he wants us to do? Question words that lead in different directions than those already evident in our lives and ministries. Scripture demands us to preach the Gospel and make disciples. No subsequent (after or following) word can be allowed to deny that command. Scripture Commands Unity.

Do my concrete realities go along with the word? Reality checks could save us a great deal of headaches and confusion if only we would take the time to pray and examine. When receiving guidance or direction, we need to consider if concrete realities are embedded in the revelation itself, this will confirm the accuracy of what is being spoken. Confirmation! (A true word will confirm something we have already alive in our hearts). Nowhere in Scripture can this be found. We have to beware that what is already in the heart (feelings, considerations, thoughts) of the one the word is for is not being sensed, reflecting feelings as a word from God without discerning the difference between what comes from the heart of God and what has its source in the heart of the person. The Word has to have an impact that accomplishes the purpose of God and connects all who hear with Jesus. Our livelihood and nutrition flows from the Holy Spirit and the authoritative and perfect revelation of the Bible. So the word given cannot add to or subtract from Scripture, prophecy cannot be made into a key for interpreting the Bible.

When reading the bible it is important that we have an understanding of the context of the passage we are reading with the verses surrounding it. Without context revelation for understanding cannot be formed. When we lift a verse from its context not only can we miss the revelation, but we often also distort its true understanding entirely. Diverted from the perfect, reliable, true, unfailing life of God's message we do not have the right of changing, spiritualizing, making it say anything other than it is originally intended to say. Absolutely no level of supposed Holy Spirit inspiration can be allowed to supersede these considerations, or else we have allowed ourselves the right to make the Bible say whatever we want it to say. God is not going to give up his throne for us, so when we do this we separate ourselves from him. Careful that arrogance does not sneak in to personal revelation, prophetic words, dreams and visions. Never stop expanding your understanding, or filling your heart. But never do it at the expense of altering the Message.

I will not rest on anything 'I' have already done, anything 'I' am doing or anything 'I' will still do. I will however rest on what Jesus has done for me on the cross, and on his finished works of the forgiveness of my sins. God does not accept my personal ideas on how to get right with him. I might have the best intentions in the world, but sincerity is not enough – it does not bridge the gap. I look at independent thinking as a good thing. I need to be careful, because an independent spirit can also be very self-centered. So my aim is to only hear 'God's Voice,' and pray to obey it completely. Asking for help to get rid of my worldly nature, so my heart is always at home in heaven, while still living here on God's created earth. Letting only the Will of God be my strength. Revelation 21: 27 Nothing impure will ever enter it, nor will anyone who does what is shameful or deceitful, but only those whose names are written....In the book of life.

Now as we gather as a group for instance for a meal, or a meeting, I have heard it said, "lets open with a little prayer." Always beware and aware that there is no such place as a "little" prayer. Prayer enters us into the lions' den bringing us before the Holy One, where it is uncertain whether we will come back alive or hey even sane. For it is a great honour, courageous respect, to find the boldness and in awe enter into the Living God. No matter what the reason for our approach.

A lot of folks both inside and outside the church think prayer as a harmless but necessary starting pistol that shoots blanks and gets things going like projects, conversations, plans, performances. This is an actual outrage and blasphemy to adjust prayer to accommodate. We don't leave space for prayer we wrap what we are praying over with a blanket of God's Will, leaving space for what is being prayed for in the prayer. The worst part is when we do place prayer in the apparent first place we contribute to its actual diminishment. By simply uttering a prayer in the belief it will get thing started we justify that everyone is now free to go their own way without including God any more. That now, (prayer) at least is out of the way; now we can get on to the important things at hand that require our attention. We have pleased God with our piety (loyalty) and are free to get on to the things concerning us. Psalm 33: 11 Let all the earth fear the Lord; let all the people of the earth revere him. For he spoke and it came to be; he commanded and it stood firm. The Lord foils the plans of the nations; he thwarts the purposes of the peoples. But the plan of the Lord stands firm forever, the purposes of his heart through all generations.

All speech in prayer is answering speech because all of us have been spoken to before we intercede, our appeal. Scripture is one place that speaks to us, because it is the Living Word, and no word of God can go unanswered. The word of God now then is not complete when uttered, it is complete when answered.

It is not to learn a specific answer that is required from us, but that we acquire fluency in a personal language that is accurately responsive to what we hear God saying to us from his Word out of the Scriptures and from Christ for our ever changing situations and various levels of faith. Our vocabulary needs to be personal and wide, ranging to answer everything that God says from whenever we happen to hear it within every developing stage of this pilgrimage across the entire spectrum of our lives. Do you view prayer as being a specialized and incidental language to get by on during those moments when we happen to pass through a few miles of religious country? Here is a newsflash: When our entire lives are involved with our Father we need fluency in the language of the country we are living in at any given time.

My biggest hope in this life is to receive a righteousness that is completely acceptable to God. Psalm 17: 15 But because I have done what is right, I will see you. When I awake, I will be fully satisfied, for I will see you face to face.

Here is the life line prayerfully that will form the stages of my life. The most amazing part of this our Fathers life for us is that it is unending, because God's time and lifeline is so different, than the worlds time and lifeline where we pass through each stage only once if we are even lucky enough to get to all the stages and then life ends.

1: Genesis is the prenatal word of God. Where we discover great energies gathering together, hope in an enormous birth is swelling in the womb of Genesis.

2: Exodus is this birth and infancy, Exodus shows how it's infant people were drawn out of the dangerous waters, and taught them their first baby steps as a people of worship. So in return they could attend and respond to the God who gave them birth and being.

3: Leviticus is childhood, children of God learning to read his purpose for their lives from his word for the first time. Studying the ABC's for the reason of their creation under the mercy and judgement of God.

4: Numbers is adolescence reaching for adulthood, awkwardly rebelling against authority. In the stage of restlessness and wallowing impatiently in a no-man's-land of confusion.

5: Deuteronomy is adulthood, here is where love interacts all that develops in us as we grow from a hope in the womb, to birth, infancy, through childhood, into adolescence and presents that wholeness for an intimate and faithful personal relationship , with each other and with God.

Fivefold Word of God that comprehensively calls us into existence of our purpose in God's creation, from new birth to mature love, requiring thoroughness in our response. Every prayer is restored to proper context in the word of God.

Thank You Father for giving me a unique relationship with you, I wish I may/I wish I might, always trust in you to maintain it. Revelation 21: 3 I heard a loud shout from the throne, saying, "Look, the home of God is now among his people! He will live with them, and they will be his people. God himself will be with them.

In wilderness function there is rest. What you say, are you talking about woman? Yes the wilderness is a place of loneliness, reflecting, suffering, even temptation, but it is also the place God intends to position us for rest and in a situation to find him. Learning how to peacefully embrace solitude and loneliness, no one else can truly understand what we are going through, our depth and our hunger for God. Resting is to yield to this place of deprivation into which the Holy Spirit has led us, to surrender to the wilderness and allow it to do its work. The wilderness is the place where God blesses by not blessing. In the wilderness you do not learn what you can do rather you learn what you cannot do until you come to rest in God.

In heaven everything is living and everything is pure, a total resting place in God. This is the place wilderness prepares us for. 1 Corinthians 2: 9 That is what the Scriptures means when they say, "No eye has seen, no ear has heard, and no mind has imagined what God has prepared for those who love him."

I should never wonder what "I" am going to do or say, but rather be observant and a vessel for what the risen Christ is doing or saying that is moulding a gospel story out of every life. Everything we walk in on, there is something already going on, we are just a part of what the risen Christ has already set in to motion, already brought into being. How blessed are we?!

Holiness cannot be dictated it must grow, and grow from the inside out. No one knows how Jesus is going to appear in a person, let alone a whole congregation.

As a congregation we should be working together with environment of heaven and earth functioning as one unit, everything harmonizing together in certain rhythms in all dimensions, in its full magnitude.

It is time we stop trying to improve our religion, stop serving our religion. Instead what we should be doing is destroying our religious nature, so we can deal in faith with a Living Saviour. Instead of accusing evil, or denouncing sin and wickedness, we need to call into question the future. Like Jonah did when he entered the city and after walking through it for about a day, simply said, "In forty days Nineveh will be destroyed." Now it is up to us to choose our future, by ceasing to sin, or endure the consequences. Now blame is no longer possible.

Is our present belief strong and true? Or are we to secure and obsessed in the ways of this world, and religious beliefs? Are we willing to grab hope at its core, live in faith, examine pure truth in periods of testing the reality of our lives, and with genuine certainty believe that God is skilfully shaping and wisely guiding our lives? Accepting my life as c. womb, pregnant with new beginnings? Are we allowing each day to be a training ground for living in worship by faith, in a preparation for discovery of obedience to the cross? Our hearts need to absorb the Message of God as a proclamation of hope, not a prediction of doom, seeing in the destroyed religion another way of life, faith in our Father.

Repeat after me, "I believe in the Holy Spirit!" If this is really true why are we still moonlighting as efficient experts in religion? We cannot nurture the life of Spirit in any form or time, or by managing or controlling the development of souls. The moment tidiness (order) and conduct (behaviour) become dominant, true Spirit is restrained, and our souls come to be viewed as energies managed, objects to control, moulding into what we want not who we are.

We can have nothing to do with blue prints on which people are made good and comfortable at the expense of their freedom, at the cost from God. We are constantly being formed into an image, an 'image' of God. Found in the gift of 'image'-ination. Capacity to make the connection between visible and invisible, seeing heaven while here on earth, seeing eternity as it is in its true form of "NOW". Here in imagination is where we find the means to see reality at its whole.

A major evil is following a fixed plan performed in a fitted and systematic way to the imagination. Our imagination is among the chief glories gifted to human creation. If it is healthy and energetic it ushers us into adoration and wonder into the mysteries of God. If it is sluggish it turns us into copycats, and couch potatoes. It is imagination that is the tool which connects us to the visible and invisible, material and spiritual, heaven and earth.

Do/re/me/fa/so/la,la,la, I am warming up to sing so you might want to use your imagination to catch the sound from heaven. "I Surrender All". Ok, all done with the singing! How many times are we suppose to surrender? I am wondering if surrendering and forgiving have the same mathematical formula? I was at church, this is now years after my adoption into the kingdom, we were blessed by special guests who blew the shofar (a rams horn blown as a trumpet) over me. So many prayers seemed to miraculously be answered as I fell into a guided brokenness. Once again I surrendered this time to the rebuilding from this brokenness in the Holy Spirit, the forming of the Will of God in my life and on my life was strengthened once again to a level of total awe. God is good my friend, God is good. This phrase really does not even come close to what God indeed is.

Anyone who is walking intimately with God, having a fellowship and spiritual union with God, receives God's revelation and clearly knows what moves they should take. This behaviour will receive no sympathy from men, for others cannot know our walk with Christ.

Holy Spirit must be completely enhanced and have total control, or the soul will constantly war against him. The soul needs to completely lose its place and submit entirely to Holy Spirit. Then we can realize the basic difference between spiritual and soul experience. One begins with God, the other from man.

Nothing is of any value in Christian life except being in the Spirit. Everything has its own function, so it is for the Spirit to discern the things of God, and the things from God. God does not want us to grow in our own knowledge, eloquence, or gifts. God only wants us to grow in his Spirit, though his wisdom, vigour, provisions. God's Will is that our new life in Christ, resurrection from death to the world, will grow, in the way we were created to be. Leaving the developed creation (the one of flesh which equals sin) to be buried. This is a lifetime journey with again a constant surrender to our Father, always moving forward in the Will of God, trusting only the daily bread of God's Will. Becoming nourished in God's mercy and grace, and enjoying the full banquet of love. Ephesians 1: 17 I keep asking that the God of our Lord Jesus Christ, the glorious Father may give you the spirit of wisdom and revelation, so that you may know him better.

In fellowship with God, he gives revelation. And only in receiving revelation in the spirit do we positively know God. Everything else is just the activity of the mind. The mind of man is surely different, one from the other. But the Spirit of God is always the same and in unity with Christ no matter in whom it is born. And the Spirit can only grow through faithfulness and obedience to God, not in any knowledge that can be achieved with the mind. Colossians 1: 9-14 For this reason, since the day we heard about you, we have not stopped praying for you and asking God to fill you with the knowledge of his will through all spiritual wisdom and understanding. And we pray this in order that you may live a life worthy of the Lord and may please him in every way; bearing fruit in every good work, growing in knowledge of God, being strengthened with all power according to his glorious might that you may have great endurance and patience, and joyfully giving thanks to the Father, who has qualified you to share in the inheritance of the saints in the kingdom of light. For he has rescued us from the dominion of darkness and brought us into the kingdom of the Son he loves, in whom we have redemption, the forgiveness of sins.

If God, When God, Why God, How God? Strange/strange just plain outlandish that, pure love, total victory, gets blamed for what the world has become. God started creation in a perfect environment, and he never changed this: God made everything and he declared it to be good. Free will is what was, and still is separating us from this good, not God. God wants us to choose him, he needs us to choose him and have everything perfect. God will never give up on us and even though we ruined his plans he is still sticking to his promise and purpose for us. Remember that as long as we are doing things in our own strength, we do not allow God in our hearts to be saved. God can only save us when we give up trying to help ourselves. We must realize we are helpless sinners so we can ask God for help and in this approach we can be released from exhaustion to rest.

When Jesus was born, the shepherds were in the fields minding their own business, tending their sheep as they always did life as usual. Until the angels came, and then their whole world was turned upside down into the glory of God. Luke 2: 15-17 When the angels had left them and gone to heaven, the shepherds said to one another, "Let's go to Bethlehem and see this thing that has happened, which the Lord has told us about." So they hurried off and found Mary and Joseph, and the baby, who was lying in a manger. When they had seen him, they spread the word concerning what had been told them about the child.

Christ responded to Satan by quoting the Bible. God's written (living) Word he said it is more important to follow God than to take care of physical needs. This is very important to crab a hold of, many folks are so concerned about their physical life that they totally ignore their spiritual life, and then wonder where the balance in life is. Mark 8: 36 What good is it for a man to gain the whole world, yet forfeit his soul?

Jesus himself was tempted so we cannot accuse, when God finally judges all mankind, "God you don't get it!" Jesus was not born to us in a palace; and us in dirt. Jesus was tempted; even more than us. We can never ask, "How can you judge me when you never faced what I faced?" Because we my friend have never faced that cross that he bore for our sin. Hebrews 4: 15 For we do not have a high priest who is unable to sympathize with our weakness, but we have one who has been tempted in every way, just as we are - yet without sin.

It is important to know that Jesus did not come to earth to judge it. Instead he came to save the world from all the tragedy that sin, Satan, and self, bring. John 3: 17 For God did not send his Son into the world to condemn the world, but save the world through him.

That is why the first step we take to accept God is to recognize our sinfulness. Mark 2: 15-17 While Jesus was having dinner at Levi's house, many tax collectors and sinners were eating with him and the disciples, "Why does he eat with tax collectors and sinners?" On hearing this Jesus said to them, "It is not the healthy who need a doctor, but the sick. I have not come to call the righteous, but sinners."

We cannot make ourselves acceptable to God by fixing up our outward appearance we also cannot be accepted on our actions from the outside. We can maybe impress others with what we show on the outside, but God knows what we are really like.

If we do not believe God, and have our own idea about how to get rid of sin we cannot be made right with him. We need to trust the Lord to be our Saviour this is what our Father wants. God tells us over and over again in the Bible to trust the Lord Jesus as our Saviour. Proverbs 28: 26 He who trusts in himself is a fool, but he who walks in wisdom is kept safe.

In contrast to religion, the Bible says that the only true way to God was provided by God himself: John 14: 6 Jesus answered, "I am the way and the truth and the life. No one comes to the Father except through me."

friends (you) with the Fire. Dancing in God's glory is spectacular, but even better is dancing in God's glory with a friend. So right now my prayer is that whoever is reading this will be filled with this fire, so we can have one big Holy Spirit bonfire for eternity.

The first and third heavens are not separate places they are actually the same only on different plains. One is as close to the other as close as the breath blown to warm cold hearts. The Garden of Eden still is, it is out of reach until we get reconciled to Jesus, leaving a part in us still dead and being trapped under the third heaven in this first heaven, but still connected with God. It is exciting though to know that when we come alive and awake through submission from a connection to God to a full relationship with the Father, Son, and Holy Spirit, the doors of the Garden of Eden will be opened to us and we can freely partake of the first fruits. Come on let's go!

Ok, now how do we wake up? We must decide that we are hungrier for a relationship with the Father, Son, and Holy Spirit, than to witness or even perform the purist of miracles, signs, wonders, anointing, and gifts. In a true and trusting relationship we can stop choosing fruit from the wrong tree. Realizing that anything and everything comes from God, we do not have the power to satisfy this hunger unless we are totally surrendered to the Throne of God, and allow the heavens to be as they really are 'ONE'. So, before we even approach the gates of the garden we have to be clean, awake, and alive. Then with a smile, will the cherubim open the gates for us to enter.

Matthew 13: 44-46 "The kingdom of heaven is like a treasure hidden in a field. When a man found it, he hid it again, and then in his joy went and sold all he had and bought that field." "Again, the kingdom of heaven is like a merchant looking for fine pearls. When he found one of great value, he went away and sold everything he had and bought it."

So when we totally surrender everything back to God, because it is God's in the first place, now we can be richer than we ever imagined in a true relationship in the Trinity, from where every blessing flows.

To enter into the third heaven, and going into the Throne Room, is not a matter of flying off somewhere is space. It is a simple step into faith and a belief is our bridge between the plains, a belief in our faith, a faith in our belief, a full circle step into whole creation, because everything, what we know and what we don't know was created within the third heaven. Actually our spirit man walks in the spirit realm on a regular basis it being its home, fellowshipping freely. While our natural man walks her on earth, sees, tastes, smells, hears, feels from earth. So the two are one, one is the same as the other so guess where you already are. Where is your natural man going to follow? Because it will follow the spirit man either to the beautiful voice of Abba Daddy, or into the Lake of fire.

There are times in our life that it all seems.....I am not honestly sure how it seems, but man things can get to a point where holding on is hard. We can fill in a lot of stories here but instead let's stop and forgive each story, and surrender them all into God's hands. Because I think we have a hard time understanding that God is so big that this huge universe cannot contain him. We have to get over the idea of a little God flitting around in this big universe sort of waving his hands and trying to get things to behave. And when we can understand this we will see how powerful we are with the light of Christ, as it shines through the darkness of this world and Satan.

John 7: 38-39 Whoever believes in me, as the Scripture has said, streams of living water will flow from within him. By this he meant the Spirit, whom those who believe in him were later to receive. Up to that time the Spirit had not been given, since Jesus had not yet been glorified.

Speaking words of true life is when we are sharing what comes from the heart in love, not the mind in our opinion.

64

Demons are beings of spirit not flesh, and they only respond to words that are spiritual. The words from our mouth need to have the power of light to have the ability to drive out darkness, words that come from the heart that is joined together with God's heart. The fullness of the spiritual ability we are equipped with is measured to the degree that God dwells in us.

1 John 2: 26-27 I've written to warn you about those who are trying to deceive you. But they're no match for what is embedded deeply within you - Christ's anointing, no less! You don't need any of their so - called teaching. Christ's anointing teaches you, the truth on everything you need to know about yourself and him, uncontaminated by a single lie. Live deeply in what you are taught.

This does not mean we are not to receive teaching from people, for the Lord gifted teachers to his church for that purpose. It's the Holy Spirit working through the people we must recognize, so really we are not taught by people but by the use of people for his teaching. It is not just the words 'Of' the Lord we are after, but hearing the word Himself. John 16: 13 but when he, the spirit of truth, comes, he will guide you into all truth. He will not speak on his own; he will only speak what he hears, and he will tell you what is yet to come.

If we don't know how to listen how can we hear his presence and power, that which is truth?

The Father works from the inside out remember not from the outside in. This is why the thing we want to accomplish, tend to work slower than we are willing to accept.

The greatest produce of ministry is produced when it is being developed to be Christ like, and doing the work of the Father. This is how people are drawn to the kingdom. A single Christian has more power than all the armies of this earth. This is because God dwells in his people, and as we search and find God's living truth rather than doctrine the world as well can get to witness and learn this truth.

The Church (presence of God) is already much greater than anything Satan can counterfeit. Another wakeup call here people of God, as we sound the alarm multitudes will come and be blessed with the true bread from heaven. If it is adventure you are seeking then seek the true Christian life, because there is no greater or longer adventure available.

The church as it is now is coming to an end radical change is on the way. Genesis 35: 16-18 They left Bethel. They were still quite away from Ephrath when Rachel went into labour - hard, hard labour. When her labour pains were at their worst, the midwife said to her, "Don't be afraid - you have another boy." With her last breath, for she was now dying, she named him Ben-oni (son-of-my-pain), but his father named him Ben-jamin (son-of-good-fortune).

Just as Rachel died giving birth to Benjamin, who was the last born to Israel, when the last day of ministry is born the same will happen to the church.

When it comes to the fun stuff everyone seems to be there, but a few come to endure the discipline, the scourging correction or to focus devotion on what is required to be proven trustworthy.

Matthew 4: 8-9 Again, the devil took him to a very high mountain and showed him all the kingdoms of the world and their splendour. "All this I will give you," he said, "if you will bow down and worship me."

This same temptation is still being used by the devil on us to this very day, especially those who are called. The unfortunate part is many fall for it.

Jeremiah 6: 16-20 "Go stand at the crossroads and look around. Ask for direction to the old road. The tried and true road. Then take it. Discover the right route for your souls. But they said, 'Nothing doing. We aren't going that way.' I even provided watchmen for them to warn them, to set off the alarm. But the people said, 'It's a false alarm. It doesn't concern us.' And so I am calling in the nations as witnesses: 'Watch, witness, what happens to them!' And, 'Pay attention earth! Don't miss these bulletins.' I'm visiting catastrophe on this people, the end result of the games they've been playing with me. They've ignored everything I've said, had nothing but contempt for my teaching. What would I want with incense brought from Sheba, rare spices from exotic places? Your burnt sacrifices in worship give me no pleasure. Your religious rituals mean nothing to me."

Again I would like to testify how God took an absolute insecure time in our family and made me whole. It just amazes me when we get to the point of "How low can you go?" And I cry out to God how my prayers for me to stay connected with him are answered in a heartbeat, because that is where he wants us in the first place. This time again the Spirit descended upon and in me, and I experienced Father God with my entire being, holy fire filling me so full that it had to be released in shouts, groans, whines, bubbling in pure most incredible joy. My fingers and toes tingled, it's not the situation/circumstance that is important, it is how God does what he does in the midst of it, the fingers and toes tingling, is what needs to empower us.

Another poem I would like to share with you, some of you might know it and hope you enjoy it once again, and those of you who are reading it for the first time I pray the title takes hold on you: The Difference:

I got up early one morning
 And rushed right into the day:
I had so much to accomplish
 That I didn't have time to pray.

Problems just tumble about me,
 And heavier came each task.
"Why doesn't God help me?" I wondered.
 He answered, "You didn't ask."

I wanted to see joy and beauty,
 But the day toiled on, gray and black;
I wondered why God didn't show me.
 He said, "But you didn't seek."

I tried to come into God's presence.
 I used all my keys at the lock.
God gently and lovingly chided.
 "My child, you didn't knock."

I woke up early this morning,
 And paused before entering the day;
I had so much to accomplish
 That I had to take time to pray.

God is the inescapable depth and centre of 'All' that is. God is not a being superior to all other beings. God is the Ground of Being itself. So let us proclaim him not explain him. 2 Corinthians 5: 15-21 And he died for all, that those who live should no longer live for themselves but for him who died for them and was raised again. So from now on we regard no one from a worldly point of view. Though we once regarded Christ in this way, we do so no longer. Therefore, if anyone is in Christ,

66

He is a new creation; the old has gone, the new has come! All this is from God, who reconciled us to himself through Christ and gave us the ministry of reconciliation; that God was reconciling the world to himself in Christ, not counting men's sins against them. And he was committed to as the message reconciliation. We are therefore Christ's ambassadors, as though God were making his appeal through us, we implore you on Christ's behalf; be reconciled to God. God made him who had no sin for us, so that in him we might become the righteous of God.

Being a disciple of Jesus requires me to be empowered by the Holy Spirit, to invite the presence of Jesus by living fully, by loving wastefully, and by having the courage to be all that God created me to be. This does not mean we turn away from life to make contact with the holy, because our life is created with the holy already in us. We are not able to commune with our Father, live life in love, while being separate from the family. We cannot be a worshiper to God without being simultaneously an agent of life with someone other than ourselves. This is the pathway that opens up the realities of 'in giving we receive, in forgiving we are forgiven, in love we are loved'. We can only fully serve Christ by seeking to build a world in which all barriers to full humanity for every person is being removed. This is why absolutely no prejudice can ever be allowed to be present within the entity which has come to call itself "The body of Christ." For any prejudice no matter what it stems from, causes division. 1 Corinthians 1: 7-9 Therefore you do not lack any spiritual gift as you eagerly wait for our Lord Jesus Christ. God, who has called you into fellowship with his Son Jesus Christ our Lord is faithful. I appeal to you, brothers, in the name of our Lord Jesus Christ, that all of you agree with one another so that there may be no division among you and may be perfectly united in mind and thought.

God is easy to please, but hard to satisfy.

The finality of the church is changeless. The church exists to display witness of Christ and carry the gospel in its way of life. The form of thought for the church and its course of action: taking seriously Christ's mandate to make him know to all men, to the ultimate bounds of human habitation. In doing so the community of Christ will in the love of God for the love of men, form great love for one another, making available worldwide, a reality to a totally new type and dimension of community.

There is nothing surer on this earth than the truth that Abba Daddy hears prayers and answers prayers, with only minimal requirement for this, and that is we receive of the abundance he blesses us with. Psalm 37: 4-6 Delight yourself in the Lord and he will give you the desires of your heart. Commit your way to the Lord, trust in him and he will do this. He will make your righteousness shine like the dawn, the justice of your cause like the noon day sun.

Do we delight ourselves in the Lord? Do we know the desires of our heart? Or are they repressed? As we search the Scripture for clues, and proclaim God's presence we end up claiming Psalm 16: 11 You have made known to me the path of life; you will fill me with joy in your presence, with eternal pleasures at your right hand.

Spiritual eating, works in the opposite way from physical eating. If we don't eat physically we get hungry, once we consume food the hunger disappears and we feel satisfied. If we don't eat spiritually we can lose our appetite. The less we eat spiritually, the less hungry we become. But the more we are nourished by the Word of God the hungrier we become for spiritual food.

The Bible is a menu, a map, a compass, whatever it needs to be from the heart of God. It makes available everything we need to know and equip us for this journey. It gives direction ; it teaches; it corrects; it trains; it encourages. It is God's Holy Spirit-breathed book for us to read, study, and meditate on. With a consistent in-take we will grow strong. Here is where we will find the revelation of our heavenly Fathers character, and discover his love for us. The reason for us spending time with Abba Daddy and his word should be because we want to and it brings the joy and delight of our hearts, not because someone told us to, or because we think we are suppose to.

We are responsible for the whole Word of God. When we stay sensitive to the Holy Spirit's leading and cooperate with them, we can trust he will guide us into the truth and help us grow up as a Christian. This means the licence we have is to uphold the Whole of Scripture, we are an accident waiting to happen when we are ignoring parts. On this journey we will partake of the entire menu for our nourishment. Every word big or small is for each one of us on a personal level today, because the living Word will never die. Prayer is two-way communication, just as true friends require equal participation from each member, so does our relationship with God. In order to experience the fullness of our kingdom relationship we must allow the Father to express his love, will, and truth to us. And we must be totally honest with him, now when we read the Word, picture it, and share his peace from it we can be joined in harmony with Colossians 3: 15-17 Let the peace of Christ rule in your hearts. Since as members of one body you were called to peace. And be thankful. Let the word of Christ dwell in you richly as you teach and admonish one another with all wisdom, as you sing psalms, hymns and spiritual songs with gratitude in your hearts to God. And whatever you do, whether in word or deed, do it all in the name of the Lord Jesus, giving thanks to God the Father through him.

A huge step for me to enter into the Holy Place is to forget about myself all together, to focus solely on the God of peace. Mostly when the focus lies on me I see myself as a small dirty object, instead of the sheep equipped from the great Shepherd with everything good for doing his will, working through me the work that is pleasing to our Father. So yah it is better to forget me and just become a part of the glory in which we are all united forever and ever.

Each day should be started with a definite decision: Am I going to walk in the spirit? Or live to please myself? Every time a sin is committed, confess it on the spot. Then keep going. If going through hell don't stop! Go ahead, do not stop! If you are serious about walking in the Spirit, no one is standing in your way, and if there is it is you.

"All things work together for good!" Christians love to quote this verse to others who are having problems. But how many of us truly believe it? What is the important condition of this quote? "Those who love God?" let's see: 1 John 4: 19-21 We love because he first loved us. If anyone says, "I love God" yet hates his brother is a liar. For anyone who does not love his brother, whom he has seen, cannot love God, whom he has not seen. And he has given us this command: whoever loves God must also love his brother.

So the kind of love that will work everything together for good comes through the command: All in unity one with another; is how all things will work together for good. Never let circumstances take away your peace. Let the love for one another through Christ always fill you with joy. Because my friend it is God who is our circumstance. All things that happen go through God first and everything even out of our understanding is for his glory. Things like disappointments, frustrations, even tragedy. Not just comfortable cozy things. So the main question of life is not why, but a prayer that as everything is uncovered we will have our trust on our Father for complete survival.

For me religion is just not enough, I need a person, someone who understands, who cares someone who will help me up from the ground when I am down, to try again. And you know, Christ is willing to do all this plus more.

We are related to the living God, always at work in us, and we need to be willing to respond to his love with love and trust of our own. Ok, so, when we become bitter against life, against the church, even against God, we cut ourselves off from the resources we need most. Knowing God loves us and will help us.

God allows us the freedom to make decisions, to be individuals. Even though we are different (in the same image) God works on us all for our own good, which is the good for all, with Christ as the model. Let's say here that the moral of this story is: No matter what is happening, through it the Father has a plan, a purpose, and above all love.

It is ridiculous for Christians to feel that they should be delivered from accidents, sickness and death. The Bible does not promise escape from suffering. Instead God promises his presence in all our lives situations, bad and good alike. Every cloud does not have a silver lining, (ouch). But, behind every cloud the sun (Son) is always shining! Hurray.

"The Christ that dwells within you," is the key to Sanctification,' set apart as holy, made pure and having power to live a Christ like life. Jesus was sent not to die but to arise and live for us to be able to believe him, trust him, walk with him both here on earth and in the spirit. In this we respond to his love with our own. This is the difference between Christ (like)ian and settling for religion.

God is never on trial. He runs everything according to his will. He is sovereign. We are his creation. So, we have no business judging him, or questioning how things are done. We are not to be critics of our Father. Each and every one of us will stand their own trial.

Gods will and man's will both have meaning, interesting meaning at that. An exploration of a particular way in which interaction of wills (Gods will, my will, my neighbours will, etc.) take shape in the everyday doings, is by taking seriously every person, however obscure, unimportant, out of it, different.....

Forgiveness, it does not undo the wrong committed. Forgiveness is to free me from the claims of their control by the action that was performed. Releasing them from the bondage to my spirit back into Gods will. Now I can step forward, continuing on the journey home. God willing with a new brother or sister.

One thing that needs to be recognized is that there are many who do not identify that they have anything in common with what they hear at church, in the preaching-teaching, praise and worship, in the time set aside for relationship building, not finding any similarities between their inner life and their community of faith. Worse yet by selective observation and listening, feel secluded, because someone who feels rejected believes they are being excluded. Now they will feel unnoticed drifting away and becoming embittered, concluding in the thought that they are being rejected. These individuals listen to the large story but fail to find their place in it, not being able to see where they fit.

So for anyone who can step in to this last paragraph please accept the gift of faith I am praying for you as you read. Because it is faith that sees the invisible, believes the unbelievable, and receives the impossible. Ezekiel 37: 5-6 God, the Master, told the dry bones, 'Watch this: I'm bringing the breath of life to you and you'll come to life. I'll attack sinew to you, put meat on your bones, cover you with skin, and breathe life into you. You'll come alive and you'll realize that I am God."

Biblical revelation does not explain or eliminate suffering. Instead it shows God entering into the life of suffering humanity, accepting and sharing the suffering. Scripture is not a lecture from God, pointing the finger at unfortunate sufferers, or a program from God providing step by step elimination from suffering.

Suffering is very individual, and many times very spontaneous. So we must be very attentive in our suffering, paying attention to everything God says, and everything the suffering is bringing us through. Now in not understanding any of this going into prayer and placing the entire matter over to God, then obey his reply for his will. Staying thankful that God cares for us, trusting Gods love through suffering breaks through any indifference, and intensifies the relationship of love, where we are lifted to faith and hope. Isaiah 9: 2 The people walking in darkness have seen a great light; on those living in the shadow of death a light has dawned.

Sin needs to be taken seriously, even the ones we look at as little ones you know the ones that don't really matter, let's call them the little white sins. You have no idea how nice this would be if it were true, it would make so much easier. But nope, every sin hinders us from entering into the presence of God. So no matter what the temptation I need to be brave and stay relaxed and focused as God will work it all out.

We tend to exalt those who have strong outward experiences, as if they were more holy, more spiritual, more gifted, or more prophetically reliable than others. What a dangerous unbalance and improper focus. It is better to hunger after simple and pure intimacy with the Holy Spirit than to lose our focuses on any given result of that intimacy or means of receiving revelation. In the Bible it is prayer, meditation and worship that seem to be the key means of finding that intimacy. Take Jeremiah for example when God called him as a prophet he did not promise mystical experiences. Jeremiah 1: 9 Then the Lord stretched out his hand and touched my mouth, the Lord said to me, "Now I have put my words in your mouth."

When striving after the mystical realms in an unbalanced way, we open ourselves to delusion and even the possibility of demonic counterfeit. It is much better to reach after intimacy with the one who gives dreams as he chooses to give us dreams. So I read it in Ecclesiastes 5: 7 "In spite of many daydreams, pointless actions, and empty words, you should still fear the Lord."

It is always the Father's love; the people of the world need to accept and experience the love of the living God. Better to long to be included in the intimate counsel of the Lord, because when answers to prayer and release of power depend upon the accuracy of our words, then we have left the realm of prayer and entered into magic. What began as relationship has degenerated into something mechanical – a casting of spells – as if we could push the right buttons and move God to act. God acts because he loves us, not because we got our words right. It is, however, important to discern the will of God to the best of our ability and align ourselves with it. 1 John 5: 14 We are confident that God listens to us if we ask for anything that has his approval.

In the call to hear and reveal the Will of God for prayer, intercession is to reveal the places where sin hides and to lead in repentance. 2 Chronicles 7: 13-16 I may shut the sky so that there is no rain, or command grasshoppers to devour the countryside, or send an epidemic among my people, who are called by my name, will humble themselves, pray, search for me, and turn from their evil ways, then I will hear their prayers from heaven, forgive their sins, and heal their country. My eyes will be open, and my ears will pay attention to their prayers at this place. I have chosen and declared this temple holy so that my name be placed there forever. My eyes and my heart will always be there.

Immature people who are filled with the sense and power of the Lord's Word – need our patience, even though sometimes full of themselves remember we were once young and then grew up, so will they. Even when they tend to overestimate the boundaries of our so thought authority in prayer, giving themselves more credit than we think they have been given, here would be a good time to give it all over to God and in harmony start praising and worshiping letting him sort it all out. Mature vs. Immature: 1 Kings 18: 36-37 When it was time to offer sacrifice the prophet Elijah stepped forward. He said, "Lord God of Abraham, Isaac, and Israel, make known today that you are God in Israel and that I'm your servant and have all these things by your instruction. Answer me Lord! Answer me! Then these people will know that you, Lord, are God and that you are winning back their hearts."

An immature person would have commanded fire to come from heaven, but not Elijah, no! His prayer was in the form of a humble request of one who understands himself to be a servant exercising their position of relationship with God who loves them. Not one word of command! Just humbly asking God to glorify his own name by sending fire, and God responded.

The Spirit of God in us is required to please God. The Spirit of God in us is required to know God. Let's show the person who has not reached maturity the blessing it is that if you are with the Spirit, the fire of God, now, what a revival. Praise the Lord! Not to say that only certain people can be in the kingdom, or enter heaven. Just sharing my excitement of how I do not think God will love me because I am good, but that God that makes me good because he loves me.

Alive in faith is not "done" to us, but "develops" in us by commanding and blessing words that are completed in words of obedient agreement and willing praise. All the parts of our lives and our history are addressed by God and then answered by us. The all-encompassing, every-penetrating Word of God establishes, appoints then drafts the environment in which we live. We need to stay awake to this language and giving to every word. Not all at once, but all the time, for there is nothing in our lives that escapes the creative and saving word of God that invites answers in faith and obedience, language and prayer.

Sleep is God's ingenious plan for giving us the help he cannot get into us when we are awake. So when the day's work comes to an end, nothing essential stops. As we prepare for sleep it should not be with a feeling of exhausted frustration because there is so much yet undone and unfinished. But with expectancy, the day is about to begin! God's fresh newly anointed Words are about to be spoken again. During the hours of this sleep, how will God prepare to use my obedience, service, and speech when morning breaks? Sleep is to get out of God's way for awhile. To get into the rhythm of salvation, in sleep, great and marvellous things far beyond our capacity to invent or engineer, are in process!

We can hardly avoid stopping our work each night as fatigue and sleep overtake us. But we can avoid stopping work on the seventh day, Sabbath-keeping often feels like an interruption, an interference with our routines. It challenges theories we gradually build up that our daily work is vital in making the world go round. Exodus 20: 8-11 "Remember the Sabbath day by keeping it holy. Six days you should labour and do all your work, but the seventh day is a Sabbath to the Lord your God. On it you shall not do any work, neither you, nor your son or daughter, nor your manservant, or maidservant, nor your animals, not the alien within your gate. For in six days the Lord made the heavens and the earth, the sea, and all that is in them, but he rested on the seventh day. Therefore the Lord blessed the Sabbath day and made it holy.

Sabbath keeping is commanded so that we internalize the being that matures out of doing. Deuteronomy 5: 15 Remember that you were slaves in Egypt and that the Lord your God brought you out of there with a mighty hand and an outstretched arm. Therefore the Lord your God has commanded you observe the Sabbath day.

The consequence to, "Never a day off," is no longer being considered a person, but rather a work unit. Not someone created in the image of God, but work equipment. Humanity defaced.

The moment we begin to see ourselves in terms of what we do or accomplish, rather than what we are, we mutilate humanity and violate community. Our lives are so interconnected that we inevitably involve others in our work whether we intend to or not. Sabbath keeping now becomes basic kindness. Preserving the image of God in our neighbours so that we are able to see them as they are, not as we need them or want them to be.

If our Father did have a fear I think it might be for us. Us slipping away from the adoption into his family. We all have the same privileges of the house hold, and have been blessed with everything that is given to Jesus while he was here with us. And we have been trusted with equal demands of duties, responsibilities, and love. May I have the courage and strength from heaven the same faith Jesus had to honour this at all times causing my Father nothing but peace and joy for me.

Romans 5: 3-5 There's more to come: We continue to shout our praises even when we're hemmed in with troubles, because we know how troubles can develop passionate patience in us, and how that patience in turn forges the tempered steel of virtue, keeping us alert for whatever God will do next. In alert expectancy such as this, we're never left feeling short changed. Quite the contrary – we can't round up enough containers to hold everything God generously pours into our lives through the Holy Spirit.

In wilderness function there is restoration: When God sets out to build a great work, he digs a deep hole for the foundation. Sin is judged and cleansed. Strongholds of thought, behaviour, and emotion that rise up against the true knowledge of God are broken, transformed and brought under the blood of Jesus. Our Father is more concerned with character formation, than building great ministries for us. He wants to restore us to himself, by granting us the realization of a list of character changes. Restoring me back to the me God created. Hosea 2: 14-15 "That's why I'm going to win her back. I will lead her into the desert. I will speak tenderly to her. I will give her vineyards there. I will make the Valley of Achor (Disaster) a dove of hope. Then she will respond as she did when she was young, as she did when she came out of Egypt.

In wilderness function there is preparation. We all long for the Lord to come into our lives with power, failing to realize this requires a significant period of preparation. Reducing us to a singular longing where nothing will satisfy but God alone. Being with God becomes more important than success or recognition. All bumps must be smoothed out of his highway, the potholes filled and the surfaces levelled. Isaiah 40: 3-5 A voice cries out in the desert; "Clear a way for the Lord. Make a straight highway in the wilderness for our God. Every valley will be raised. Every mountain and hill lowered. Steep places will be made level. Rough places will be made smooth.

Suffering often magnifies temptation. Be aware of these possible wilderness dangers: anger and bitterness; and does God really expect for me to embrace this relentless pain without bitterness? The answer is yes. We must seek God's grace to surrender to the process without bitterness. Wounding put into God's hands will prepare us for the wonder of our destiny by refining and changing our character. Here is where genuine faith takes root and we minister from a base of true rest in him.

The wilderness is the necessary preparation for high calling, but be careful that wilderness unbelief and despair don't render you incapable of recognizing, receiving or believing the promise when at last it comes. It is in love, my Father God disciplines me in this wilderness by leaving me to fight more difficult battles than I could possibly bear in my flesh, so I will break, and in the brokenness unbelief will be refined out of my character. I need to fall before I can succeed in order to restore visible favour over my life. All of it, every part and parcel, is an expression of his favour over my life, but in the end it is up to me to believe it. Matthew 24: 14 "Therefore many are invited, but few are chosen to stay."

Agape: a "stick to it" kind of love; a love that won't let go. Being committed to somebody does not make a relationship joyful. Phileo: demonstrates natural/tender affection. It is my obligation to demonstrate the love of God, no matter if anyone gets it or not I must keep demonstrating.

The tool we have to connect us with material to spiritual, visible to invisible, earth to heaven, is imagination. We have a pair of mental operations actually, Imagination and Explanation, designed to work together. When the gospel is given robust and with healthy expression, the two work in graceful relation. In robust I am thinking not so much loud, as each person giving it their all. Explanation pins things down so that we can handle and use them – obey and teach, help and guide. Imagination opens things up so that we can grow into maturity – worship and adore, explain and honour, follow and trust. Explanation restricts, defines, and holds down: Imagination expands and lets loose. Explanation keeps our feet on the ground: Imagination lifts our heads into the clouds. Explanation puts us in harness: Imagination launches us into mystery. Explanation reduces life to what can be used: Imagination enlarges life into what can be adored.

Two more preconditions for spiritual direction; Unknowing and Uncaring. Unknowing: spiritual direction is not an opportunity for any one person to instruct another. Yes, teaching is an essential ministry - knowing Scripture and receiving the revelation of God is super important. But there are also times when diligent instruction is not required and a slow relaxed gentle comfortable pause before mystery is. None of us know in detail what God is doing in someone else. Actually what we don't know here, far exceeds what we do know there are times in life when this vast unknowing to us must be what we offer to represent the needs of someone else, and it is when this takes place that Spiritual Direction is in motion. Uncaring: spiritual direction is not an occasion for one person to help another in compassion. Yes, compassion is an essential ministry, when we get hurt, rejected, we do require the loving and healing help of others. But there are also moments when caring is not required, when detachment is appropriate. Because what the Holy Spirit is doing in others far exceeds what we ourselves are doing. There are times when we need to just get out of the way to become aware of the "Silent music." When this takes place, spiritual Direction is in motion. This my friend is very hard, because knowing and caring are in such high demand. Spiritual direction just does not hold up well under logical investigation.

Spiritual as I understand it means that which is not material, not ordinary, where direction makes no distinction between religious and secular, because we should be readily spotting God everywhere and anywhere, the mall as in the sanctuary. A remark from a child carries as much immediate weight as an oracle in Isaiah. Spiritual direction deals with prayer and Scripture and service, but it also deals with groceries, leisure sports, work. In your whole entire living not just where it is convenient.

Direction carries an obvious significant intention of taking charge and showing the way. But spiritual direction is likely to be quiet and gentle, submissive and restrained (unemotional). Because the characteristics of spiritual direction is to "get out of the way" to be un-important, un-influential.

The normal of God's Word in providing direction is to cultivate the deep places of the spirit where the spirit creates the 'new things.' Not busily trying to figure out what is wrong with others so that we can help solve their problems. But looking for God in others - listening, worshiping, loving, attending.

God not only loves us objectively, but he communes in a way we can grasp what he is saying and he touches us with love in a way we can really feel it, with his power, gifts, the Bible all in harmony. One is as essential as the other, (love, communication, Words, touch,) to equal the presence of God.

The most crucial thing in Christian life is to walk according to the Spirit. Once the Spirit has made his function known, it is very important that we join steps immediately. We must not slack in concerning the Spirit, even if it is a minute by minute matter. When we receive the teaching of the Spirit we must be extra cautious to follow his leading, or failure in our spirituality will occur. If we are truly walking in 'the way of the cross,' we are walking according to the Spirit. In order to walk according in the Spirit, all self-will must be put to death. So if we want to play follow the leader, the Holy Spirit is required for the role as the leader. Another cool game is (Simon says) Holy spirit says. Who says I am not having a blast living in Christ?

As believers we should be determined to do the will of our Father found in following the guidance of the Holy Spirit, yet we lose our boldness to step forward, because things of the world make us uncertain of the trustworthiness of the Spirits leading. In dancing one must lead and the other follows.

The best way to obtain revelation is to know the will of God, and the best way to know the Will of God is through revelation, see we are dancing again, now we can be pleasing to our Father. Staying ignorant to the ways of the world will bring us in perfect harmony with the Spirit. The working of the Holy Spirit is not to be treated as an occasional happening or the most wonderful experience of a lifetime. As we follow the calling of God on our life, we see that spiritual experiences are an ordinary daily part of living.

It is our soul that can be affected by the outward world, not the spirit. So now we have a great reason to learn to live only in spirit, surrendering our soul on a regular basis. Holy Spirit moves on his own, unlike the soul which depends on outward influences, and moving in result of outward emotions. This is why in the Spirit we can continue to work, whether our soul has any feeling or our body any strength, because we live according to the continually active Spirit. Galatians 1: 15-17 But when God, who set me apart from birth and called me by his grace, was pleased to reveal his Son in me so that I might preach him among the gentiles, I did not consult any man, nor did I go to Jerusalem to see those who were apostles before I was, but I went immediately into Arabia and later returned to Damascus.

The revelation is in the believer's spirit as testified in the Scripture. Revelation 1: 10 On the Lord's day I was in Spirit, and I heard behind me a loud voice like a trumpet.

There are times in the spirit we do not confer with flesh and blood, or the thoughts and arguments of men's opinions. We just have to follow the leading of the Spirit all the way. When we obtain the revelation of God and start to understand the Will of God, we no longer need other proofs. Even according to Paul the revelation in Spirit was sufficient to guide him, don't forget preaching the Lord among the gentiles was unheard of back in Paul's generation. But it is a good thing for us today that Paul only followed the Spirit and did not care for the opinion of men, even the most spiritual apostles. So, we must, also stay bold and in direct guidance of the Lord himself. This does not mean however that the words taught by the spiritually mature are of no use. NO! They are still of great profit (prophet). And this journey is not of one alone but as a whole body in Christ. Praise the Lord! Amen.

So be careful not to let anyone normalize you, not even the church, stay in the love God has called us in as one for him.

The privileged blessing from God is a gift of no return. God loves us because he created us (we are wanted, not some accident). We were created for the simple reason for us to know each other, a Father/child, turning into a Father-in-law/bride, as we mature into the bride for his only Son. There is no gift he wants from us all he wants to do is enjoy us and us to enjoy him our love for each other forming a wellspring, for all kingdom enthusiasm, and releasing it into a fountain of an intimate worship.

Now we come back to choice. Jesus wants to deliver us out of the darkness of sin into the life of eternal living. John 8: 12 When Jesus spoke again to the people, he said, "I am the light of the world. Whoever follows me will never walk in darkness, but will have the light of life."

So really 'our' choice is as simple as to follow while Jesus does all the difficult work in our stubborn souls. I can hear the angels praying that all of God's creation will make this choice, but it is up to us to love even those who cannot. For those of us who have made the choice we are not accepted back simply as a friend, but are now placed into God's family as a full member. We are adopted: A child once said, "The difference between having a baby and adopting a baby is one you grow in your mom's tummy, and the other you grow in mom's heart." So as a whole family we must pray for everyone. Ephesians 2: 13 But now in Christ Jesus you who once were far away have been brought near through the blood of Christ.

There is only one way to be saved from the consequences of sin. Jesus is the only door to eternal life. Just as there was only one door to safety in Noah's Ark - Just as there was only one door to the Temple - Just as there is only one door to the sheep pen - So Jesus is the only way to God.

There are belief's out there that you can come to God in various different ways, but the Bible makes it quite clear that there is no other ways to God. This may be viewed in a prejudice way of thinking of this day and age, but over and over again Scripture allows no room to ignore the Bibles echo's of this theory. Jesus is the only way. Acts 4: 12 Salvation is found in no one else, for there is no other name under heaven given to men by which we can be saved.

We might not like this Biblical narrow-mindedness, but it is the truth, it is what the Bible teaches. The Bible also says that if we don't approve of God's chosen ways, we can reject them. God allows us that freedom but then we must also pay our own dept. We can also deny the existence of God and ignore the Bibles message entirely, though frankly in my opinion this is a hazardous decision.

We are all drowning in the world. If we think we are floating just fine, we will reject all help. Then there are those who know they are sinking but are too proud to ask for help, all the same drown they will. Others might see that I am drowning, but they are unable to help until I allow them to. We have to see ourselves as helpless before we can be helped.

Here are two choices: #1 Unbelief. In this frame of mind we believe there may be many ways to be accepted by God – if there even is a God. Jesus may be a way, another way would be to live a good life and do my best then God will not reject me. Having chosen our own way, we will find we are in a spiritual wilderness, grabbing for truth confused with no purpose – Lost sheep. #2 Belief. In this frame of heart we believe that when Jesus died on the cross, he died in our place as our replacement paying for my sin-debt. I trust in him alone to save me from sins consequences. Jesus as the Good Shepherd, has found me and has given me new life and heart, eternal life, God's heart, forgiveness, purpose for living, freedom from guilt and shame, and this my dear friend is just the tip of the iceberg, there is so much more.

My hope is for everyone to choose and put their trust in Christ, the reason I can have such High Hopes is because the Bible says God will lead us, step by step. And if someone like me can dance to this music from heaven anyone can. Do you want to hear a secret? In its own right it is already half happening because God walks with each and every one of us, let's pray that every one's chooses to follow. If you do not already read the bible on a regular basis it is a journey worth taking, you can take my word for it. The road will not always be smooth, I can promise you that, but on this path on God's Word you will learn to realize that God is always with us all, every step of the way.

It is not what any of us have prepared for living it is what God has planned, now letting go of our prepared life and stepping into God's planned life, watch the blessings rain. Let's not be predictable in our worship or service let God take over in this area as well, better put on the life jackets because now for sure the flood gates are bursting. Hebrews 13: 20-21 May the God of peace, who through the blood of eternal covenant brought back from the dead our Lord Jesus, the great shepherd of the sheep, equip you with everything good for doing his will, and may he work in us what is pleasing to him, through Jesus Christ, to whom be glory forever and ever. Amen.

Blame is an act which will only entice us to curse ourselves. We alone are responsible for every sin we commit, and it is our sin that brings judgment of death upon us. Jesus summed it up in an easy formula, following this formula we cannot go wrong. First: Love God, it is through love we honour our Father, our Creator it is when we remove ourselves from this love we will find ourselves more open to sin. Second: Love others, if we do not love everyone we are not honouring Jesus, friends, brothers, sisters thinking we are better than they are. Third: Love ourselves, if we can't do this we are calling God a liar, because we don't believe we are worthy of God's love.

Sin means stepping out of the protective hand of God, because we have allowed this sin to separate our relationship. If we are not in the protective hand of God where are we? God does not step back or away, we do.

The anointing and promises of God linger over the world, waiting for gifts to be claimed by the family lines they were gifted to. Each family line has a fountain of blessings, a calling on their lives, stemming back to the very beginning. If the chosen person does not claim the calling, it just lays dormant waiting for someone to rise up and fulfill it. If the family lines die off before it is claimed, anyone can then claim it, it does not go Void.

Now curses also go back as far as the beginning, and will stay over a family till cancelled by breaking its power in the Name of Jesus.

Both are active, waiting for us to choose our way, the power of deliverance has been gifted to break the curse, along with the honour to receive the privilege of claiming our anointed gift. The world could be free if we would simply claim our promises from God given to us through Christ's sacrifice and resurrection.

Jesus' death was to reclaim the deed of the Garden of Eden, to return it back to man who it was created for. So let's believe and receive this truth so we can co-labour with our Father. Let's do our part so God's part is accomplished to its complete success, and the sacrifice of Jesus was not in vain.

Fear and faith are in direct conflict and each one has the need to be fulfilled. Fear offers us lack while faith offers us provision. It is fear that will lead us to sin and faith that will lead us back to Christ.

The Father has his church in the palm of his hand, protecting her through everything. So as the fear in our lives is overcome, the reward is to eat the fruit from the Garden of Eden once again. It is important, actually fatal to realize God's provisions in all things through faith. Remember that fear will always show us our lack, pushing us away from the promises provisions from God, so enter back into faith and our struggles will be overcome by the First and the Last, by the one who died but is now alive, right by our side, it is in trust we will watch every temptation successfully be overcome.

We began as spirits with God. He prepared a body for us and we were born, however it becomes a body filled with generational spirits from conception. The requirement of being cleaned and deal with fear of lack, temptation of the flesh, pride and boasting, slander and destruction, compromise, seduction and lust, and dead works. In order to be able to receive the over-comers reward for our lifetime, these things need to be dealt with not just as the saying goes swept under the carpet. When we deny our emotions, we limit the experience of his love we are able to receive.

Luke 7: 43-48 "That's right," said Jesus. Then turning to the woman, but speaking to Simon, he said, "Do you see this woman? I came to your home, you provided no water for my feet, but she rained tears on my feet and dried them with her hair. You gave me no greeting, but from the time I arrived she hasn't quit kissing my feet. You provided nothing for refreshing up, but she soothed my feet with perfume. Impressive, isn't it? She was forgiven many, many sins and she is very, very grateful. If the forgiveness is minimal, the gratitude is minimal." Then he spoke to her: "I forgive your sins."

Confirm the celebration that takes place each time heaven observes that someone has been forgiven. Confessing of sin is very hard, making the acceptance of the creation of God, to be the forgiveness from the act committed. The Father commands that we love each other at all times, but the act has to have consequences filled with hope through forgiveness.

Hebrews 6: 11-12 We want each of you to show this same diligence to the very end, in order to make your hope sure. We do not want you to become lazy, but to imitate those who through faith and patience inherit what has been promised.

The greatest and truest test of true faith may be faithfulness. Full assurance in faith and patience is needed to inherit the promises. We seem to hunger greatly for the faith movement, but there are very few that have been head of the patient movement never mind hunger for it. So it does not matter if you are nine or over ninety it is our obligation to be the ears which can hear the sound of the trumpet, and we are required to be the hearts which are drawn to the sound of the battle.

What is true success? True success is doing our Creators Will, using each talent that has been entrusted to us. Now we will find that people whom no one would follow unless they are anointed with God's presence seem to be chosen for leaders. They have denied the Lord and fled from him when he needed them most. They do not have a great plan or program, other than the fact that the Lord has appointed them, their authority is strictly in the fact that the King of kings lives in them.

If we were to build the church to attract God and not people what would it look like? The teachings from God's Word are the true foundation of Christian truth. When we see God in everything, is when everything will make sense. The strength of the congregation is dependent on how strong every individual's personal relationship is to the Lord. We need to know who we are in Christ, instead of who he is in us.

"The Way," is not just fundamental truths about the Lord – "The Way", is the Lord! In order to be all God has called us to be, we have to open our hearts to all of him.

Jesus does not beg man to 'accept him,' Jesus calls us, and we must step towards the choice (all of God's creation is called), Luke 9: 23 Then he said to them all: "If anyone would come after me, he must deny himself and take up his cross daily and follow me."

When Jesus does call us to be disciples he requires total commitment, and giving up everything to follow him. We do not change to fellowship with God instead we are changed by our fellowship with him.

We must not confuse the fact that even though God's authority is based on love and service, it still contains discipline and judgement. A huge problem in the church today is that most are to earthly minded to be of any spiritual good.

Hebrews 11: 27 By faith he left Egypt, not fearing the kings anger: he persevered because he saw him who is invisible.

True spiritual vision is seeing from the eye of our heart; so we can see what is invisible to others. The Message should not be delivered in word alone, but be united with the demonstration of the power in the Spirit.

The apostolic church which is now being born will turn the world upside down again, or turn an upside down world right side up again.

Am I valued? I am valued! Is God with me? He is always here/there/he is never out of our presence.

God is 'pure' everything and anything else we label God is just wrong.

2 Corinthians 10: 3-6 The world is unprincipled. It's dog-eat-dog out there! The world doesn't fight fair. But we don't live or fight our battles that way – never have and never will. The tools of our trade aren't for marketing or manipulation, but they are for demolishing that entire massively corrupt culture. We use our powerful God-tools for smashing warped philosophies, tearing down barriers erected against the truth of God, fitting every loose thought and emotion and impulse into the structure of life shaped by Christ. Our tools are ready at hand for clearing the ground of every obstruction and building lives of obedience into maturity.

Once a barrier is gone and strongholds destroyed, we are ready to receive the Father's love. It may come on a private basis. But more often it comes by the intercession of others, and many times in the laying of hands.

In the midst of the collapse of a traditional faith, we need to refrain from seeking any control over our destiny, knowing that these tactics cannot work. And to embrace our fragile reality. And come to grip with our existence over which we have no power is impossible.

In prayers people have uttered in the past, we can see the presence of human hopes, and human fears. We are witnessing the loss of confidence in religious enterprise coming into clear focus. Genesis 32: 24-28 So Jacob was left alone, and a man wrestled with him till daybreak. When the man saw he could not overpower him, he touched the socket of Jacob's hip so that his hip was wrenched as he wrestled with the man. Then the man said, "Let me go for it is daybreak." But Jacob replied, "I will not let you go unless you bless me." The man asked him, "What is your name?" "Jacob," he answered. Then the man said, "Your name will no longer be Jacob, but Israel, because you have struggled with God and with man and have overcome."

Yet, despite a sometimes frenzied, but at least persistent effort. We cannot seem to make prayers, as it has been traditionally understood, have meaning for us. Before we are able to move beyond all this past religion we must be willing to declare bankruptcy of what we know. But then in total revelation and trust and then obedience our first prayer is, "Lord, teach us to pray."

Person A: A well known, Christian diagnosed with cancer.

Person B: A sanitation worker. Same diagnoses is not religiously oriented.

Person A: Has prayer groups and individual petitions in hundreds of churches.

Person B: Has only angels praying.

Person A: Goes into remission. And the people of the church acknowledge, "Our prayers are working!" They claim, "God is using our prayers to keep this disease at bay."

Person B: Has had no human prayer, prayer groups as we know them, praying for him. Would this affect the cause of their sickness? Would they live less time? Endure more obvious pain? Or face a more difficult dying?

Everyone is being prayed for at all times, be it in the earthly realm or spiritual realm, none of God's creation is ever left alone or without prayer covering. We should never attribute a behaviour pattern based on human status. Not in God's world and this is God's world. Luke 17: 20-21 Once, being asked by the Pharisees when the kingdom of God would come, Jesus replied, "The Kingdom of God does not come with your careful observation, nor will people say, 'here it is' or 'there it is,' because the Kingdom of God is within you."

Praise the Lord for airplanes, which bless us with a pre destination of a planned flight from beginning to end. Now you are wondering what is this lady talking about? But let's look at life as a Bus: Well on a Bus we can come and go as we please, so if the ride gets uncomfortable we can step out at the next stop. But on a plane once we are in, we are in, no matter how rough things become we cannot exit till we reach our destination. So see what I mean Thank-you Lord for airplanes because when things get rough and I want to run for comfort, or let my will enter into God's Will. It is on the plane where we are secure while we are carried to where God needs us, wants us, or smarten us up, and sometimes just to love us.

So open up and ask for grace and peace to enter and become your Spirit. Even in the midst of a turbulent world. Trusting God can keep you calm.

We need to understand what is going on in the invisible realm of our life with God! Psalm 139: 1-7 O Lord, you have searched me and you know me. You know when I sit and when I rise; you perceive my thoughts from afar. You discern my going out and my lying down; you are familiar with all my ways. Before a word is on my tongue you know it completely. Oh Lord, you hem me in – behind and before; you have laid your hand upon me. Such knowledge is too wonderful for me, too lofty for me to attain. Where can I go from your Spirit? Where can I flee from your presence?

Sometimes instead of answering our questions God will reveal himself to us and some of the mysteries he is. Like he did for Job, this, my friend is an answer to prayer.

Once we inquire anything from God whether spiritual or natural, we must no longer be fretful otherwise it is just an exercise of uselessness. Do we really believe the Word of the Lord in Ephesians 1:11 In him we were also chosen, having been predestined according to the plan of him who works out everything in conformity with the purpose of his Will.

This is why we must pray by faith only. We need to believe God means just what he says, and then as we act upon the Word (faith requires action) we need to understand it, we need to take hold of it, we actually make it our own. Why do we need to see how? Really all we need is to believe and carry on – on the basis of the assured promise in God's Word. Deuteronomy 30: 11-14 Now what I am commanding you today is not to difficult for you or beyond your reach. It is not up in heaven, so that you have to ask, "Who will ascend into heaven to get it and proclaim it to us so we may obey it?"

If it is time to work, get on with your job; if it is time to go to bed, go to sleep in peace. Give the Lord your worries.

We must always be aware of transformations. One way is by thanking God for the reality behind the symbol of the broken bread. First we embrace the sacrifice of Jesus on the Cross, his body broken for us all. (let's proclaim in harmony everyone reading right here, Just For Me.....). Second we realize the way in which his life continues to sustain us today; Jesus' body, the Living Bread. Third we look around and recognize those who are worshiping with us; seeking the essential oneness. Seeking to find Jesus in each and every one this way it is formed into a love feast as well as a memorial service, and the celebration of a continuing life of the Lord through us all.

How odd that God humbles himself to be seen in the most ordinary beauties, the everyday taken for granted stuff of creation. Romans 1: 20 For since the creation of the world God's invisible qualities – his eternal power and divine nature – have been clearly seen, being understood from what has been made, so that men are without excuse.

If our hearts are straight with God then every creature will be to us a mirror of life and a look of holy doctrine.

To the God, my God, who restores dignity I would like to thank God at this time for the teachings he has sent for me from the heart of some very special teachers united to the Spirit with truth of the Word.

Authority is not control: Authority is serving. There are differences in us all we were created that way, not one of us are the same, but we are all equal in the love of God, serving in many different roles as one united in Christ.

An act of dominance is an act of sin; do not mistake headship as being in control, headship is to carry the weight, the cornerstone carries the weight. It is in our responsibilities that mark our strengths the source of obedience with harmony.

Now when we submit let it be in agreement, harmonizing with the source, blending into a very special relationship, as we yield to each other as long as no principles are broken.

Take Pharaoh for example: He was not rejected because God decided to be mean, but because he refused to acknowledge the Lord.

The problem is never with a Holy God but with sinful man. The miracle is not that God does not reject sinful man, and that he is merciful to those who scarcely deserve it. The miracle is that God has not yet destroyed this world!

God saves individuals: the correct question is not "Has God discarded his people?" No! It is, "Who is responding to God's gift of Salvation in Christ?" From the beginning God's terms were personal responsibilities and individual faith, and through Christ binding these together in unity to form one body that is the "Bride of Christ."

If God does not rule then our belief about God matters very little. If God is not in charge how can we lean on him? The Lord is King he is to be worshiped not used. He is to be adored, not merely made attractive his wisdom is far beyond us. We can do little else but acknowledge that God is God.

Is your cart before the horse? Do you fume and fret about what God is calling you to do? (Service.) Are you spiritually unprepared to do it? (Character.) In order to serve God he needs a guarantee that he really has you!

It's not too hard while we are sitting in church to promise God our soul and spirit. After all, it is proper for God to have these things. God does not just save your soul. He saves you – your total self.

A trap that snares a lot of us is the old duel standards: One set of rules for our outward behaviour and another standard for the mind. Here is where you will find the game rules to learn to play Church-ianity. You learn not to do certain things or so we would like others to believe, the real trick is not to get caught doing them. Show up to church often enough to be labelled 'active' and 'faithful' making you look pretty spiritual, meanwhile your thought life is running wayward hither and dither, feasting on materialism, greed, hatred, jealousy, etc.

God Word, inward witness of the Holy Spirit, outward circumstances when these three things line up move ahead until then wait! Waiting is hard, but it is the best even safest thing to do.

There is only one way we can say we are seeking God's Will, and that is by knowing it. The Living Word of the Bible must be alive in us. The Bible is not just to be used as an answer book or escape book, casually paging through, trying to find just the right verse to help out. Every word in the Bible is God's Message, not just the ones we want.

We have made "I'll pray", something of a cliché. Maybe we should change the phrase to, "Let's take this to God and see what he says about it," because true prayer is talking with God not at God. Our Father is not some button to be pushed when we find the time or when things get inconvenient and we need it stopped to make our life easy.

How can we even evaluate circumstances if there is no guidance from God's Word and Spirit? No, God's Will does not drop out of the sky in a special delivery letter, when we have time to receive it. But he has written everything we will ever need to use in his Word.

When we enter this Word it is a good idea to look at the principle of the Scripture, find the authors intentions, then open your heart to see how it can be applied for us to honour God now. Stay open and alert to the context of the text you are reading making it available to receive the revelations as they are gifted.

We need to be ready, willing, and able to evangelize, take Paul for example he was released from prison as he walked through those doors he climbed through God's window and started evangelizing. Now I myself am not an evangelist but that does not give me the right not to evangelize when God asks me to. We do not only use the gifts we were blessed with we do as God directs always in truth. Another reason to be ready to help one another, because if God ask me to evangelize it is a blessing when someone with that gift is in harmony to unite any differences, now God's window has been opened for us to work together as one.

The gospel which boldly sets the cross at the center of its message also courageously accepts discipleship as part of daily routine. Difficulties and suffering are not problems for which the gospel provides an escape, but a reality that we experience and in which a faith is shared by encouraging one another in hope.

Although Jacob walked with a limp, he walks with a purpose, with meaning, with integrity. A wounded healer. The night at Peniel held despair before God and confidence in God in a tight embrace. In the morning there came a blessing.

We tend to look at suffering as a deficiency, trying to deny the affliction and the sense of pain, acting as it should not be, and we devalue the experience of suffering. But this myth denies our encounter with reality. The first approach is usually to find the cause of the suffering and then to eliminate it. Suffering as such has no value or meaning; it is only a sign that things have gone wrong, and a challenge to humanity to set things right again through goodwill and ingenuity (ability.)

We have no business interfering with another's sorrow, or manipulating it. Suffering is an event in which we are particularly vulnerable to grace, able to recognize dimensions in God and depth in the self. To treat it as a 'problem' is to demean that person.

Though by that person 'sharing' the suffering, help can begin, but this does not solve it or eliminate it. But a basic observation seems to stand; when suffering is made into a community act, whatever individual elements there are get incorporated into the community. This is the Biblical style. When Biblical people wept, they wept with their friends. The Biblical way to deal with suffering is to transform what is individual into something corporate. No single person's sin produced the suffering consequent to Jerusalem's Fall and no single person ought to mourn them; response to suffering is a function as a congregation. The suffering person is joined by friends who join their tears and prayers. They do not hide the sufferer away from view but bring them out into the public square in full view of everyone.

When private grief is integrated into communal, several things take place. For one thing the act of suffering develops significance. If others weep with us, there must be more to the suffering than our own petty weakness or selfish sense of loss. When others join the sufferer, there is, "consensual validation," that the suffering means something. The community votes with its tears that there is suffering that is worth weeping over. When the community joins, the outpouring of emotion is legitimized in such a way to provide for renewal.

Studying the Bible is hard work, the godliness provides for our needs it does not produce profit. The bible should be replacing the manuals we have so neatly numbered all our rules to be good enough to be part of our family we claim to be God's; but is it? Our obligation is to lead, people to love who Jesus is, from a grateful heart, from there they will be led into the life God has them purposed for. A Christian life is not dull it is very busy constantly producing a constant labour in the fields of Christ. Joyfully being productive not idol.

Whenever prayer is needed (which is always in everything) an elite body of intercessors to pray is not called in. NO! In all forms of support needed the church in full is to pray, because we are all called upon to be a people of prayer. And in unity and all different styles of prayers, we step into faith together knowing that Jesus who lives forever is always in our midst. Hebrews 7: 23-25 There was a long succession of priests because when a priest died he could no longer serve. But Jesus lives forever, so he serves as a priest forever. That is why he is always able to save those who come to God through him. He can do this because he always lives and intercedes for them.

Authority to pray effectively lies within the entire body of Christ whose very lifeblood is prayer, not an elite group, always with Christ as the head.

The term "Prayer Cover," sounds logical but when misused serves to exalt our fleshly sense of importance. As if we the people or the prayers themselves is what protects us or prosper our ministries. Wrong! We inflate ourselves at Jesus' expense, and allow ourselves to become puffed up in our sense of importance. Jesus alone is our rock and our Salvation. He allows us to participate with him in what he is doing because he loves us and loves to be in relationship with us. I love to be supported in prayer. But I refuse to attach a magical significance to it that will credit people to my protection rather than the hand of Jesus, my Rock and my Salvation. 2 Corinthians 1: 8-11 Brothers and sisters, we don't want you to be ignorant about suffering we experienced in the province of Asia. It was so extreme that it was beyond our ability to endure. We even wondered if we could go on living. In fact, we still feel as if we're under a death sentence. But we suffer so that we would stop trusting ourselves and learn to trust God, who brings the dead back to life. He has refused us from a terrible death, and he will rescue us in the future. We are confident that he will continue to rescue us, since you are also joining to help us when you pray for us. Then many people will thank God for the favour he will show us because many people prayed for us.

It can be easy to forget where the Word must originate, in immaturity and fleshy need to feel powerful. We cannot over look the source, in which all revelation, and affirmation stem. God's Word not ours, create reality and accomplishes the purposes of heaven. All authority in heaven and on earth is given to Jesus. Apart from Jesus we stand empty. We must never determine what we want to see happen, no matter how good, loving or appealing it might seem.

Meditation: Our own Christian gift of Spirituality. It is a gift, however, that has been stolen and twisted by others, leading a lot of Christians to have little or no interest in meditating, because of a misdirected reaction and use of it by the world. The church seems to have a habit of abandoning good things to the enemy just because the enemy has adopted and twisted them, assuming falsely that if the enemy does something, then we cannot. The enemy is not a creator and can seldom be credited with originating anything. He can only steal from us what God has made and then twist and distort it. But our Book (the Bible) teaches about meditation, and it's time for us to reclaim it and do it right.

I ask myself how do I appear among an unbelieving world, as bright as the wings of a butterfly, as happy as a sparrow's afternoon song, as beautiful as a garden filled with flowers? I hope I pass this test! Because this is what will make the outsider want to look in, it is not my preaching and opinions but the true knowledge of God being shown in our way of life.

Instead of grace/work we make it work/grace. Instead of working in a world God calls everything into being with his Word and redeems his people with an outstretched arm, we rearrange it as a world we preach the Mighty Word of God and in afterthought ask him to bless our speaking.

"Sabbath" - Uncluttered time and space to distance ourselves from the frenzy of our own activities so we can see what God has been (and is) doing.

"Sabbath-keeping" - Quieting the internal noise to hear the still small voice of the Lord, removing the distractions of pride so Christ can discern the presence of us as we seek him.

"Sabbath" - Uncluttered time and space to detach ourselves from the people around us so that they have a chance to deal with God without us poking around and meddling. They need to be free from depending on us. They need to be free from our guidance that always tends towards manipulation.

"Sabbath-keeping" - Separating ourselves from the people who are clinging to us, from the routines from which we are clinging to for our identity, and offering them all up to God in praise. Ephesians 2: 1-10 As for you, you were dead in your transgressions and sins, in which you used to live when you followed the ways of this world and of the ruler of the kingdom of the air, the spirit who is now at work in those who are disobedient. All of us also lived among them at one time, gratifying the cravings of our sinful nature and following its desires and thoughts. Like the rest, we were by nature objects of wrath. But because of his great love for us, God, who is rich in mercy, made us alive with Christ even when we were dead in transgressions - it is by grace you have been saved. And God raised us up with Christ and seated us with him in the heavenly, realms in Christ Jesus, in order that in the coming ages he might show the incomparable riches of his grace, expressed in his kindness of us in Christ Jesus. For it is by grace you have been saved, through faith - and this not from yourselves, it is the gift of God - not by works, so that no one can boast. For we are God's workmanship, created in Christ Jesus to do good works, which God prepared in advance for us to do.

The two Biblical reasons for Sabbath-keeping developed in side by side Sabbath activities of praying and playing. The Exodus reason directs us to the study and reflection of God, which becomes prayer. The Deuteronomy reason directs us to social leisure, which becomes play. Praying and playing are harmonious with each other and have extensive inner connections. Psalm 92:1 It is good to give thanks to Yahweh, to play in honour of your name, Most High.

Sabbath-keeping involves both praying and playing. The activities are alike enough to share the same day and different enough to require each other for complementary wholeness.

Psalm 92 sets praying and playing in sequential order and then works out the equal actions with three comparisons, Psalm 92: 1- 3 What a beautiful thing, God, to give thanks, to sing an anthem to you, the High God! To announce your love each daybreak, sing your faithful presence all through the night, accompanied by dulcimer and harp, the full-bodied music of strings.

Music: Playing and praying are like the musicians art that combines discipline with delight. Music arouses something deep within us. Our bodies absorb and digest the sound and rhythm and experience aliveness. Taking us beyond our exterior selves into understanding and yearnings eagerly stretching us into beauty. And anytime we are beyond ourselves, by whatever means, we are close to God.

Psalm 92: 10 But you have made me as strong as a wild ox. You have anointed me with the finest oil.

Animals: We are delighted when we see animals in their natural environment - leaping, soaring, prancing. An eagle plummets to its pray; a grizzly carelessly rips through wilderness turf; a deer vaults a stream. Praying and playing must become like that, undomesticated. We need to shed poses and masks, becoming unself-conscious.

Psalm 92: 12-14 But the godly will flourish like palm trees and grow strong like the cedars of Lebanon. For they are transplanted to the Lord's own house. They flourish in the courts of our God. Even in old age they still produce fruit; they will remain vital and green.

Sylvan (forest like) close to my name Sylvia which means (forest maiden): Praying and playing share this sylvan quality. They develop and mature with age, they don't go into decline. Prayerfulness and playfulness reverse the deadening effects of sin – determined lives. They are life-exchanging, not life-diminishing. They infuse vitalities, counteracting fatigue. They renew us they do not wear us out. Praying and playing block boredom, reduce anxieties, push, pull, direct, prod us into fullness of our humanity by getting our body and spirit in touch and friendly with each other.

Psalm 92: 5-9 O Lord, what great works you do! And how deep are your thoughts. Only a simpleton would not know, and only a fool would not understand this: Though the wicked sprout like weeds and evildoers flourish, they will be destroyed forever. But you, O Lord, will be exalted forever. Your enemies, Lord, will surely perish; all evildoers will be scattered.

This Sabbath-psalmist is not of smelling the flowers, dreamily detached from the terrible plight of the people. He is horrified and dismayed that the wicked are thick as weed and at how the evildoers flourish. But he goes ahead and keeps a Sabbath of praying and playing, convinced that these practices are God's Will not only for us but the battered world as well. As we set this day aside for praying and playing despite the compelling pressure to do something practical, was not the most practical thing at all to do.

Sabbath-keeping is quite easy to understand. We simply select a day of the week and quit work. We are always threatening to do this but never seem to get around to it, too busy I guess. Matthew 14: 5-8 One man considers one day more sacred than another: another man considers every day alike. Each one should be fully convinced in his own mind. He who regards one day as special, does so to the Lord. He who eats meat, eats to the Lord, for he gives thanks to God: and he who abstains, does so to the Lord and gives thanks to God. For none of us live to himself alone and none of us dies to himself alone. If we live, we live to the Lord, and if we die we die to the Lord. So, whether we live or die, we belong to the Lord.

A day apart for seeking and silence, not doing, just being. The dedication of time to be set apart for being not using. A day to watch and be responsive to what God has done.

Sabbath-keeping is not something 'we' do, but what 'we' don't do. In the practice of Sabbath-keeping we find ourselves in Luke 24: 32 They asked each other, "Were not our hearts burning within us while he talked with us on the road and opened the Scriptures to us?"

It is this kind of unassuming exchange in attention and prayer that happens quietly but increasingly intense, when we get the rhythm right, we realize that without directly intending it, we have time to pray and play.

The Bible (God's Word) should be our guide on how to behave, leading us into faith and good conscience, restoring proper behaviour that has gone astray. Stay clear of false teaching they are demonic.

God wants all to be saved we are to be praying everywhere, lifting up holy hands in unity with heaven. Run from wrong teaching, have a good testimony to an unbelieving world. Do not let your prayers be hindered by ungodly ways, or disagreement. Do not pray in anger or dispute but be in total unity and agreement, this will connect us to the Will of God. Trusting, then stepping through the opened heaven as we pray.

God refuses to bless any plans but his own. There is no way around the wilderness (or any season for that matter) there is one way and one way only to get over it and that is by humbly and obediently going through it.

In the darkness of the soul, you can hear the plead that sound something like this: "Lord, if I hurt any worse, if just one more thing comes down on me, I'll break!" and then you hear Abba Daddy answer: "Right! Isn't that the point?" Because when the dark night of the soul comes to an end in the new light of a new-day eternal fruit is produced, fruit that is clearly the Lord's and not of human origin. We who have suffered the dark night have been made ready to surrender everything so that we take no personal ownership of the blessing, anointing and even fulfillment. It is all about the Kingdom of God not about us.

Be honest with God about your feelings. Serve God. Keep listening, keep worshiping, remain in fellowship, no matter how painful it may seem. Walk by faith even when blinded and exhausted. Luke 17: 7-10 "Suppose someone has a servant who is ploughing fields or watching sheep. Does he tell his servant when he comes from the field; have something to eat? No. Instead, he tells his servant, "Get dinner ready for me, after you serve me my dinner, you can eat yours. He doesn't thank the servant for following orders. That's the way it is with you. When you've done everything you're ordered to do, say, 'we're worthless servants. We've done our duty.'"

The very important purpose of the dark night of the soul is to bring about abandonment of any hope of personal reward for loving or serving God. Our love must be so focused on God, so simple and pure that obedience becomes its own reward. There is no space for personal reward at any level. We must serve for love alone, and pursue our calling from a base of rest in the Lord.

Humility forms the basis for the defeat of defensiveness. This flows from the security in Jesus, and it leads to transparency and vulnerability. No longer needing to protect or conceal those tender places inside by putting up a false front or strength.

I may be different, I may be apart. But I am very much one with the family I have been sent to serve. When you have nothing to hide, people cannot use hidden sin against you. Hebrews 4: 9-13 Therefore, a time of rest and worship exists for God's people. Those who entered his place of rest also rested from their work as God did from his. So we must make every effort to enter that place of rest. Then no one will be lost by following the example of those who refuse to obey. God's Word is living and active. It is sharper than a two-edged sword and cuts as deep as the place where soul and spirit meet, the place where joints and marrow meet. God's Words judge a person's thoughts and intentions. No creature can hide from God. Everything is uncovered and exposed for him to see. We must answer to him.

In a plea for self-control we find (our) self belongs to God and as for control it's all about Salvation, control of choices over true teaching or false doctrine. The safest way to live and conduct our self is by doing everything in the glory to God, and live like you are always standing in the presence of God.

Declaring the word of the Lord, serving into our community so it will be restored back to the kingdom. And even though we are in the midst of great trials, still we are the voice in the desert, shouting, prepare the way of the Lord!

If the church ceased to exist would the community miss you?

In the new generation of leadership which is emerging. Prophetic people being the forerunners. This leadership will both understand and minister from a base in the Sabbath rest of the people of God. The key will be we have rested from our own works because we suffered exposure of every thought and intention of the heart that does not have a hold on that rest. The flesh is useless and helpless in the Spirit of God's rest. 1 Thessalonians 5: 14-28 We encourage you brothers and sisters, to instruct those who are living right, cheer up those who are discouraged, help the weak, and be patient with everyone. Make sure that no one ever pays back one wrong with another wrong. Instead always try to do what is good for each other and everyone else. Always be joyful, never stop praying. Whatever happens give thanks, because it is God's Will in Christ Jesus that you do this. Don't put out the Spirit's fire. Don't despise what God has revealed. Instead, test everything. Hold on to what is good. Keep away from every kind of evil. May the God who gives peace make you holy in every way. May he keep your whole being – spirit, soul, and body – blameless when our Lord Jesus Christ comes. The one who calls you is faithful and he will do this. Brothers and sisters pray for us. Greet all the brothers and sisters with a holy kiss. In the Lord's name, I order you to read this letter to all the brothers and sisters. The good Will of our Lord Jesus Christ be with you.

No one has the gift to dominate, we were, both genders, created for equality in unity. To teach God's truth does not require on to be male or female, it requires a humble demeanour which in a submissive context is being guided by the Holy Spirit. So it is not accurate when it is said women should not be teaching, or serving God. In any manner where the Spirit is the leader, both men and woman alike are to be following in a Godly manner.

There are times when a teacher is required, but mostly all that is required is to enter into reality that is already God in and around us.

Most of our words can be set in one of two categories: Words for communion and words for communication. The communion words are used for storytelling, love making, nurture intimacies, developing truth. The words of communication are used in business transactions, marketing skills, teaching of math, read etc. Both these categories are necessary, but the one to shine through in spiritual direction should be the words of communion.

Let's take a troubled marriage for example: the truth is as the husband and wife learn to communicate more clearly, it often leads to divorce rather than reconciliation. The reason for this being that words used as mere communication are corrupt and impure. So here is where words of communion replace or at least work together with communication, a place where a part of the one party enters a part of the other party. Now beware because this requires the risk of revelation, the courage for getting involved. At the center of communion there is sacrifice. Working at the core, it is not words that are used to give something but we actually give a piece of ourselves. Communion words are not words to be used for determining meaning but to pull up the mysteries. Oh/oh now we did it we have entered into a loophole of unknown and we find safety being pushed out of the way as we step over to a risky unknown. The Eucharist uses the simple words of – this is my body, this is my Blood (given to you) – these words plunge us into the depth of pure love, venturing into what is not tied down, a fresh dance of freedom, from words of description, to words that point, reveal, they reach.

Authentic spiritual direction flows out of the act of worship. Coming through God alone, coming before our Father as listeners, and believers, as singers and pray-ers, as receivers and followers that bring about common worship in our ordinary lives.

Our human need is very visible, our awareness of human needs crowd out and then takes priority over our attention to God's presence. So watch out for the eager, well meaning helpers, nine out of ten times they only get in the way, by meddling where they have no business, consequently the final moments of clarity getting muddied. Romans 8: 18-22 I consider our present suffering insignificant compared to the glory that will soon be revealed to us. All creation is eagerly waiting for God to reveal who is children are. Creation was subjected to frustration but not by its own choice. The one who subjected it to frustration did so in the hope that it would also be set free from slavery to decay in order to share the glorious freedom that the children of God will have. We know that all creation has been growing with pain of childbirth up to the present time.

Don't let comfort deceive you from your goal. Know God's truths and way's no matter how wayside or off path they may seem. 2 Chronicles 32: 10-15 "This is what King Sennacherib of Assyria says: why are you so confident as you live in Jerusalem while it is blockaded? Isn't Hezekiah misleading you and abandoning you to die from hunger and thirst when he says: The Lord our God will rescue us from the King of Assyria? Isn't this the same Hezekiah who got rid of the Lord's places of worship and altars and told Judah and Jerusalem, worship and sacrifice at one alter? Don't you know what I and my predecessors have done to the people of all other countries? Were the gods of these nations able to rescue their people from my control? My predecessors claimed and destroyed those nations. Is your God able to rescue you from my control? Don't let Hezekiah deceive you or persuade you like this. Don't believe him. No god of any nation or kingdom could save his people from me or my ancestors. Certainly, your God will not rescue you from me!"

When we find ourselves up against a wall and the realization that life is not always fair is facing you as a tall mountain, you could run away and try to hide let the old self decide or, you can be strengthened from your circumstances with a prayer. I used to think the best thing for me to do when everything is falling apart is to praise the Lord, but the truth turned out to be the only thing for me to do when everything is falling apart is praise the Lord. See how there is always something to be learned even when we are so sure we "Got It!" When our heart is broken in two, maybe even three or more pieces just raise your hands and say, 'Father, you are all I need, you are everything for me, and I give this pain to you. When it feels like you just can't go on and you seem so all alone don't forget to praise in thanksgiving. Raising your hands and proclaiming greater is He who lives within me! With joy in your hearts is how you can praise the hurt away. It is in the blood of the Lamb we will overcome. With the words of our testimony we will watch the darkness disappear, to make room for the light where faith begins to grow. How can we be lonely, we are never alone.

Galatians 4: 19 My dear children, for whom I am again in the pains of childbirth until Christ is formed in you.

Like Paul we must endure the apostolic travail so that Christ can be formed in the church. And for this to take place means, "to be in pain." But even in this pain God gives us a wonderful promise. 2 Corinthians 4: 7-11 But we have this treasure in jars of clay to show that this all surpassing power is from God and not from us. We are hard pressed on every side, but not crushed: perplexed, but not in despair; persecuted, but not abandoned; struck down, but not destroyed. We always carry on our body the death of Jesus, so that the life of Jesus may also be revealed in our body. For we who are alive are always being given over to death for Jesus' sake, so that his life may be revealed in our mortal body.

The time in this life is for the 'Will of God,' not for our own happiness, serving God brings us the greatest joy and peace that we on our own can ever know. 1 Peter 4: 1-2 Therefore, since Christ suffered in his body, arm yourselves also with the same attitude, because he who has suffered in his body is done with sin. As a result, he does not live the rest of his earthly life for human earthly desire, but rather for the Will of God.

Again! Church is the Lord Himself moving in our midst it is the living relationship with Jesus. In the real belief that the testimony of Scripture is: What Was, What Is, and What Is Too Come. God wants us to see Jesus as he was, and then present Jesus as he is, then watch as he appears.

We Christians have doubt over the type of unity God wants built by his church (bride.) We need to swallow our pride, false understanding, judgment, and a whole lot more and always remember this: 2 Peter 3: 8 But do not forget this one thing, dear friends: With the Lord a day is like a thousand years, and a thousand years is like a day.

So in God's time the church will tower in to heaven, with the common purpose and common language to gather men together in unity, in the true Gospel of Jesus Christ.

Church Government should be formed with a solid foundation of doctrine, which promotes liberty not conformity. This enables the hearts of men to a freedom of the power of truth and a true conviction of the Holy Spirit.

In order for true obedience to exist there has to be the freedom of disobedience. This is why leader's of God's church come to this great position because of their love for the truth, not for any lust of power. A true leader does not come out of compulsion, but something much deeper – a heart that loves God and God's ways above anything else.

When we submit under the Headship of Jesus, is when our ultimate unity will come.

There is only one place living water can come from, our most innermost being, the heart, a true apostolic church must come from what the Lord has spoken in the heart of his people. This is why authority is not to be considered a position of privilege instead as a responsibility for serving.

A main purpose for the church is to be an instrument for God to Reach, Redeem, and Restore the lost what a sweet tune.

God is supernatural, making Christianity a supernatural experience. So it would be in our best interest to become comfortable with the supernatural, if we are going to walk with God. We are living in enemy territory. So as we live Godly in the world we will do it in persecution, being conformed to God's image. 1 John 5: 19-20 We know that we are children of God, and that the whole world is under the control of the evil one. We know also that the Son of God has come and has given us understanding, so that we may know him who is true. And we are in him who is true - even in his Son Jesus Christ. He is the true God and eternal life.

Someone of True Faith doesn't just believe the events written in the bible are true - they believe that through their lives today, the same works of God are being done.

The meaning of 'The Head'? Is it authority? When we are in covenant with someone we are betrothed to many. Our behaviour today will account for the appearance of Christ. When we are born again we are now engaged to our future title Bride of Christ. Engaged is the preparation for marriage.

The word head means source of creation. In every action you do it must honour your source.

Ester 6: 11-13 So Haman took the robe and horse; he robed Mordecai and led him through the city square, proclaiming before him, "This is what is done for the man whom the King especially wants to honour!" Then Mordecai returned to the King's Gates but Haman fled to his house, thoroughly mortified, hiding his face. When Haman had finished telling his wife Zeresh and all his friends everything that had happened to him, his knowledgeable friends who were there and his wife Zeresh said, "If this Mordecai is in fact a Jew, your bad luck has only begun. You don't stand a chance against him you're as good as ruined."

Is there really 'free will?' Or is it just rebellion? If it has all been done from the beginning in his perfect presence and we are to honour our source in every action, were we not created to do his purpose? So again just outright rebellion if we do not do that purpose. So to be tired of church is rebellion, because it is the connection as a family connected with God, just to worship and commune with God. Just us and our Daddy preparing us for the Bride Groom, don't let attitude, pride, anger, confusion the list goes on and on and on.........rob you from this.

If believers do not have the concept of the church being the body of Christ, and are making their own group their foremost concern, then their spirit has dwindled and became narrow. A spiritual believer considers God's business as their own business and the whole church is the object of their love. If their spirit is open, the river of life will flow everywhere. If our spirit is not big enough to include all of God's children, it means our spirit has been poisoned.

Anyone who seek for only joy in their feelings, and does not realize that the burden of sin laid on the cross is also a major source in spiritual calling, and is afraid of taking up any duties for the church are living for themselves. The promise from God himself in the Bible confirms that when God gives us the responsibility of a burden, it is always manageable, even light is how it is put in Scripture. We should not be fooled into thinking that we have fallen or that we have committed an error. No! We should rejoice and in God's strength carry this task through in the Joy of the Lord!

God's life is not like the tide of the Sea which rises and falls; it is like a river which flows forever with living water. John 7: 38 Whoever believes in me, as the Scripture has said, streams of living water will flow from within him.

God's life is not like the tide which must ebb after a certain time. The source of life within us is God; He never changes, and within him there is no shadow of turning, and we must always be waiting on the Lord, and have no resistance toward the Lord, then we can walk with him.

God wants us to be bold to step forward because of his power. To witness for the Lord, to suffer pain, to bear shame, to love everything, to rely only in God, and to trust in his love, wisdom, power truthfulness, and promises.

There are teachings that only reach the believer's mind they have no root in the Spirit. Behind a true teaching the Spirit should touch another's spirit, not give others dry rotten and infested manna in the mind, but rather fish and bread on the fire of coals in the Spirit. Only if our spirit is in the Lord, are we fit to meet others. All we have needs to continually be new from our Father. John 6: 57 Just as the living Father sent me and I live because of the Father, so the one who feeds on me will live because of me.

A believer should keep their spirit in a condition of being one with all believers. Not being joined only with a small group of those with the same opinions, but with the entire Body of Christ.

1 Corinthians 2: 9-13 However, as it is written: "No eye has seen, no ear has heard, no mind has conceived what God has prepared for those who love him," - but God has revealed it to us by his Spirit. The Spirit searches all things from God. For whom among men know the thoughts of man except the man's spirit within him? In the same way no one knows the thoughts of God except the Spirit of God. We have not received the spirit of the world but the Spirit who is from God, that we may understand what God has freely given us. This is what we speak, expressing spiritual truths in spiritual words.

I wonder if God is telling us that this does not refer only to heaven or the things to come in the life hereafter. But the Holy Spirit takes the deep things of God, that God has prepared for us, even in our lives now, and reveals them to us.

May every single thing we act to react in bringing glory not shame. Let's look at being the glory: being the glory equals the existence of one who brings praise and honour to the other.

Marriage is a covenant of relationship. We see the big picture of abuse quite easily but the hidden ones or the ones that don't suit our ways to change, we don't want to bring into reality but here are a few that might end the reading of this book, a good time to say thank you for staying this long if you are still around, but God says to teach his way, not tickle the ears of his people. I have choices, but they must honour my husband's agreement or it is abuse. But at the same time we are free to serve not dominate. There is a mutual dependence between men and women, not one can exist without the other. Male and female are both the image of God, man is the glory of God woman is the glory of man. Now we can see why being one in unity connects us in completeness in the whole principle of mutual oneness in Christ this is the importance unity replacing abuse.

So yes even though we are in Spirit, we are still planted here on earth. Creation is based on love and relationship one with another they are the only thing that really matter. In Abba Daddies love he created us. Free choice was given to us because of love. Jesus gave his life to redeem us from our wrong choices, in love Abba Daddy raised Jesus back to an eternal life for his choice in love to reconcile everything back to the way it was created. He provides all our needs because of love, and the Father loves everyone! So if we are angry with someone and take that anger into hate (which is sin) I am hating Jesus' friend. God's love requires us to be in relationship, with him and his friends.

Are we aware enough to be ready to recognize and repent from our sins, ok free-spirits let's start dancing because it will only be God's fire falling on us, a refined fire of growth.

The struggles of truth and lies always seem to surround us. Truth is, knowing we can do nothing without God, nothing exist without God. Truth is the gift through love of free-will, even though we are going to mess up. From the very beginning God set in place the plan of redemption this is why he can always be trusted.

So both good and evil only have the power to control our lives as much as we choose to allow them to, I don't know about you but I am going to take a risk and head up the what might seem the tougher road and pick truth, now discovered low and behold as the power is given to God it ends up being the carefree load. The lies seem to be waiting in the ditch so let's help each other stay on the path.

What is the veil between heaven and the third heaven? It is simply our lack of love for God and the understanding of how much God loves us! The simple, stark, honest truth about God's love and his abundance towards us has been buried under the devastation of wars, starvation, rape, murder, abuse, lack, poverty, hardship, evil.................God is a merciful God and wants nothing more to give us the desires of our heart, God has the perfect plan in operational order already he is just waiting for us to follow it for it to work. 2 Thessalonians 2: 9-12 The coming of the lawless one will be in accordance with the work of Satan displayed in all kinds of counterfeit miracles, signs and wonders, and in every sort of evil that deceives those who are perishing. They perish because they refuse to love the truth and so be saved. For this reason God sends them a powerful delusion so that they will believe the lie and so all will be condemned who have not believed the truth but have delighted in wickedness.

We need to let God bring us back to the purity of Eden before that first lie and sin separated the spirits. Are we to wrapped up in our time, that we are missing this time with God to walk in the spiritual and natural realm, and co-labour with our Father. What time is it? It is no-o'clock! It is time to become one in spirit and union with Father, Son, Holy Spirit and each other.

Walking through the veil between the heavens, we will be able to walk out of the third heaven as a new creation, with a new full relationship with Abba Daddy. Jesus went to the cross for this very relationship to be regained. And now the body of Christ with the fullness of the Godhead living in us, we are the best friend, in one corporate body, soul and spirit.

Heaven is a complex open to everyone, to congregate with groups of angels, all are doing something different, but still these sounds and sights are tremendously in union.

It is hard to imagine or try to picture God as not being one-denominational. Because that is all our knowledge enables us to grasp. It is in revelation only we can trust, he is everywhere every second of everyday, in every situation, (this makes me exhausted just trying to imagine it) then to top it all off he is aware of what is going on in every corner of his whole creation. God knows that sin has touched every life but he wants nothing more than to be able to catch the tears personally into his tender truth and love.

Good works, truth, faith, belief come to life when we get into the right position, step away from what we are doing and follow Christ, because in the way of God, in the time of God, everything is different from what sin has made this world. Righteous and sin have to be opposites, in order to take a side, now we need to make sure we balance ourselves on the righteous side of things. It's not the words we know, it's the word we apply to our lives that will bind us together from our individuality. We are all individual, no one should be looked at and seen as the same, but in the Word we blend the individualities, together forming a Body in Christ's image.

1 Chronicles 29: 10-13 David blessed God in full view of the entire congregation: Blessed are you, God of Israel, our father from of old and forever. To you, O God, belong the greatness and might, the glory, the victory, the majesty, the splendour: YES! Everything in heaven, everything on earth; the kingdom all yours. You've raised yourself high over all. Riches and glory come from you, you're ruler over all. You hold strength and power in the palm of your hand to build up and strengthen all. And here we are, O God, our God, giving thanks to you, praising your splendid Name.

In order to be trusted with revelation of things to come, we must get our roots sunk in deep, into Scripture and history. Then we can be the mainstream of what the Lord is doing here on earth. We cannot isolate ourselves from crossing national and denominational barriers, or we will drift further and farther from the River of Life which is always bringing forth "Cross-pollination" of the Spirit.

"The Messengers of God's power" are being prepared. These are the most supernatural powerful people ever to walk the earth at one time. The walking "Coals of Fire," from the very throne of God, to release revival and moves of God wherever they are sent. It is hard to find a handful together in any one place of these messengers. So if a congregation has just two of these coal walkers it is exceptional. But unfortunately the congregation cannot stand the fire that is on them, and either have, or try, to drive them away. Luke 7: 31-35 "To what, then, can I compare the people of this generation? What are they like? They are like children sitting in the marketplace and calling out to each other: We played the flute for you, and you did not dance; we sang a dirge, and you did not cry. For John the Baptist came neither eating bread nor drinking wine, and you say, He has a demon. The Son of Man came eating and drinking, and you say, here is a glutton and drunkard, a friend of the tax collectors and sinners. But wisdom is proved right by all her children.

These "special forces" sent by God, are so different they do not fit into the typical church life. Places however are being prepared for them so they may worship God in total freedom. They even fear becoming known because this would compromise the ability to do their job. Their life has but one purpose: to do what they were put here on the earth to do. Recognition actually frightens them.

Elderly are going to start growing young, as their physical bodies are going to be quickened. Just a single touch from God can renew us as no oil of olay ever could. There is no one alive whom is too old for what is taking place or coming.

Just imagine the church if we would start doing things like Jesus, instead of saying, "Stop playing God!" Come on let's get out there and show the world what Jesus can do. This practice will prepare us for our purpose on earth. This is especially important in the ways leaders are prepared then released.

Jealousy within the church is one of the greatest battles for its survival, the fastest to destroy it. But how can jealousy live is my question after reading Psalm 95: 4 In his hands are the depths of the earth, and the mountain peaks belong to him.

Taking offence to the word "elite" is another huge obstacle for the preparation in the church of today. But the dealing with things like jealousy and words like elite, is part of the training itself. There is an "elite force" of Christians being released, who are and must be very different from the typical lukewarm Christians that are in the church right now. Not only will they have higher standards they will have much higher standards.

Many lukewarm Christians will let jealousy drive them into becoming opposed of what is happening. But then others will be pricked in their hearts by the focused devotion of these elite and wake up out of their lukewarm state. This has to happen, because the 'messengers of power' need the gifts and spiritual expertise of the entire church. A lot of the greatest spiritual exploits will be done by the ones slugging it out day by day on the front lines of their local church(es). Philippians 3: 12-14 Not that I have already obtained all this, or have already been made perfect but I press on to take hold of that for what Christ Jesus took hold of me. Brothers, I do not consider myself yet to have taken hold of it. But one thing I do:

90

Forgetting what is behind and straining toward what is ahead. I press on towards the goal to win the prize for which God has called me heavenward in Christ Jesus.

Expect great things from God. Attempt great things for God. No greater endeavour in the universe can compare to the opportunity of attaining Christ.

This is why we have been called to run, and in order to win we must rise above the pursuit of our own rank and position. Because in order to win we have to become empty to self ambition, and full of love for God and our fellow soldiers of the cross, so that everything we do is for the glory of God and the benefit of these soldiers, not for any position we might gain. We need to grow into a pure love for our fellow man, and should be willing to give our own place to them. Because if we seek our own lives we are losers, to be winners we have to be willing to lose our lives for God and his sake. The highest rank is really for the purpose of being the servant to All!

A very daring thing for my mind to reverse was learning to relate to God, because I was waiting for God to relate to me. I heard it said once that we cannot co-labour if we do not know the purpose. I found even when I was aware of the purpose it was still so very hard to release it into the church, because of fear of the unknown and the uncommon, from both me to give it, and the church to receive it. So the only possible thing that can be done is to walk it through hand in hand with the Father and watch as his exact will is released. Awakening my passion, which is holding the ones who came to receive the gifts of heaven, watching and witnessing them be formed into the relationship they were purposed for and celebrate your Will for us All, in praise and worship, my personal preference form of prayer.

God will say to all creation! Isaiah 35: 3-7 Strengthen the feeble hands, steady the knees that give away; say to those with fearful hearts, "Be strong, do not fear; your God will come he will come with vengeance, with divine retribution, he will come to save you." Then will the eyes of the blind be opened and ears of the deaf unstopped. Then will the lame leap with the deer and the mute tongue shout for joy. Water will gush forth in the wilderness and streams in the desert. The burning sand will become a pool, the thirsty ground bubbling springs. In the haunts where jackals once lay, grass and reeds and papyrus will grow.

This is the portrait the presence of God in human life that manifests itself in wholeness. This is what God is and prayer is the experience of meeting God. Prayer is the conscious human intention to relate to the depth of life and love and therefore to be an agent of the creation of wholeness in another. Prayer is the offering of our life and our love through the simple action of sharing our friendship and our acceptance.

Prayer is my purpose (spiritual creation) calling with another's purpose, this gives one another the courage to dare to risk, and to venture into a whole new way, a new beginning in Christ. Prayer is also an act of opposition to prejudice and stereotypes that can diminish our purpose for God. Prayer is taking the proper political action to build a society in which opportunities can be equalized and no one will be forced to accept the status quo as their destiny. Prayer is the active recognition that there is a sacred core in every person that must not be violated. Prayer is the facing if life's urgent requirements; pressing needs, which involves us all in the realization that we live subject to and wide and array of circumstances over which we have no control. (Big breath here.) Ok let's continue. Prayer is not cowering before these circumstances, but under the covering of the Lord and in the name of Jesus be willing to meet them with courage and boldness. Prayer is the ability to embrace the fragility of life and to transform it, placing it in God's hands, even as we are victimized or killed by it.

Prayer is called out of childish dependency into the spiritual maturity. 1 Thessalonians 5: 16-24 Be joyful always; pray continually; give thanks in all circumstances, for this is God's Will for you in Jesus Christ. Do not put out the Spirit's fire; do not treat prophesies with contempt. Test everything. Hold on to the good. Avoid every kind of evil. May God himself, the God of peace, sanctifying you through and through. May your whole spirit, soul and body be kept blameless at the coming of our Lord Jesus Christ. The one who calls you is faithful and he will do it.

Are we living as if everything we say and do is a prayer? Calling others towards God, towards love, developing them to an awareness of their purpose to creation. Just imagine that when life is lived in this fashion the enormous amount of energy released from heaven.

Let's reconnect to the true agent and energy which brings healing and wholeness to us right here on earth. Love, concern, caring, expresses the opportunity of the difference this makes for our living.

Open up wide my heart Lord, as you close my eyes to anything in another that is not of you, that I may not grab this opportunity for judgment. As my heart sees only all that is best for your kingdom leading me home and developing these fantastic bests from you into an uncontrolled unity so I might not miss the revival as it is rains from your throne.

Another influence that has turned meditation into a practice that seems to have been left behind is our culture of action and entertainment. It seems that no one ever sits still anymore. And as for silence I wonder how many remember what it sounds like? When the opportunity is presented to us to be still who knows what to do with it. It is hard enough when this is put into our routine, but when it occurs uncontrolled it is a lost art. Our minds and hearts have taken on the pulse to the rhythm of constant stimulation and entertainment. God is a God for fun and games, prayer, worship, a God of everything.... but there are times when we surrender to meditation in order to hear the voice of God who often does speak in whispers, so don't make your Creator assert his unwillingness to compete with the noise of our world. Meditation is heard more in the Old Testament, another possible reason modern Christians neglect this practice, what a shame. Because really the foundation for our spiritual life is laid in the Old Testament, which the New Testament writers regard as the Word of God which is still enforced. Remember the Word of God for Jesus was the Old Testament, Jesus became the New Testament. So one does not exist without the other, it would be like being born without a mother, impossible. 2 Timothy 3: 14-17 However continue in what you have learned and found to be true. You know who your teachers were. From infancy you have known the Holy Scriptures. They have the power to give you wisdom so that you can be saved through faith in Christ Jesus. Every Scripture passage is inspired by God. All of them are useful for teaching, pointing out error, correcting people and training them for a life that has God's approval. They equip God's servants so that they are completely prepared to do good things.

Meditation is the form of prayer in which after we have actively engaged ourselves in conversation with God, meditation becomes the purest position we place ourselves in. A passive receiving mode, where we enter into the state of peace and rest in our Father. It is here in meditation the flow moves between heaven and our heart that receives God's laws, promises, instruction, and his approval. Allowing them to resonate there assurance to us of being safe and sound. This is the pulse that needs to be penetrating through us, expressing itself frequently without forethought or effort like an echo. A kind of inner environment of God speaking to us and us listening to him. Joshua 1: 7-9 "Only be strong and very courageous, faithfully doing everything in the teaching that my servant Moses commanded you. Don't turn away from them. Then you will succeed where ever you go. Never stop reciting these teachings. You must think about them night and day so that you will faithfully do everything written in them. Only then will you prosper and succeed. I have commanded you, Be strong and courageous! Don't tremble or be terrified, because the Lord your God is with you wherever you go.'"

Another key concept to meditation is repetition, this is a practice of repeating a concept (also referred to as chanting). It is to take a word or verse from God to one's self until it takes on a life of its own, causing the meaning to take root in our heart and understanding springs into a gushing of revelation. Causing the mind, the heart, spirit to ponder what God is saying to us in order to unlock the depth of a given truth at every one of these levels of our being.

Transformation to destiny. What a way to live our lives. Just before this transformation took hold of me I had a vision: In this vision I was pregnant (don't forget I am over fifty) and a very proud Oma. I was in labour in tremendous pain, but as I proceeded to try to give birth in the labour room of the hospital, birth would not take place. So I left the hospital to find myself in a parade, well, as the labour pains started again all the spectators on the sidelines watching the parade gave birth to babies as I continued moving along the parade route each one as I passed them gave birth to a new born baby.

Shortly after the vision I entered into the transformation of my destiny, an exciting attraction on the journey home. And here I received a spoken promise to my heart. "Take my hand. Trust, understand, believe ME! I Love You, I have chosen you. We have many works to do together. Your job Knecht Sylvia is in me and with me. As we impart be ready, we are going beyond faith, beyond anything understood to you and the world. Thank you Knecht Sylvia for coming with me. I Love You. And together it is this love we are going to bring to my creation everyone a true love conceived in heaven that will be born on earth!" Psalm 16: 11 You made the path of life known to me. Complete joy is in your presence. Pleasures are by your side forever.

God also changed, well more like added to my name here through this transformation. He added Knecth, I was familiar with this word from a Christmas poem I memorized when I was young. But never really knew the meaning so it was an honour to find out that God has made me his servant. Yup! Knecht means servant. Psalm 28: 8 O Lord, I love the house where you live, the place where your glory dwells.

When we get a tendency to thinking we are "No Good", always failing, not accomplishing anything. If this is the boat you find yourself on 'abandon ship,' right now. God has accepted you. You are of great worth to your Father. Don't sell yourself, or the Lord Jesus short!

These words are heard frequently among Christians, 'loving God,' 'loving one another.' What does all this 'loving' talk mean? Hopefully it means we quit playing let's pretend, quit being phoney. Loving mankind not humouring mankind. Romans 12: 14 Bless those who persecute you, bless and do not curse!

Even though we hate what is wrong, we are the church and we stand as one. Romans 12: 9-13 Love must be sincere. Hate what is evil; cling to what is good. Be devoted to one another in brotherly love. Honour one another above yourselves. Never be lacking in zeal, but keep your spiritual fevor, serving the Lord. Be joyful in hope, patient in affliction, faithful in prayer. Share with God's people who are in need. Practice hospitality.

This means more than just trying to stay out of trouble. It means getting involved with trying to develop things for the better.

We seem to be surrounded by so much evil and sin in this day and age, we seem to just grow accustomed with it. Not being shocked, just getting along, keeping ones mouth shut so we don't cause trouble. Is it really enough just to avoid evil? Or should we be hating it? Is it enough to just support the good? Or should we be fighting for it? Let's not make Christianity a passive compromise towards sin. Or just the plain opposite to evil. It is so much more. Let's take Christianity to the limits.

The power and motivation to conquer evil is more than doing good and being good! It is love, genuine love. Don't just pretend that we love others. Really love them. This is probably the hardest thing we are asked to do. That is why we will not do a perfect job of unselfish loving. And endure being laughed at and criticized.

But to try to love others unselfishly and at the same time have concerns over standing up for our rights is a contradiction. You cannot serve God and self. We need both hands on the Bible, not just one while waving your person design for life in the other. Or by posting up a list of laws that must be followed. It is setting up goals to aim at, to set your sight on. So walking in the spirit is not some quaint religious experience, it is the street that we live on.

We are all missionaries, because a missionary is someone who is sent to bring and to be the Good News to others. No more pretending to love others, we have to truly love them. How? Together with Jesus as we over look faults, going out of our way to help by taking the guff, by refusing to retaliate.

To obtain genuine love, we must sincerely and unselfishly offer our daily life to God. God then proves, tests, tempers our sincerity and unselfishness by sending us out to live with other people many of whom are not that loveable. It is in this living, loving, and serving, in the daily routine of life, that we have countless opportunities to be a living sacrifice, or a burnt offering.

I heard through the grape vine that mistakes need to be our victory not our condemner. Well my friend let me tell you that you are taking to the most victorious person alive. Alive being the key word here, alive to serve God, because mistake after mistake as long as I have breath I am planning to continue listening step by step. How do I serve God? Well, by serving his creation all his creation not just the easy ones; or the ones I chose, nope, every single one God plants in my path, and also with praise by worship to God for everything and everyone.

An authentic sign that we have become the house of the Holy Spirit is that we are spontaneous. Unpredictable is openness, freedom, expectancy, willingness to be surprised, and the declaration of the many-splendored things we call life. True spontaneity is the result of surrendering our wills to the indwelling Spirit so the natural qualities by which we respond to life are his. It becomes an unbound excitement in us when the Spirit is given complete freedom to express himself through us...God has so much to reveal to us every day. So often we miss the beauty around us, because of our fearful effort to defend, protect and preserve ourselves.

Spontaneous is the result of the fire of the Holy Spirit alive in us. The key to spontaneous living is to feed that fire with complete trust. "Don't Quench the Fire," this means not to extinguish, smother, or stifle God's love.

When the fires of the Holy Spirit are fuelled by our willingness for God's Will, an uncontainable enthusiasm for the Gospel is developed. The key to great living is formed through this enthusiasm. Authentic, enthusiasm is a gift! It is not the result of our own efforts. So my friend this sounds like a good time to learn how to receive gifts from heaven. Colossians 3: 12-17 Therefore, as God's chosen people, holy and dearly loved, clothe yourself with compassion, kindness, humility, gentleness, and patience. Bear with each other and forgive whatever grievance you may have against one another: Forgive as the Lord forgave you. And over all these virtues put on love, which binds them all together in perfect unity. Let the peace of Christ rule in your hearts since as members of one body you were called to peace and be thankful. Let the word of Christ dwell in you richly and you advice one another with all wisdom, and as you sing Psalms, hymns, and spiritual songs with gratitude in your hearts to God. And whatever you do, whether in word or deed, do it all in the name of the Lord Jesus, giving thanks to God the Father through him.

In these verses maybe Paul was simply saying, since you are Christians act like Christians. And we are all greatly loved. "Dearly loved by God" so we should be clothed in Christ like virtues, 'garments of grace.' But these clothes are only available from heaven, God's one-of-a-kind glory outlet mall, now here is where I want to do my shopping hope to meet you there. Nowhere or no one on earth can create such a wardrobe. There is only one true way to show compassion or patience towards someone and that is in the belief and trust that God is compassionate and patient with us. Even when I slip on a slippery patch of sin on this road home, or the storm gets so strong it doesn't seem like God's compassion, patience and forgiveness will make it through, but still it gets poured out to me unquenchably, this is how I hope to be with all of you my brothers and sisters, ma's and pa's, and even more bold you with me. Titus 2: 11-15 For the grace of God that brings salvation has appeared to all men. It teaches us self-controlled, up-right and godly lives in the present age, while we wait for the blessed hope – the glorious appearing of our great God and Saviour, Jesus Christ, who gave himself for us to redeem us from all wickedness and to purify for himself a people that are his very own, eager to do good. These, then, are the things you shall teach. Encouragement and rebuke with all authority. Do not let anyone despise you...

Kingdom destiny has been established for us from the beginning, so man what an awesome adventure like a treasure hunt to actually go and discover the blessings of our purpose for us and others, through the process of revelation, obeying, trusting, listening, be only in God's Will, grace, hope, praying, submission. Jeremiah 1: 5-8 "Before I formed you in the womb, I knew you. Before you were born, I set you apart for my holy purpose. I appointed you to be a prophet to the nations." I, Jeremiah, said, "Almighty Lord, I do not know how to speak. I am only a boy!" But the Lord said to me, "Don't say that you are only a boy. You will go wherever I send you, you will say whatever I command you to say. Don't be afraid of people. I am with you, and I will rescue you." Declares the Lord.

Only God can work out his purpose, not me for me, or you for me, or me for anyone else, and what God has done, is doing, and will do, for me, he will do for you. Choice in following = Victory. Psalm 29: 11 The Lord will give power to his people. The Lord will bless his people with peace.

Church cannot adequately function if it is limited to private individual consolation. The congregation must gather, so that if anyone of its family members happens to be suffering it can come to be realized that the pain they cannot resign themselves to, is know and even experienced by the rest of the family, then be placed before God in common prayer.

It is so human to wall ourselves up in pain; so we want to be abnormal and open up our suffering for others to walk us through it taking it back to Jesus where in his time and will the purposed healing will be granted. God suffers with man! Why? In order to strengthen the bonds between creator and creation. Jesus chose to suffer in order to better understand man, and so God can be better understood. But those of you who insist on suffering alone, such suffering shrinks you, diminishes you. Friends, that is just downright cruel.

Yahweh is our portion, and we must stay bound together in him, (suffering things are learned things.) We have a communion with a merciful God that is unable to be lost because it cannot be touched by the dislocation of external circumstances. Deuteronomy 10: 6-9 The Israelites traveled from the wells of the Jaakanites to Moserah. There Aaron died and was buried, and Eleazar his son succeeded him as priest. From there they traveled to Gudgodah and on to Jotbathah, a land with streams of water. At that time the Lord set apart the tribe of Levi to carry the ark of the covenant of the Lord, to stand before the Lord to minister and pronounce blessings in his name, as they still do today. That is why the Levites have no share or inheritance among their brothers; the Lord is their inheritance, as the Lord your God told them.

To someone who is unacquainted with the holy history of which God's blessing is articulated, or someone who fails to participate in the pilgrim worship in which God's bounty is remembered, blessing can easily be supposed to more than a commodity available for purchase or trade. A religion that promises the fulfillment of all 'needs' is distorted into a religion that manipulates God for the satisfaction of all 'wants.' The fact is that everything that is done and spoken in the Name of God is not, "Sweet, soft and cosy, easy, understandable." Everything that happens does not turn out "all right," if only we put on a happy face. Mark 13: 21-23 At that time if anyone says to you, "Look here is the Christ" or "Look there he is!" Do not believe it. For false Christ's and false prophets will appear and perform signs and miracles to deceive the elect – if that were possible. So be on your guard. I have told you everything ahead of time.

ITS time/ITS Time/ITS TIme/ITS TIMe/ITS TIME! To put on the blindfolds towards prejudice and work from following the direction of a God's heart. The colour of our skin, the ways of our culture, our sexual preference, the religions that are practiced are irrelevant to our opinions. Our opinions are safest when we just throw them into the trash, even better put them into God's dirty laundry hamper. We are all here because God put us here and God wants us to get along and unite, yes, unite into harmony. No one knows it all, yes Jesus is the way to heaven this is true, but he was sent for the Whole World, so we need to get over ourselves and our opinions every one of them from every one of us. From the North, South, East, West, we are all found on the same compass, and were all created in the same heaven from the same Father. What we do or where we go is not the all in all of importance, but to do it as someone who lives in the whole earth united to one another, not just our small corner separated from one another, letting God be our leader, how can this turn out wrong? Yes there is good and evil and I know where I pray to be blessed to stand. But no one knows it all but we all know some. This is why we need everyone together to know it all.

Thoughtful, studious, analysis involves a couple of matters: One is openness to words that reveal. And another is a submission to words that shape. Words are double dimensioned: they carry meaning from their source and they carry influence to their destination. God's decision to use words as a means of revealing himself and shaping us means that we need to pay attention both to what he says and how he says it.

Spiritual direction takes place when two people agree to give their full attention to what God is doing in one (most probably both) of their lives and seek to respond in faith.

Our slowness to engage in the not so glamorous, mystical work of spiritual direction is not new. It is the more public, appealing, impulsive appearance of ministry have always been more attractive. 1 Corinthians 4: 15 Even though you have ten thousand guardians in Christ, you do not have many fathers, for in Christ Jesus I become your father through the gospel.

It is easier to tell people what to do than to be with them in a discerning prayerful companionship as they work it out. The unfavourable ration of "guide" to "fathers" does not seem to have altered. If anything it is aggravated by the mass marketing of spiritual helps. People who are seeking guidance look towards paperback best-sellers, magazine articles, google, television talk shows, the further from a personal touch the better it seems. When the true nature of the life of faith requires a personal touch and an understood agreement is when we are going to mature: not only wisdom but a person to understand "us" in revelation to the wisdom. In order to grow we need to become vulnerable and ready to accept counsel that is sincerely offered.

There are so many different ways of engaging in this work as there are fingerprints. Our individuality and the individuality of the other increases in these encounters making it impossible to predetermine what should be done or said. But there is a basic stance that we can take: It would be unwise to forget for a moment that we are sinners dealing with sinners, so the primary orientation is looking towards God for grace.

Doctors have a saying among themselves, that the doctor who is his own doctor has a foolish doctor. Tells us that taking care of the body is a complex business and requires cool detached judgment. All of us, doctors included want coddling not healing. We prefer comfort to wholeness. And we are endlessly deceiving ourselves about ourselves.

If those entrusted with the care of the body cannot be trusted to look after their own bodies, the same goes for those entrusted with the care of souls looking after their own soul. Nothing is more harmful than trying to direct oneself – we should never allow ourselves to follow our own desires without seeking counsel. Proverbs 11: 14 For lack of guidance a nation falls, but many advisers make victory sure.

Scripture teaches us that we should not establish ourselves as our own guides, not to consider ourselves wise, never think we can direct ourselves. We need one another's help! We need guidance to lead us to God's grace. There is none more defenceless than a person who has no one to guide them along the road to God. A person who has no one to guide them will at first have great enthusiasm about fasting, keeping prayerful watch, silence, obedience etc. Alone however after a short while the fire goes out, and having no guidance and support they grow cold falling back into "the way they were."

Feed your fruit and gifts to everyone God brings to eat. We have been equipped to be sent out for just this very purpose. Ephesians 4: 7-13 God's favour has been given to teach us. It was measured out to us by Christ who gave it. That's why the Scripture says, "When he went to the highest place he took captive those who had captured us and gave gifts to people." Now what does it mean that he went up except that he also had gone down to the lowest parts of the earth? The one who had gone down also went up above all the heavens so that he fills everything. He also gave apostles, prophets, missionaries, as well as pastors and teachers a gift to his church. Their purpose is to prepare God's people to serve and to build up the body of Christ. This is to continue until all of us are united in our faith and in our knowledge about God's Son, until we become mature, until we measure up to Christ, who is the standard.

Let's look at the church: what is the role of the church? The church provides a loving and nurturing environment, safety. The church provides an opportunity to receive healing. The church provides teaching, mentoring, God's tools for the preparation of discipleship. The church provides opportunities to mature in gifts and callings. It provides encouragement. And after all this provision the church recognizes who you are and then sends you out. Psalm 42: 8 The Lord commands his mercy during the day, and at night his song is with me – a prayer to the God of my life.

Church as a family! Why do I need friends? God intended the family to be an incubator in which we grow the maturity, tools, abilities we need. Once this job has been fulfilled, we are suppose to encourage young adults to leave the nest and connect to the outside world. To establish a spiritual and emotional system of their own. An adult should be free to do whatever God has designed for them.

This is why friendship apart from family is so important. We should have the freedom even though we have a home church to visit, participate, and be involved in friendship (other churches). When we live God's love to the fullest we will grow the most.

We are to accomplish God's purpose by living his love into the world. Matthew 28: 19-20 Therefore go and make disciples of all the nations, baptizing them in the Name of the Father and Son and Holy Spirit, and teaching them to obey everything I have commanded you. And surely I am with you always, to the very end of the age."

So if we just stay in the comfort zone of our family, we frustrate the purpose. How can we make a difference to the world if we never even leave the same street?

Now we can absolutely be friends with our family members as well. But to become an autonomous adult, we must be willing to separate as well, and become the individual God created us to be.

God through his people must be the source from which the world will return to the way it was created. Ephesians 4: 14-16 Then we will no longer be infants, tossed back and forth by the waves, and blown here and there by every wind of teaching and by cunning and craftiness of men in their deceitful scheming. Instead, speaking the truth in love, we will in all things grow up into him who is the Head, that is Christ. From him the whole body joined and held together by every supporting ligament, grows and builds itself up in love, as each part does its work.

Change can be frightening, but hopefully it will be a comfort for you to understand that if you are frightened you might just be on the right road. The road of faith and growth. Hebrews 11: 8 By faith Abraham, when called to go to a place he would later receive as his inheritance, obeyed and went, even though he did not know where he was going.

We were not created to stand alone. Ecclesiastes 4: 9-10 Two are better than one, because they have a good return for their work: If one falls down, his friend can help him up. But pity the man who falls and has no one to help him up!

So church be a family, but a family with friends. Learn to be in unity one with the other.

Faith: Sure and certain of what we believe and do not see. My desire is to bring this into reality not just leave it hidden in my dictionary. Imagine receiving our birth to our destiny, then leaping in to the arms and character of God.

So the burning question now becomes, "What is sin?" In Hebrew "chatta'ah" meaning an offence. It comes from the root word "chatta" which means to miss. So sin is then the offence of missing the relationship with our Father, in return forcing his relationship with us to be missed. Isaiah 58: 5-14 Is this the kind of fast I have chosen, only a day for man to humble himself? Is it only for bowing one's head like a reed and for lying on sack cloth and ashes? Is that what you call a fast, a day acceptable to the Lord? "Is this not the kind of fasting I have chosen: to lose the chains of injustice and untie the cords of the yoke, to set the oppressed free and break every yoke? Is it not to share your food with the hungry, and to provide the poor wanderer with shelter - when you see the naked, to cloth him, and not to turn away from your own flesh and blood? Then your light will break forth like the dawn, and your healing will quickly appear; then your righteousness will go before you and the glory of the Lord will be your rear guard. Then you will call, and the Lord will answer; you will cry for help, and he will say here I am. "If you do away with the yoke of oppression, with the pointing finger and malicious talk, and if you send yourself in behalf of the hungry and satisfy the needs of the oppressed, then your light will rise in the darkness, and your night will become the noonday. The Lord will guide you always; he will satisfy your needs in a sun-scorched land and will strengthen your frame. You will be like a well watered garden, like a spring whose waters never fail. Your people will rebuild the ancient ruins and will rise up the age-old foundations, you will be called Repairer of Broken Walls, Restorer of Streets with dwellings. If you keep your feet from breaking the Sabbath and from doing as you please on my holy day, if you call the Sabbath a delight and the Lord's holy day honourable and if you honour it by not going your own way and not doing as you please or speaking idle words, then you will find your joy in the Lord, and I will cause you to ride on the heights of the land and to feast on the inheritance of your father Jacob." The mouth of the Lord has spoken.

Pretending that we are walking in the way of the Lord has to stop, and repenting needs to take over, in the realization in how far off we still are. Jesus was in communion with the Father continually every day, even in the midst of business, tiredness, whatever. This is what is required of us as well in order to be qualified as Christians.

The Hebrew word for repent is from the primitive root, "nacham," literally meaning 'to sigh.' To breathe strongly and to be sorry. God gives us our breath, God gives us his breath. To repent is to expel our breath, in return inhale his breath, we can never be separated or we will be suffocated.

The Greek word for repent is "metanoes," meaning to change one's mind (heart) for the better, to amend heartily of our sins.

So in mouth-to-mouth resuscitation from God, and the willing act to make amends, we will become completely vulnerable, and so ending up humble!

God does not want theology, God wants us to tell; "My Heart." God misses his creation. Don't forget, God is not ours there to do our will. No! We are his here to do his Will.

Let's pray: Spirit of repentance, come upon your people now. Give us the revelation of our sins, and the Lord's mercy and grace. We need to be completely yours Father, knowing without a shadow of doubt, that your desire is towards us all the time because you Oh Lord, love as so very much and you alone know what lives in our heart. Bless us please, Lord. With a new concept to this life you blessed us with. Life in your kingdom, with you as our guardian, looking after your only Son's Bride.

We need to stop doing things our way and begin doing things completely your way. We need to let God be God! Being showered with the release of truth and love from God. Amen.

Authority for the anointing: To enforce God's mercy, grace, healing, love, into the created world, after being called, and accept being saved. We need to be disciplined, so we are one body in accomplishing God's Will. Luke 4: 17-19 The attendant gave him the book of the prophet Isaiah. He opened it and found the place where it read: "The Spirit of the Lord is with me. He has anointed me to tell the Good News to the poor. He has sent me to announce forgiveness to the prisoners of sin and the restoring of sight to the blind, to forgive those who have been shattered by sin, to announce the year of the Lord's favour."

The outer court of the tabernacle is the largest section, the closest to the exit as well this is also where most people will be found. It is important to know that once we enter the tabernacle we can go as far in the Lord as we desire. It is a calling! (Are you willing to answer?) Once we answer and go into the holy of holies, the standards become very different. Things that were acceptable in the outer court can get you killed in the holy place. The way is open for us all, who are willing to go to the Altar and die, go to the laver and be cleaned, and understand that once you enter the Holy Place no natural light exists. The only light here is the anointing of the Holy Spirit. And still proceeding on into the final smallest compartment, the only light is that of the Glory of the Lord, which explodes into eternity.

It is hard to minister in the anointing and in God's glory. But we must learn to stand and do what is required of us by God even in Jesus' manifested presence. It is good to be 'slain in the Spirit,' when we are released to do so. But the mature have to learn when not to fall down. We need those who can stand – stand in the Spirit's presence, so we can in turn stand against any onslaught of the enemy. Jeremiah 23: 18-22 But which of them has stood in the counsel of the Lord to see or to hear his voice? See, the storm of the Lord will burst out in wrath, a whirlwind swirling down on the heads of the wicked. The anger of the Lord will not turn back until he fully accomplishes the purpose of his heart. In days to come you will understand it clearly. I did not send these prophets, yet they have run with their message; I did not speak to them, yet they have prophesied. But if they had stood in my counsel they would have proclaimed my words to my people and would have turned them from their evil ways and from their evil deeds.

The only foundation for human lives is Jesus the cornerstone of creation. As we firmly place our lives to his Will, instead of the will of the world, we come too truly know our God, not just about him. All fear can be cast out in God's perfect love, as changes in our personality come from his power within through faith, no longer from our power. Jesus prayed – John 17: 21 That all of them may be one, Father, just as you are in me and I am in you. May they also be in us so that the world may believe that you have sent me.

The religious institution the world is trying to build is degrading and confusing. However the church God is building will astonish the world with its unity. A true unity that transcends covenant and agreements; a unity that's only possible through the One who holds all things together by the Word of his power, Abba Daddy! To find this unity we must seek unity, by seeking God and God alone because that is the only place this type of unity can be found.

As spiritual principles are at work in the spiritual realm, so there are natural laws at work in the natural realm. The spiritual principles will work for anyone who uses them. Even the powers of Satan are completely dependent upon God. Satan did not create the principles God did. Satan does however bend them for his own purposes. So trust in faith and know the voice of God. Genuine faith is by having peace in whatever circumstances the Lord has us in.

True ministry even Christianity is not to gain God's approval; but from obedience to God.

Never must we cast stones at others who fall short of God's glory, for we have all fallen. If we judge a servant or congregation of the Lord, we are actually judging God, and are in effect saying, God's workmanship does not meet our standards -- we could do better! Exodus 16: 8 Moses also said, "You will know that it was the Lord when he gives you meat to eat in the evening and all the bread you want in the morning, because he has heard your grumbling against him. Who are we? You are not grumbling against us but against the Lord.

The greatest reason for the church's lack of light, power, and a closer relationship with the Lord is her critical spirit. So let's open our hearts to God's Word for us in James 4: 11-12 Don't bad-mouth each other, friends. It's God Word, his Message, his Royal Rule, that takes a beating in that kind of talk. You're supposed to be honouring the Message, not writing graffiti all over it. God is in charge of deciding human destiny. Who do you think you are to meddle in the destiny of others?

Why do we seek God's Word? Well speaking for myself I like to be fed, and I love to drink from the glory of heaven, which nurtures me more and more into the image of Christ. To be refreshed in revelations to facts heard over and over. Psalm 62: 5 Wait calmly for God alone, my sole, because my hope comes from him.

We are brought together by the blood and body of Jesus. Bread and wine just symbolically represent communion. We must be in communion/harmony with one another, to be blessed, healed and changed to God's glory, as we testify our belief and trust to this ceremony, and of the love Jesus has for all of us. 1 Corinthians 10: 16-17 Is not the cup of thanksgiving for which we give thanks a participation in the blood of Christ? And is not the bread that we break a participation in the body of Christ? Because there is one loaf, we, who are many, are one body, for we all partake in the one loaf.

So for my life I pray to be able to undergo and stand up under the extreme discipline of God's pure love. We are always under construction in becoming the masterpiece of God. The new church is being formed in truth, by God alone. We can only see what we know, God's creating the predestined church that only God knows, and we are here to receive and release. And if we have any questions don't be afraid to ask for answers because my friend God can answer any question, he is very secure. Praise, rejoice, give thanks in everything, the victory is God's, "SHOUT GRACE!"

A pastor has a God-given nature to protect the flock. Were as being a visionary by nature the prophet may often be a bit reckless. So balance is essential. Without a prophet a pastor will tend to stagnate and may become set in their ways. As without the influence of the pastor the prophet may drift into extremes. So here we see how the one compliments the other and the importance of them being in harmony, to keep us in balance.

For sure and no doubt we are 'bearers,' people that carry and support with authority, wisdom, victory, encouragement, honour, a vegetation of holiness producing fruit of truth, faith, integrity, goodness, righteousness, light. Psalm 99: 9 Highly honour the Lord our God. Bow at his holy mountain. The Lord our God is holy!

Take time to be holy?!?! For some reason to do this we withdraw into periods of time which we named quiet days, pilgrimages, and retreats. Each one of these time periods seem to reveal hidden assumptions. "Quiet days," assume that God cannot be found in the business of life, but rather is discovered primarily in an experience of being quiet and still, so we feel it is a must to withdraw into silence to be in a holy place. "Pilgrimage," assumes that we have to depart from our normal routines of life to visit a holy place. "Retreats," imply that we have to step back from life in order to visit the holy.

Nothing we do or accomplish on our own brings us closer to God. It is in our relationship with our Father, his Son, and the Holy Spirit, we are the bearers of what is given. In living strictly with Abba Daddy for his kingdom the things we do and say come out fresh and clean from our heart, because in this way of life all we want to do is please Abba Daddy, wanting to do right, not having to do right.

Now if we are in the holies twenty-four-seven and choose to partake in such activities as quiet days, pilgrimages, retreats, it can be most uplifting, and powerful, but they should not be the only times we find ourselves in the Holy. These are defiantly times to focus and for preparation and are still essential, but not the only place we seek communion with God. Our holy time, our commitment to be praying people, still should come throughout our entire day. It comes in our living and in our engaging with the lives of others. Prayer is the process of being open to all that life can be. Especially when our prayer is formed into entering the pain or joy with another person. See praying is never separate from acting. God is the presence in whom our beings come alive. Our prayers are an essential part of whom we are. Romans 10: 1-8 Brothers and sisters, my heart desires and prayer to God on behalf of the Jewish people is that they would be saved. I can assure you that they are deeply devoted to God, but they are misguided. They don't understand how to receive God's approval. So they try to set up their own way to get it, and they have not accepted God's way for receiving his approval. Christ is the fulfillment of Moses' teachings so that everyone who has faith may receive God's approval. Moses writes about receiving God's approval by following his laws. He says, "The person who obeys laws will live because of the laws he obeys." However, Scripture says about God's approval which is based on faith, "Don't ask yourself who will go up to heaven," (that is, to bring Christ down). "Don't ask who will go down into the depth," (that is, to bring Christ back from the dead). However, what else does it say? "This message is near you. It's in your mouth and in your heart." This is the message of faith we spread.

Worship is a self-conscious awareness that all of us are God-bearers. And our deepest task for Christ is to give ourselves away to him for him! It should involve the acceptance of God's promise for comfort for our tears, not from our tears, and light to guide the way. In the midst of pain and sorrow, not instead of pain and sorrow, strengthening us to laugh, to shine in the darkest day, not without the darkest day, and voila giving our lives away become both natural and desirable. Worship is not oriented toward an external God, but to the world of our human community. This, however, is not to result in a shallow humanism but in a recognition that the place where God is ultimately found is in the depth of humanity. Heaven right here on earth. So our worship is not an attempt to escape life, instead every attempt to expand life.

God is the heart of life, available to everyone, and not as a special possession of the religious institution. This is why worship is a prayer for the secular. Worship needs to be a freedom in spirit towards God, be it loud or soft, full of action or submissive. It must not be a denominational agenda or territorial war. It is a privilege, or a right laid down to the royal images of glory. A sole channel of divine grace, speaking to God and for God. Rejoicing with those who are hungry for God, who thirst for righteousness. Now watch and see how heaven and earth are one right here, right now. Causing change! This change will begin by focusing on the God experience itself, not on the explanation of God experiences that rise out of yesterday's consciousness. This new awareness will include acknowledging that the God experience carries us into new senses of awe and wonder, into a state beyond limits or time.....Who was, Who is, Who is to come!

Everyone has to come to the Lord on their own. When we are constantly chasing others we are robbing ourselves from our purpose, and we are putting out the glory of the Fires from heaven. All we can do is stay hand in hand with Jesus ourselves, proclaiming God's love, promises, grace, mercy, stability. But the gift has to be accepted it cannot be forced. And when it is WOW! It is beyond anything they could have ever imagined. Yes we must always be moving forward, always proclaiming, but for everyone, not just one or the other. Then allowing them to take the step into Glory, I did so can they.

So my family, let's go Beyond! Living our life for God in his world. Like the song (beware I am going to sing) "This is my Fathers World).

I remember a prayer evening very exciting for me that I would like to share. God showed me as each prayer was offered how it has already been answered (put into place) it was amazing seeing each word that was spoken getting released into action. Psalm 100: 3 Realize that the Lord alone is God. He made us, and we are his. We are his people and the sheep of his care.

Now the Word of God can begin to flow spontaneously. Psalm 119: 17-24 Be generous with me and I'll live a full life; not for a minute will I take my eyes off your road. Open my eyes so I can see what you show me of your miracle-wonders. I'm a stranger in these parts; give me clear directions. My soul is starved and hungry, ravenous! – insatiable for your nourishing commands. And those who think they know so much, ignore everything you tell them – let them have it! Don't let them mock and humiliate me; I've been careful to do just what you said. While bad neighbours maliciously gossip about me, I'm absorbed in pondering your wise counsel. Yes, your sayings on life are what give me delight; I listen to them as to good neighbours!

There are times that require us to deliberately seek stillness. Stop what we are doing, not finish what we are doing, STOP! what we are doing, coming away from the pervasive noise around us. Begin to repeat a particular truth, desire, or concept letting it echo until it takes root and grows to be a part of you. Tell your mind to be still, empty yourself of all concerns, anxieties, purposes and plans that have filled this day and burdened your spirit. Psalm 116: 7-8 I said to myself, "Relax and rest. God has showered you with blessings. Soul, you've been rescued from death; Eye you've been rescued from tears; And you foot, were kept from stumbling."

Focus into your stillness, Jesus is before you. Touch that, feel that, own that. Let Jesus resonate within you as if he were a wonderful, vibrating and pulsing sound. He is there, having filled you with his Spirit. You need only to become aware of him. Come into the quiet you have entered and wait for him with no other agenda or goal than to rest in the Lord's presence. Then bring this back into what you were doing when you stopped! Psalm 62: 1-2 God the one and only – I'll wait as long as he says. Everything I need comes from him, so why not? He's solid rock under my feet, breathing room for my soul, an impregnable castle: I'm set for life.

Now ponder: Think deeply, feel intuitively, sense the truth and let it resonate within you. When pondering you do not bully your mind for answers or strive to think things through. You simply let an issue, a matter of God's Word roll around inside you until it begins to make sense and the revelation is released. Psalm 77: 1-6 I yell out to my God, I yell with all my might, I yell at the top of my lungs. He listens. I found myself in trouble and went looking for my Lord; my life was an open wound that wouldn't heal. When friends said, "Everything will turn out all right," I didn't believe a word they said. I remember God – and shake my head. I bow my head – then wring my hands. I'm awake all night – not a wink of sleep; I can't even say what's bothering me. I go over the day one by one, I ponder the years gone by. I strum my lute all through the night, wondering how to get my life together.

We are created in God's image? Then why do we all look different? We are created perfect and yes in total likeness of God, but because of sin which is upon us at the time of conception: we need to realize that we were conceived at conception, changed from pure into sin. Creation is perfect so I am hopeful that when we are changed back into the kingdom as we walk forward into our purpose here on earth till it is complete, once we return home again in perfection we will all look the same once more. A revelation that was enlightened through a gift blessed to me from my Father: That at one point on this journey back home, right here on earth we are united and harmonized and we do all look alike, even if it is just for a split of a second our time. There have been many a time I have been mistaken for someone else. Psalm 37:7 Quiet down before God, be prayerful before him. Don't bother with those who climb the ladder, who elbow their way to the top.

God's mercy is indeed meant to be a transforming grace. Philippians 4: 4-9 Celebrate God all day, every day. I mean, revel in him! Make it as clear as you can to all you meet that you're on their side, working with them and not against them.

Help them see that the Master is about to arrive. He could show up any minute! Don't fret or worry. Instead of worrying, pray. Let petitions and praises shape your worries into prayers, letting God know your concerns. Before you know it, a sense of God's wholeness, everything coming together for good, will come and settle you down. It's wonderful what happens when Christ displaces worry at the center of your life. Summing it all up, friends, I'd say you'd do best by filling your minds and meditating on things true, noble, reputable, authentic, compelling, gracious – the best, not worst; the beautiful, not the ugly; things to praise, not things to curse. Put into practice what you learned from me, what you heard and saw and realized. Do that, and God, who makes everything work together, will work you into his most excellent harmonies.

When we chose "Glad," over "Sad," we and those around us become richer as a result. We are all capable of increasing our state of cheerfulness. Being of good cheer is an attitude of the mind made possible by God's enabling power within us. We need to remember that Christ our firm foundation never moves or wavers, we do. But still in partnership with him, make choices about habits of the mind that produce attitudes of cheer.

2 Peter 3: 17-18 But you, friends, are well-warned. Be on guard lest you lose your footing and get swept off your feet by these lawless and loose-talking teachers. Grow in grace and understanding of our Master and Saviour, Jesus Christ. Glory to the Master, now and forever! Yes!

Here are two poor attitudes that cause spiritual insensibilities and keep us from moving on with God. First: Having unrealistic expectations may defeat us before we even begin. Being human gives us the in-built tendency to blame others for their imperfection and the distress this causes us. Keeping the focus off of our own imperfection and even the distress this causes them. We think that if things would just change I could grow spiritually and then we can get ourselves in shape to begin to trust God. WRONG! The world isn't perfect; our family isn't perfect; our friends aren't perfect; we are not perfect. None of this takes God by surprise. Why it should surprise sinners that we are imperfect is a mystery. But there are Christians that can't believe that God has done much until situations become absolute perfection – which it hardly does on earth. Bad unrealistic goals based on our views on how things ought to be rather than on how they actually are. We need to learn to live in a real world with real problems; with a real God who is capable of meeting our human needs for now and eternity. Setting values straight now because now is already in eternity. In view of how we view eternity I wonder if what we count of supreme worth will be seen as trivia? We need to give all we know of ourselves to all we know of God and continue to grow in the knowledge of both. Becoming a channel for the outflow of Christ's character. Not waiting for life to change, but by living the life we now live (in all it entails) by faith.

Second: We may have an inadequate concept of freedom, which makes us afraid to give ourselves completely to anyone, least of all God. The key to giving ourselves to others is in the abandonment of our personal selves to God. But we are afraid. And so we hold on tightly to ourselves, afraid to lose our life because we are bent on saving it. Freedom involves living the way we were intended to live, in the life we were given, according to our nature. And who best know this nature of our freedom? Me, I, would sooner give God that wisdom than claim if for myself.

I am finding that the most effective form of prayer is obedience. When we are obedient and release the will of God here on earth, it is amazing to watch as people and their situations change into joy, peace, healing, acceptance, understanding, revelations from heaven. And be uplifted filled with hope, receiving God's promises even though nothing outward seems to have changed.

Psalm 42: 1 As a deer longs for flowing streams, so my soul longs for you, O God.

We need to train people in robust acceptance of what God gives us. Not to passively submit to the trashy merchandising of religious sales people. We must confront the breezy, irresponsible nonchalance that avoids difficulties and shuts eyes to the worst suffering. Assuming that being on God's side carries with it the comfortable wisdom that will solve all of our difficulties. God is the living center of everything we are and everything we do. He is before, behind, over, beneath, 'Everything,' if we separate any part of our lives from him we are left holding an empty bag. Nothing can stand on its own apart from God. Anything that is wrenched from its context in God's creation and God's Salvation is without substance. It is either God or nothing. No idea, no feeling, no truth, no pleasure can exist on its own. Jeremiah 9: 23-24 This is what the Lord says: "Let not the wise man boast of his own wisdom or the strong man boast of his strength or the rich man boast of his riches, but let him who boasts, boast about this. That he understands and knows me, that I am the Lord, who exercises kindness, justice, and righteousness on earth, for in these I delight," declares the Lord.

Whatever else wisdom does, it does not qualify anyone to function on their own apart from God. There are times when we simply just shut up and let God speak.

Miracles are evidence that there are dimensions to God that with all our knowledge we are not able to anticipate. Believing in a miracle is only a way of saying God is free. Free to do new things. Not bound to a master/slave creation of natural cause and effect. Not trapped in a universal apparatus. Free above and beyond what we observe of his way. Free to implement whatever he wills. Miracle is the word used when describing something that is a surprise to us, events that are outside our expectations and beyond our abilities.

We don't live in a godless, inhuman, ruthless world ruled by necessity; a random world ruled by chance; we live in a world ruled by the God of a journey filled with promises. God does things in us that neither we or our friends and family have supposed possible. God has no limits, he is not swayed by anything you think you know about him; God is not boxed into any dimension, never mind our ignorance or despair. Isaiah 43: 19 I am doing new things! Now it springs up; do you perceive it? I am making a way in the desert and streams in the wastelands.

How can I perceive to apprehend 'our' if I live only for myself in a watertight compartment? How can I acknowledge God to be my 'Father' if I do not endeavour each day to act like his child? No matter how spiritual we are portrayed, or perceive to be, we cannot say 'who art in heaven,' if we are laying up no treasures there. How can I proclaim 'hallowed be your name,' and not strive for holiness? In order for me to announce 'thy kingdom come,' I need to be full of your power willing to release it for the preparation of that wonderful day. I cannot say 'your Will be done,' if I am disobedient to his Word. How can I stand in the gap of 'on earth as it is in heaven,' if I will not serve him and serve for him here and now? In order to say 'give us this day our daily bread,' I must be honest, no room for looters. How can I receive 'forgive us our trespasses,' if I am holding a grudge? How can I stand firm in 'lead us not into temptation,' if I deliberately lay myself in its path? I cannot ask 'deliver us from evil,' if I do not put on the entire armour of God. How can I assume the blessings from 'yours is the kingdom,' if I do not give to the King the loyalty due him as a faithful subject? I cannot attribute to him 'the power' if I am afraid of what men may do. I cannot ascribe to him 'the glory,' if I am seeking honour only for myself. It is impossible to imagine 'forever,' if the horizon of my life is bound completely by the things of time?

Psalm 23: 1-2 The Lord is my shepherd. I am never in need. He makes me lie down in green pastures. He leads me beside peaceful waters.

When a person who has dared to begin to think with personal passion about God, comes to us for spiritual direction. We should not get into a theological discussion, but rather find the friendship in one another in this spiritual context. Prepared to engage in honest, open, shared, inquiry after God.

These inquiries however are always an implied threat, for we never know when their relentless searching will expose some undetected shallowness, some unexamined characteristic in us. We invent methods and roles that allow us to function smoothly and successfully, with as little pain, anguish, possible.

We learn routines that give an appearance of expertise in spirituality. This is why reputations do not count in spiritual direction. Experience is not enough. Stories brought up to illustrate an experience, the insight we use to explain or clarify personality developments, however impressive, will sustain the probing of a troubled soul. Only a life devoted to spiritual adventure, honest and alert searching prayer is adequate for the task. Our mind departure from the straight and narrow causes that which is wrong with the world. Human despair is rooted in wrong thinking. We think that if we can just fix a person's theology they can be changed (fixed). Searching out what is wrong with their belief system. Once we find this we would be able to instruct them in what to believe so they can be whole!?!

Belief cannot be imposed (forced). In spiritual direction we enter a desirable place to observe the endless revisions grace offers, the fantastic richness (pregnancy), of the divine Spirit bring faith into creation. But we can never know just how Christ will be formed in someone else.

There are times for just plain idle chit-chat, and just plain listening. Something does not always have to be done. People need a friend who will pay attention to who they are. Not a project manager providing temporary relief.

Someone is needed who is secure enough to absorb, reflect, tolerate the uncertainty of their troubled despair and temptation and strong enough not to do something to them or for them. Providing space for the Holy Spirit to initiate the new life.

God is killing us for him, and maybe even for the good of ourselves, this is why we give thanks for and thanks in every circumstance, rather than blaming Satan, our parents, the church....... (the list goes onnnnnn), for thing that have gone wrong. Who knows it could be all Jesus making things right!

Psalm 90:2 Before the mountains were born, before you gave birth to the earth and the world, you were God. You are God from everlasting to everlasting.

If we expect we need to accept.

In order for a clear acceptance of the Word, which is essential. It is important that we expect our teaches to have a pragmatic nature, one that is realistic, that they are concerned with the actual practice of what is accepted in their everyday affairs, not just with theory or speculation; practical so to speak.

Evangelist are focused in reaching the lost, but they tend to forget to raise and mature them, as they in passion go along the path of life to rescue more lost souls. This is why we work in harmony one with another this way as the evangelist picks up lost souls he drops them off for the next one to begin the journey back home, and we will all have our role in this mission, so let's do our part and lead them to the next person to do their part because not only do we help the lost they teach us as well, so keep the line moving then no one will miss their mark.

As for the apostles they are called to be evangelists, prophets, pastors, and teachers, which usually give them a more balance nature. And they are given for the purpose of keeping the church on the right path. Because they understand unity, for the pure fact of all the gifts within them they can more freely accept all the gifts for what they are and who is walking in them. Psalm 133: 1-3 How good and pleasant it is when brothers live together in unity! It is like precious oil poured on the head, running down on the beard, running down on Aaron's beard, down upon the collar of his robes. It is as if the dew of Hermon were falling on Mount Zion. For there the Lord bestows his blessing, even life forevermore.

Abundance does not suggest that everything will be good. It just means there is a lot of it. This includes both good and bad my friend.

Even so many things that take place might not make sense to us, they do not have to God told me. I just have the hard part and that is to listen hahahaha... and my dear friends this I have personal experience with, I have been on an eleven day listening fast but that is another book so stay tuned. Back on track again; so even if it would be more comfortable to remove the wild life from our church, God has them place there for his purpose. Acts 20: 29-30 I know after I leave, savage wolves will come in among you and will not spare the flock. Even from your own number men will arise and distort the truth in order to draw away disciples after them.

Judas was chosen by Jesus and was included in the inner circle, this was not a mistake my friends it was God's Will. So it is no different today, even though these untamed vicious creatures still roam among us and will cause great damage and confusion, they are working out the purpose of God. All things work for the good of those who love God. Romans 8: 28 We know that all things work together for the good of those who love God - those whom he has called according to his plan.

As we are willing to step back it is amazing now how Jesus appears, and how fear disappears, now we can find the courage to trust that these disruptions will result in our becoming more dependent on the Lord, and less dependent on those who are flesh and bones.

Proverbs 4: 1-2 Listen, friends, to some fatherly advice; sit up and take notice so you'll know how to live. I'm giving you good counsel; don't let it go in one ear and out the other.

To absorb the Word of God this is how the Word should penetrate. First of all the Word is like a dancing partner who is full of life. As it enters your eyes and ears it is born into the living word, now alive it finds its way straight to the heart, then back up to your mind.

Psalm 95: 7 He is our God, and we are the people of his pasture, and the sheep of his hand.

Let's ponder again; and let appreciation flow at an ever deeper level, to where joy takes hold and fills us to overflowing. Peace settles and builds a home, and voila character changes occur. Not by magic but revealed to us from the mystery of God. What we say with our mouths is hopefully not repeatedly rehearsed in our minds, but spontaneously sprung from our hearts so it is revealing our true focus to what we believe about God, how we worship, the complete intensity and purity of our complete love. Psalm 145: 1-7 I will highly praise you, my God the king. I will bless your Name forever and ever. The Lord is great, and he should be highly praised. His greatness is unsearchable. One generation will praise your deeds to the next. Each generation will talk about you mighty acts. I will think about the glorious honour of your majesty and the miraculous things you have done. People will talk about the power of your terrifying deeds, and I will tell about your greatness. They will announce what they remember of your great goodness, and they will joyfully sing about your righteousness. Amen!

Seatbelts fastened, tight and secure because God has called us into movement once more. This one is unfamiliar to me, I am not use to traveling with my husband on this journey, but after thirty five years of marriage God must think it is time. This movement is to fulfill the prophesy spoke over us numerous times, "as a team in ministry." Now who says you have never seen a miracle, (signs and wonders even), you who look on us have even witnessed death/resurrection. God has even shown me the vision and mission for this ministry. So with rejoicing and faith, I sing, "Onward Christian Soldier."

An invitation to someone special to come as you are!

Vision: Supporting and encouraging the leaders from God, then building the church of Christ, as we abide in the vine, holding on to God's every promise, and stepping into God's plans for us to fulfill as he opens and closes the doors at the right time. Accepting the Bible as the Living Word for this day and age, now, for us! Ephesians 1: 20-23 All this energy issues from Christ: God raised him from death and set him on a throne in deep heaven, in charge of running the universe, everything, from galaxies to governments, no name and no power exempt from his rule. And not just for the time being, but forever. He is in charge of it all, has the final word on everything. At the center of all this, Christ rules the church. The church you see, is not peripheral to the world, the world is peripheral to the church. The church is Chris's body, in which he speaks and acts, by which he fills everything with his presence.

Mission: To receive God's grace, mercy, healing, love, revelations all his gifts, and then release them into the world. Living who 'we' are in Christ, so others can trust this ethnic reality, and want it for themselves. Living the Word, proclaiming God's Will through our lives, as much as with Scripture. Edifying one another and Christ our Lord. As one, with one another, not to one another, not comparing each other's gifts and anointing, but uniting them and bring beautiful harmony to life.

Ephesians 3: 14-21 My response is to get down on my knees, before the Father, this magnificent Father who parcels out all heaven and earth. I ask him to strengthen you by his Spirit – not a brute strength but a glorious inner strength – that Christ will live in you as you open the door and invite him in. And I ask him that with both feet planted firmly on love, you'll be able to take in with all Christians the extravagant dimensions of Christ's love. Reach out and experience the breadth! Test its length! Plumb the depths! Rise to the heights! Live full lives, full in the fullness of God. God can do anything, you know – far more than you could ever imagine or guess or request in your wildest dreams! He does it not by pushing us around but by working with us, his Spirit deeply and gently within us. Glory to God in the church! Glory to God in the Messiah, in Jesus! Glory down all the generations! Glory through all millennia! Oh, Yes!

This life of faith consists in just this – being a child of the Fathers house. Romans 8: 15-16 For you did not receive a Spirit that makes you a slave again to fear, but you received the Spirit of Sonship. And by him we cry Abba Father; the Spirit himself testifies with our spirit that we are God's children.

Now what is the characteristic of a little child and how do they live? They live by faith, and their main characteristic is thoughtfulness. Their life is one long trust. They trust their parents, their caretakers, their teachers they even trust people who are utterly untrustworthy because of the confidence of their nature. They provide nothing for themselves yet everything is provided. They live in the present moment, and receive their life unquestioningly as it comes to them day by day from caring hands. Matthew 18: 2-3 He called a little child and had him stand among them. And he said; "I tell you the truth, unless you change and become like little children, you will never enter the kingdom of heaven."

"Take no thought for yourselves!" Who is the best cared for in a household? Is it not the little child? And does not the least of all, the helpless baby, receive the largest share?

Psalm 18:2 The Lord is my rock and my deliverer; my God, my strength, in whom I will trust.

This life of being the Chid of God will be enough to transform every weary burdened life into one of blessedness and rest. In giving our child-heart to the Father's heart, and praying to be shown what faith involves.

Psalm 18: 33 He makes my feet like the deer, and sets me on high places.

Submission to God requires a new alignment of our lives. We could change our spiritual tires every week but find no peace or joy. It is on a daily basis (sometimes even down to the second) that we submit our lives to God. Resist the Devil and he will flee from you. Come near to God and find him right there beside you already. We need to wash our hands regularly because sin is contagious, and purify our hearts to chase away the double-mindedness.

Psalm 85: 10 Mercy and truth have met together; righteousness and peace have kissed each other.

Even when we are being pulled by the world, the flesh, the devil, and defeat seems to override victory. Coping with the constant battle of life every day. There is only one thing left for us to do, and that is become fully aligned with the Lord. Only by this can we stop running and hiding and be the warriors we were created to be in Spirit. So until we bring our hearts into proper alignment under God's Authority, we will stay worn-out believers. Utterly abandoning yourself to God's control.

Once again it would be an honour to share the prophetic Word to me released this time through my dear sister the apostle Carol: "I hear God saying that he's pleased, he's pleased. He says that, that there's been a fox that's wanted to do something, but God says you've closed the door to the fox. He's says you've said I will not listen to that and God says he's pleased, he's pleased that you have chosen to be a women of honour, that you've chosen says the Lord God to stand, that you've chosen that even though God says you may not understand all. But God says because of your heart that's being open and open to me says the Lord God, he says I am pleased with you my daughter. And is saying because of what you are doing there is healing taking place in your body and God's been healing you and he's setting you free in areas and that, that God says of divine health belonging to you God says. He says I've been delivering you and I've been setting you free he says of word curses and of pronouncements of things that have happened in your life that God says you are the new creature in Him. He says joy has been restored back into your heart, he says a hunger has been restored back to you, he says, he says, that even the principalities and the powers of darkness that are even over where you live. He says you're now standing over them says the Lord God. God's sees you've been taking hold of the Word and he says you've been trusting me says the Lord God and he says and I've been changing your prayer. He says I've been changing your intercession. He says I've been causing you to be a women of warfare says the Lord God, one that will come alongside of leaders says the Lord God, because he says I'm raising you up for a leadership position says the Lord God and it's going to come God says in due season and time says the Lord God Almighty. Because God says he's putting you through the fire and he's testing you says the Lord God. And God says (carol now breaks into song) He's answering your prayer. He's filling you, he is filling you, he has robed you with righteousness. You are free, you are free, you are free in him, to soar like an eagle, you've never seen yourself like eagle but you are an eagle. You are a prophetic eagle who is soaring, soaring, soaring, soaring, soaring, soaring...........soaring to new depths and heights, soaring, soaring, you're a carrier of revival you're a carrier of revival, revival, revival. Lord may the revival fire and the passion that she has, may it be released out of her, take her to depths of intercession oh God let the travailing and the birthing of your Spirit oh God, let it come forth Father in Jesus Name. It's time, time Lord, time, it's time Oh God for your children, your daughters of Zion to give birth to the things of your Spirit to bring forth things Oh God that you're wanting to happen in this day and hour Father, in Jesus Name.

Psalm 90: 1 Lord, You have been our dwelling place in all generations.

God is calling us to leave that temporary comfort, (little warm spot we have developed in the world) for the greater reward of getting ourselves in proper rank under Him. Romans 12: 1-2 Therefore, I urge you, brothers, in view of God's mercy to offer your bodies as living sacrifices holy and pleasing to God – this is your spiritual act of worship. Do not conform any longer to the pattern of this world, but be transformed by the renewing of your mind. Then you will be able to test and approve what God's will is – his good, pleasing, and perfect Will.

Although the realization of God's love for us, it is still possible for us to slip and fall under the burden of a low God-esteem which equals a high self-esteem. When this does happen we must be open to the discipline of retraining our thought habits. Inner self-perceptions are desperately hard to reprogram. So here are three steps that can hopefully put us back on the right path of eliminating negative self-concepts. First: Prepare spiritually for your day! Focus on God! Believe to be God's overall plan for this day he created for you to be in. Second: Positive interchange of some sort with everyone your eyes directly meet. This may be as little as the saying of "Hello," or "Please and Thank you," or even just a plain and simple smile. Third: Practice the art of praying for those you see but do not have the opportunity to talk with. This is the type of un-noticed praying that brings us joy merely because we are making an effort to get outside ourselves and relate back into God-esteem.

Psalm 32: 8 I will instruct you and teach you in the way you should go; I will guide you with My eye.

There is no magic in these ideas it is simply joy filling our hearts as we escape the bitterness of our own world. Opening ourselves to the light of Christ accepting God's purpose for our lives, in the wider world God created with infinite love.

Psalm 33: 5 He loves righteousness and justice; the earth is full of goodness of the Lord.

I WANT TO DELIGHT GOD! Scripture says that God's eyes scan the earth searching for those whose hearts are right towards Him! I'm praying that I may be one of those whom God can consistently find comfort and pleasure, and is delight with. Learning to hear God's holy laughter regarding me. To have that delight in life that only an open, intimate relationship with God can have.

Psalm 37: 3 Trust in the Lord, and do good; dwell in the land, and feed on his faithfulness.

I WANT TO "PRACTICE HEAVEN," BY ENJOYING GOD NOW: To be complete and whole as a human, is to glorify God and enjoy him forever. Experiencing the pleasures of knowing God. My entire being becoming skilled and comfortable with heaven in my life everyday freshly anointed by God, praising and enjoying everything God has to offer, now.

Psalm 37: 4 Delight yourself also in the Lord, and he shall give you the desires of your heart.

I WANT TO REMAIN OPEN TO AN UNEXPECTED, OFF-THE-BEATEN-PATH PLAN: Intending to nurture an adventuresome spirit. Fully aware that God can use people whose boundaries may be unconventional and well of the beaten path.

Galatians 2: 19-21 What actually took place is this. I tried keeping rules and working my head off to please God, and it didn't work. So I quit being a "law man" so that I could be God's man. Christ's life showed me how and enabled me to do it. Identified myself completely with him. Indeed, I have been crucified with Christ. My ego is no longer in control. It is no longer important that I appear righteous before you or have your good opinion, and I am no longer driven to impress God. Christ lives in me. The life you see me living is not "mine" but it is lived by faith in the Son of God, who loved me and gave himself for me. I am not going to go back on that. Is it not clear to you that to go back to that old rule – keeping peer-pleasing religion would be an abandonment of everything personal and true in my relationship with God? I refuse to do that, to repudiate God's grace. If a living relationship with God could come by rule-keeping then Christ died unnecessarily.

I WANT TO THINK LESS LIKE A VICTIM AND MORE LIKE A SURVIVOUR: Everyone has significant life wounds. But more than just focusing on the suffering of these pains, realizing the learning experiences from them. And seeing how they have been the builders of interior character.

Psalm 84: 2 My soul longs, even faints for the courts of the Lord; my heart and my flesh cry out for the living God.

I WANT TO REAFIRM MY DESIRE TO EXCEL IN PRAYER: Becoming more keen at hearing God's voice and seeing things not just from a human perspective but God's perspective. The only way I can make a difference in this world is by bringing God's presence into it. With total praise and thanksgiving. *Ephesians 2: 8-10* For it is by grace you have been saved, through faith – and this not from yourselves, it is the gift of God – not by works, so that no one can boast. For we are God's workmanship, created in Christ Jesus to do good works, which God prepared in advance for us to do.

Our ears only hear what God allows them to take in. That is why resting in God is so important, because in this rest the heart will be protected as the voices enter in and used to take us down God's road to reach the nations. When you know what God wants from you do not let someone sway you from those commands. Mistakes can be fixed and are definitely learned from, so don't be afraid if you make some along the way. But when you obey, what a joy to watch God's plans unfold. Many have fallen short by being mislead, so it boils down to what do I commit to the world and myself time wise and comfort wise: to what I give God? *Psalm 84:10* One day in your courtyards is better than a thousand anywhere else. I would rather stand in the entrance to my God's house than inside wicked people's homes.

Romans 12: 1-2 So here's what I want you to do, God helping you. Take your everyday ordinary life – your sleeping, eating, going-to-work, and walking around life – and place it before God as an offering. Embracing what God does for you is the best thing you can do for him. Don't become so well-adjusted to your culture that you fit into it without even thinking. Instead, fix your attention on God. You'll be changed from the inside out. Readily recognize what he wants from you, and quickly respond to it. Unlike the culture around you, always dragging you down to its level of immaturity. God brings the best out of you, develops well-formed maturing in you.

I must always cultivate an attitude of awe. I must be prepared to marvel, at every face when they are standing in front of me, with its loveliness, because even though some may be scorched with stress, hurt, anger, so many burdens, they are an image of God. So even though this nervous slouching body that I am looking at is not the beautiful body I see, I see the precious temple of the Holy Ghost. This awkward, slightly harmonically unbalanced brother or sister is a part of the Body of Christ. Making it possible now to be amazed at what God is shaping (polished).

Removing the exceedingly preoccupied blindness, who, is standing in front of me is not what I see; I see what "Christ" has said and done. Far more relevant than what I feel or think, or what this person feels or thinks, is what God has said and done. This is a person for whom Christ died, someone he loves dearly (an awesome fact), and has been guarded alive until this very moment. Am I prepared to admire? Am I prepared to respect? Am I prepared to be in God's love, in spite of my ignorance? God has been at work in every one of us since birth. Everything that has already, and everything that will, take place in our life has in some way or another taken in the context of a good creation and an intended Salvation...Everything.

How do we look at things that are happening around us? It is funny how the same incident can have such a different outlook. As an example I am going to use a thunderstorm, now very important a thunderstorm were thunderstorms are very uncommon. As the storm passed over, my thought was how awesome that God is opening up the skies and we are praising and worshiping together, I was in total awe of the whole thing. Then someone else the next day commented, because there is not enough praise and worship, so the sky stormed. So guess we can either join in, or sit back because of.

God accepts us all because he created us all. To bring the created world back into its original state, many things are created beyond our understanding. They are created to bring to pass God's Word, to fulfill the need to bring God's glory to be first and foremost. So I am so grateful for faith which allows me to move with compassion because we are moved by compassion.

God gave me this math formula: God's Math to return to love, to stay in love, to find God's love. Division = separation, subtract separation = restoration, multiply restoration = compassion, add compassion = JOY/JOY/JOY.

Difficulties develop when, yes, bad advice is given, but even worse, when taken. Difficulties develop when we listen to crazy advice, instead of putting trust in our Father who is able to work beyond our expectations. Attempts are made to find a point of leverage (advantage) at which they can pry a miracle out of God to satisfy what they think they need. (what will make them comfortable). Miracles for them have almost nothing to do with God; it is simply a demanded item that will get them what they want. In this way religion gets misunderstood as a kind of technology of the supernatural; it provides the know-how to get things done when say physicians give up, or counsellors fail, when the economy disintegrates. Come on folks, even if we learn to pray according to God's Will, using God's prayer's, grasp onto God's math formula, and wait in faith my friend, do we catch the true miracles that are being produced? True miracles are evidence of God's purpose which most of the time we don't get anyway. I am not saying we do not witness miracles, I am saying we miss a lot of them. Because what we mean by miracle and what a true miracle is evident of, is a power found in God. So unless we live through Christ, who lives through the Father, we limit our miracles.

Magic and faith: they seem to have one common denominator, they both deal with supernatural. But everything else is different. For you see magic is an impersonal manipulation and control, a way of getting. While faith is a personal response to God, inviting him in to do what He Wills in us, an offering of obedience to walk where he leads. We come to God not to get our own way but to receive his way; not to acquire a means of impressing our friends with an access to power but to let God make an eternal impression on us with his Salvation.

The Biblical usage of worship is a response to God's Word in the context of the community of God's people. Worship is neither subjective (individual) only, or private only. It has nothing to do with our feelings at all. It is how we react toward God in responsible relations with his people. It is not something we do for what we can experience, it is something to be done, regardless of how we feel about it, or even if we don't feel anything at all about it. Experience develops out of worship. Isaiah for instance, saw, heard and felt on the day he received his call while at worship in the temple. But he didn't go there to have the experience. It just happened through his obedience to worship.

Worship is meant to be the proclamation (announcement) of the Will of God and the call for our response to it, not by feelings, or weather, but by Scripture (inspirational relationship with God).

The empty tomb for example; represents what humanity does not have to do in fact it represents what humanity cannot do. I don't have to take care of God. I don't have to watch over his body. I don't have to protect him from enemies. I don't have to manage him, defend him, or tell him what needs to be done next. The tomb is empty, leaving me free to go home and go about the work to which he has called me.

My friends a gift that is not received is a gift not given. We say giving is better than receiving, but if there is no one receiving there is no one to give to anymore. Yes we give our all to Christ but he receives this when given. We need to learn how to receive if giving is to continue. God gives us in abundance, how much are we receiving? What it boils down to is the more we receive the more we have to give. 1 Corinthians 2: 6-16 We, of course, have plenty of wisdom to pass on to you once you get your feet on firm spiritual ground, but it's not popular wisdom, the fashionable wisdom of high-priced experts that will be out-of-date in a year or so. God's wisdom is something mysterious that goes deep into the interior of his purposes. You don't find it lying around on the surface. It's not the latest message, but more like the oldest – what God determined as the way to bring out his best in us, long before we ever arrived on the scene. The experts of our day haven't a clue about what this eternal plan is. If they had, they wouldn't have killed the Master of the God – designed life on a cross. That's why we have this Scripture text: No one's ever seen or heard anything like this. Never so much as imagined anything quite like it – What God has arranged for those who love him. But you've seen and heard it because God by his Spirit has brought it all out into the open before you. The Spirit, not content to flit around on the surface, dives into the depth of God, and brings out what God planned all along. Whoever knows what you're thinking and planning except you yourself? The same with God – except that he not only knows what he's thinking, but he lets us in on it. God offers a full report on the gift of life and Salvation that he is giving us. We don't have to rely on the world's guesses and opinions. We didn't learn this by reading books or going to school, we learned it from God, who taught us person-to-person through Jesus, and we're passing it on to you in the same firsthand, personal way. The unspiritual self, just as it is by nature, can't receive the gifts of God's Spirit. There's no capacity for them. They seem like so much silliness. Spirit can be known only by Spirit – God's Spirit and our spirit in open communion. Spiritually alive, we have access to everything God's Spirit is doing, and can't be judged by unspiritual critics. Isaiah's question, "Is there anyone around who knows God's Spirit, anyone who knows what he is doing?" Has been answered. Christ knows, and we have Christ's Spirit.

Deception: it cannot be kept alive, because it causes people missing prayer evening, because someone has a secret from someone else so cannot go to prayer evening because they cannot face looking at the other person. (kill deception). People asking other people to keep secrets, if it can't be spoken openly don't draw others apart by the secret don't tell anyone. (kill deception). Hurting people hurting people. Yah! A few times ok. But get help hurting people, like the rest of us hurting people did. To grow in and with Christ. We are all hurting people, does it really make it exempt to hurt? (kill deception). Psalm 62: 7-8 My salvation and glory depend on God. God is the rock of my strength, my refuge. Trust him at all times, you people. Pour out your heart in his presence. God is our refuge.

Kill Deception!

All God's people are ministers a few with a capital M. Either we are good ministers or bad ministers, but ministers we are, and we will have to take full responsibility for this ministry we have been gifted with, and not by what we know, but what we did with what we know.

Imagine if we were always encouraged about everything, because God is in it all. Amazing what life would look like. Jesus promised that the gates of hell would not prevail (conquer) against his church, because he always goes before his sheep and prepares the way. Now our job is not to second guess him, but to follow him. Acts 15: 16-18 "After this I will return and rebuild David's fallen tent. Its ruins will be rebuilt, and I will restore it, that the remnant of men may seek the Lord, and all the Gentiles who hear my name, says the Lord, who does these things that have been known for ages.

It has always taken courage and compassion to minister in any age. The Sovereignty (power) of God and the love of God provide an unbearable combination for any servant of God, against which the devil has no power.

Is the presence of God being restricted to inside the church, and in devotions? Or does that presence shine in our entire life? To be sure, the continuance of praise is a sure devise in placing our lives into one whole piece, proclaiming praise to utter out loud what is surely the truth above all truths. Great is the Lord and greatly to be praised. Psalm 73: 25 Whom have I in heaven but you? And there is none upon earth that I desire besides you.

In order to model the kingdom of God in the world, the church must not only be a repentant community, or only committed to truth, but one whole holy community that harmonizes with heaven.

God's promise both old and new, is that God of Abraham, Isaac, and Jacob, the God who became flesh in Christ, actually dwells in the presence of his people. So what is there that cannot be, well just be, everything is holy/holy/holy because the Holy God lives in our midst. 1 Peter 2: 9 But you are a chosen people, a royal priesthood, a holy nation, a people belonging to God, that you may declare the praises of him who called you out of darkness into his wonderful light.

Repeat after me and let's pray this together. Lord I open myself to your holiness/and allow myself to reflect the light of Christ/ fill my being with courage/ and renewed vision/ for the work/ of your kingdom/ may your will be done/ in and through me/ just as your will is done in heaven/ Amen.

God replies, "Christ," to every cry from you passion-filled hearts.

1 Thessalonians 1: 3 We continually remember before our God and Father your work produced by faith, your labour promoted by love, and your endurance inspired by hope in our Lord Jesus Christ.

To believe Christ (faith), to serve Christ (love), and to wait for Christ (hope): this is what it is like to find God.

But to the degree that you have not found him your passions still run out of control, (or maybe better to assume too much in control?) Just trust it out my friend, no matter how big or how small really just trust it out. We all want to explain and control; but all we are doing is reducing mystery to manageable categories and attempt to run our own life without depending on

Christ. Working on the impossible so just trust it out my friend, just trust it out. Psalm 34: 8 Oh, taste and see that the Lord is good; blessed is the man who trust in Him!

You've loved me: Personalities merge, allowing me to reach true identity. When love (the Spirit of God) comes upon a person they are transformed. Now they can no longer insist on maintaining their individuality. Our Father does not refer to a person's individuality or their isolated position, but refers in terms of the total person, the whole body.... Once our rights to ourselves are handed over to God immediately our true personal nature begins responding. Jesus is merged into our spirits he brings freedom to the total person. Praise God for this intimate fellowship, and may we merge this fellowship into one and another. Psalm 36: 7 How precious is your loving kindness, O God! Therefore the children of men put their trust under the shadow of your wings.

Here is a practice of prayer God would like released, when we get angry, frustrated, annoyed, at our brother or sister give thanks for them to God. But; I am hearing, if you only knew............ while God has a But right back at yah! But; a brother or sister was born to help in a time of need. Amen. Remember God originally placed us in our perfect environment.

God's grace is in operation and will persist. My words and gestures and actions take place in the midst of a great drama, about the details of which I know little or nothing. In no way does this mean that my part is unimportant or dispensable. But I am a supporting player and not the lead. God and only God is the center stage action. God wants to meet with all his creation; and his creation wants to meet with him, unfocused as the want may seem. I pray that I will not manipulate the conversation or construe the setting that would hinder the things of God.

Spirituality can only be conducted with the awareness that it only exists in God's active presence, this conditions the conversation into an arrangement that works two ways forming a relationship, speaking and listening to one another because my friend he is there, no matter who else is with you he is there.

Note: spirituality cannot be reduced to procedure or formula. It cannot be rehearsed because it is not accomplished so much by what we do or say, but more in our demeanour when we meet, which is hopefully prayer. Because prayer is keeping company with God, and it involves gesture and silence, meditation......again another book.

Why do we do it alone? Jesus himself uses help to build the kingdom here on earth. He is not jealous of any accomplishments, he encourages them, and through this encouragement ministries flourish allowing the kingdom to grow, because it is Jesus in us and him the enabler of our gifts and anointing so it is us blending into his ministries!!!

Neighbours of my daughters who were also friends, made some wrong choices, involved my daughter in the scheme without her even knowing what was going on, I was there when this was all taking place and I did not even realize there was something wrong taking place. But there was, and before long the police arrived at their place and shortly after that at my daughters place. My daughter was cleared right from the start but turned into a witness. It turned out to be another occurrence that I was led into by God. As soon as I went home that day after all this the Spirit entered me with a most intent mourning and prayer for the rest of the day. I was even awake at three in the morning to continue in the procedure. The next morning God wanted me to go to this couple, and tell them how much He loves them. I did and received a warm response to this message (Huge Hugs). As I left offered an open invitation to bring them to church with me if ever they wanted, and assured them they were always welcome. They showed up at my place the next morning and asked if I would pick them up Sunday for church. After they left my daughter showed up took me out to breakfast and told me, "Mom, you have no idea how much your visit meant to them." Glory to God! Sunday came and went, when I knocked on the door they were still recovering from Saturday night. But the seed has been planted, and I am positive God is sending water, sun, to complete this harvest.

Lets never grow weary to serve the Lord in everything he sends our way.

We work very hard at our faith; we agonize over it; we struggle with it; grimly and with determination setting our jaws in order to make it through as if it were to go in one end and out the other, rather than being soaked in God's promise. This brings us back to that empty tomb once again, that empty tomb that has set us free from all of this, so we do not patronize (aid) God, treating him as someone we must take care of. We get to thinking what we do actually determines his effectiveness, failing to see that, that is the position of a pagan toward an idol, not a created bowed before the creator.

Beware of becoming part of a crowd, rather than a group. Crowds; being a gathering of individuals to get lost in, and the failure to heal loneliness. No individual is complete in themselves; no matter how many people you surround yours in. To live out the meaning of humanity you must be in a personal relationship with someone besides yourself. An individual alone is not a whole person. Group; is the basic working unit in God's relations. Scripture views man and woman as person-in-community, a "people of God." Being edged out of our rugged so called individualism. In order to become the wholeness of the gospel that redeems us into whole persons complete in the community of faith.

Salvation is not only individual, it is corporate. It is in the community and because of the fellowship there in, there is joy. Joy is not a private emotion; it requires community for both its development and the release of expression. And since the community is provided and preserved by God, the response is the 'Joy of the Lord.' John 15: 9-14 As the Father has loved me, so I have loved you. Now remain in my love. If you obey my commandments, you will remain in my love, just as I have obeyed my Fathers commandments and remain in his love. I have told you this so that my joy may be in you and that your joy may be complete. My command is this: love each other as I have loved you. Greater love has no one but this, that he lay down his life for his friends. You are my friends if you do what I command.

Joy, separated from its roots in God and pursued apart from the community of faith, becomes mere sensation. Joy has no cause or motive if separated from God, just as we look at suffering as fault, or a deficiency if separated from God. The result of suffering alone is bitterness, and the result of joy without someone to share in it becomes boredom. So now we get pulled in by our culture which has seemed to have appointed entertainment and leisure the industries as guidelines to our experience of joy.

We hear the message that God gives joy, and we no joy is possible, but we seem to still lack the skill for enjoyment. Maybe we are just not listening because after hearing this message on joy, what do we do put enter back into the crowd and buy toys; instead of staying in the group and joining the party God is hosting.

We need to learn to understand ourselves as people created, provided for, ruled, and redeemed by God. Sharing testimonies, worship, praise, songs, preaching and prayers. Guarding ourselves against acts of disobedience and rebellion. Open to a marvellous return through repentance into renewal. Through it All! There is a continuous awareness that we are all spiritually unique, in a corporate reality by God's call and rule.

Somewhere along the road we have formed the church into a community of respectability, a social status for religion. The down-and-out who flocked to Jesus when he lived on earth, no longer feel welcome. How did Jesus, the only perfect person in history, manage to attract the notoriously imperfect? And what keeps us from following in his steps today? In short, Jesus honoured the dignity of people, whether he agreed with them or not. He does not build his kingdom on the basis of race or class or other such divisions. Anyone, even a half-breed with five husbands or a thief dying on a cross, was welcome to join his kingdom. The person is more important than any category or label.

We all want to be right; we call it sincerely zealous striving for the faith, and we persuade ourself that we are God's ally in defending truth. But an angry spirit or an attitude of smugness can give us away, because you see compassion and humility resist arrogance.

We long to see healing and pray for relief from pain. But if this becomes a higher priority than worship, we are creating a god who suits our human purpose, and end up devoting our life to helping people feel better about themselves, instead of walking with them down the road God paved out for them. And if we cannot take that road together put them in the hand of Jesus but never let comfort take you off God's road. Be very careful and aware of the One True God and worship Him in true faith.

As we long to connect to the supernatural, embracing mystery, falling prostrate before God in humility, and yielding ourself to no higher purpose than experiencing him! But don't let your focus be on the experience, don't demand it, or you may get caught up with your theology of finding God and the evidence that you have done so, instead of God himself swooping you into his presence where things beyond imagination are attainable. Let your passion to explain become a passion to know Christ. Let your work of faith be to always believe God is God and is good. Allowing your passion to be right become a passion to honour Christ in all that you do.

Permit warm conviction to replace cold self-evident arrogance. Give the use of your labour of love to reflect God's character at all time. Giving your passion to heal the opportunity to form a passion to give hope.

You can continue on, doing the work of faith and carrying out the labour of love, even as you are still wounded. In the desire accompanied by expectation a better city awaits!

With the patience of hope, serve faithfully now, because you know what lies ahead. Don't wait for your wounds to heal before you serve. It might just be in the serving you're healing will be granted.

As we grow a passion to connect this will become a passion to trust Christ, who will do for us exactly what needs to be done. Revealing the Father in his Time and his Way in response to our faith, labour and love, and patience of hope.

A lot of us are crawling about in a stuffy attic, trying to explain life, demanding to be right, doing our best to relieve pain, and wondering where God is. It is time to find our way back to the family room and into our Father's lap, where we can listen to His Spirit tell us stories.

Well get some rest in the family room, get familiar with the Father's voice and enjoy some quality time on Abba Daddies arms and God willing God will rejoin us into a walk with him from these steps we just dared to take. I really did enjoy our time together hope you did as well.

I would like to end this time with a new version of the story Footprints someone blessed me with, hope you are blessed as well.

Footprints

Imagine you and the Lord Jesus are walking down the road together. For much of the way, the Lord's footprints go along steadily, consistently, rarely varying the pace.

But your footprints are a disorganized stream of zigzags, starts, stops, turnarounds, circles, departures, and returns.

For much of the way, it seems to go like this, but gradually your footprints come more in line with the Lord's, soon paralleling his constantly.

You and Jesus are walking as true friends!

This seems perfect but then an interesting thing happens: your footprints that once etched the sand next to Jesus' are now walking precisely in his steps.

Inside his larger footprints are your smaller ones, you and Jesus are becoming one. (Bride and Groom).

This goes on for many miles, but gradually you notice another change. The footprints inside the large footprints seem to grow larger.

Eventually they disappear altogether. There is only one set of footprints. They have become one.

This goes on for a long time, but suddenly the second set of footprints is back. This time it seems even worse! Zigzags all over the place. Stops. Starts. Gashes in the sand. A variable mess of prints.

You are amazed and shocked.

Your dream ends. Now you pray!

"Lord, I understand the first scene, with zigzags and fits. I was a new Christian; I was just learning. But you walked on through the storm and helped me learn to walk with you."

"That is correct."

"And when the smaller footprints were inside of yours, I was actually learning to walk in your steps, following you very closely."

"Very good..... You have understood everything so far."

"When the smaller footprints grew and filled in yours, I suppose that I was becoming like you in every way?"

"Precisely."

"So, Lord, was there a regression or something? The footprints separated and this time it was worse that the first."

There is a pause as the Lord answers, with a smile in his voice.

"You didn't know? It was then that we danced!"

The Kingdom of God appears to work best as a minority movement, child like. In opposite to the kingdom of the world. When it grows beyond that, the kingdom subsequently changes in nature.

There is no point to the importance and grandeur of arrival, when the goal is on the path itself. So yes heaven is awesome and me I can't wait to get there, but we don't have to wait to enjoy its grandeur and splendour we can enjoy it on the way already. Hope to meet with you again. Great big bear hugs. XXX

OOO